MOUNTAIN

TIME

by
Paul Schullery

A FIRESIDE BOOK
PUBLISHED BY SIMON & SCHUSTER INC.
NEW YORK LONDON TORONTO SYDNEY TOKYO

First Fireside Edition, 1988
Published by Simon & Schuster Inc.
Simon & Schuster Building
Rockefeller Center
1230 Avenue of the Americas
New York, New York 10020
Published by arrangement with Nick Lyons Books
FIRESIDE and colophon are registered trademarks of Simon & Schuster Inc.

Manufactured in the United States of America

10 9 8 7 6 5 4 3 2 1 Pbk.

Library of Congress Cataloging in Publication Data

Schullery, Paul.
    Mountain time / by Paul Schullery.—1st Fireside ed. p.   cm.
    Reprint. Originally published: New York, New York : Schocken Books, 1984
    "A Fireside Book."
    Bibliography: p.
    ISBN 0-671-65953-7 Pbk.
    1. Natural history—Rocky Mountains Region.   2. Natural history—
        Yellowstone National Park.   I. Title.
[QH104.5.R6S38   1988]
508.787′52—dc 19   87-32208

Mountain Time was written in its entirety as a book; very little of it appeared in any other form before the manuscript was in the publisher's hands. It has pleased me to see several parts of the book appear in article form in the following publications.

Portions of "Home River" and all of "Geyser Gazing" have appeared in *American West*. Portions of "A Reasonable Illusion" and "The Other Wilderness" have appeared in *Rod & Reel*. Some random passages have appeared in articles and columns I have written for *The Interpreter*, the Western Interpreters Association journal for environmental communicators.

For Dianne

Table of Contents

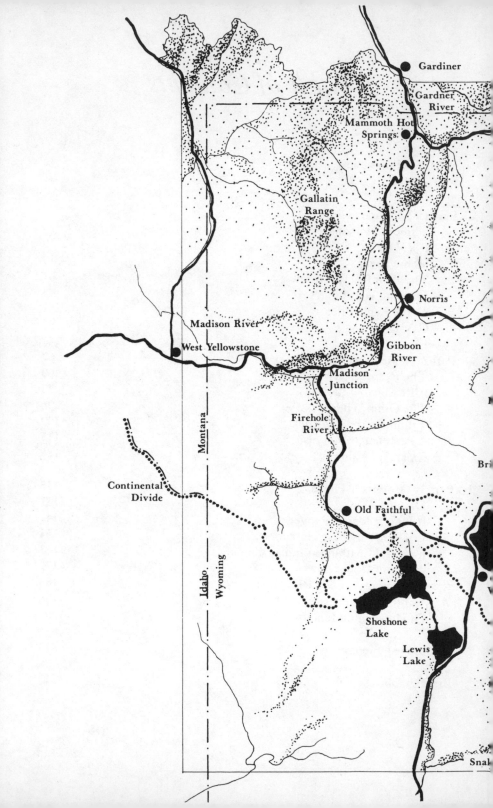

Civilization is built on a tripod of geography, history, and law, and it is made up largely of limitations.

WALLACE STEGNER, in *Wolf Willow*

Preface

A wise friend of mine, a biologist, once told me, "Whenever things are going particularly badly I take a walk in the sage above the cabin and sit there thinking about the park in geological terms. That helps keep what happens in the next hundred years in perspective." She's right. I do the same thing myself now, not as an escape, you understand, but as a restorative and as a stimulant. Workdays, schedules, deadlines . . . all this human busyness fades a bit from the perspective of mountain time. Mountain time is without zones, midnights, or seventeen jewel works. The slower something moves, the longer it lasts. Mountains outlast trees, trees outlast people. Mountains grow old, soften, weaken, and shrink, like people do, but much more slowly.

Sculptors and their admirers speak of carving a monument into the "living rock" of a cliff face. Poets and whimsical ecologists speak of the "pulse of the earth." The analogies are common, but ascribing life to a hill or a ravine is more anthropomorphism than I can handle. Mountains don't have to have life. They have time, and they have it on such a scale that I don't even register in their geologic memory unless I take tools to them and change them faster than they would be changed without me. Another wise friend once counseled some Yellowstone visitors that collecting rocks in the park was worse than picking flowers because "it takes a rock a lot longer to grow back."

Mountain time is simple enough, and poetic enough, that we don't have to call it life. Metamorphic rock is exciting and dynamic enough; anthropomorphic rock is unnecessary. There is life enough *on* the mountains—vegetation, wild animals, tame animals, people—a fast dance of life, scratching away at the surface with taproots, hooves, mandibles, Vibram soles, and road graders, all for the sake of spending a little time in the mountains.

Yellowstone was a surprise to me. As a man in my early twenties, after a childhood of steady moving (ten schools in ten years), the last thing I expected to find was a sense of place. Like many young people whose parents moved frequently, my place was with my family. Sense of place was a cliché, and not only did I not expect to find such a thing in Yellowstone, I didn't know I needed it.

But apparently I did, for within days of my arrival I felt an attachment growing—a vague comfort with my surroundings.

At the same time, growing coincident with this feeling of being home, I found a sense of wonder. Yellowstone spoke to me, sang to me, of a wild, strong, unexperienced, and good life. My previous trips to the West, little more than hasty vacations, had given a hint of this. I'd known for years that the high West had something for me. I'd felt on those earlier trips an attraction, and was vaguely aware of a need to be in the West, but I could never have identified the cause, much less trace it to this joy of surroundings I now felt soaking into me. Not only was I home, I was in love.

It seems that one barely has time to enjoy the discovery of a new love before the old fears creep in: Can it last? Will it go stale, or be lost to another? Love of wild country carries those risks. No sooner was I awakened to the joys than I began to learn the threats: the enormously complicated economic, social, political, and biological forces that constantly threaten Yellowstone. The thought of the chaotic flow of desires and motivations that compels millions of people to enjoy, use, and exploit Yellowstone gave me a sense of cause. I had come home, not only to a place, not only to a love, but to a responsibility.

Had Yellowstone, a hundred years old and thriving, been a person—a grand old lady, to follow the prevailing cliché—she would have been amused at this young ranger with his sudden commitment to defend her honor. And, because at a hundred years of age she had seen many young men transformed by her charms, she could have told me that I had a lot to learn.

PART ONE

MOUNTAIN LIVES

Three Mountains

My home in Yellowstone was at park headquarters, Mammoth Hot Springs. "Mammoth" is a small cluster of dwellings, administrative buildings, stores, and garages, a descendant of an army post called Fort Yellowstone that was here from 1891 to 1918. The most visible portion of the settlement, known as "upper Mammoth," where the museum and offices now sit, is almost all army-built; it is a permanent if generally unappreciated monument to the U.S. Cavalry's selfless contribution to the survival of Yellowstone. Down the hill to the east is a more modern housing area, consisting of four or five crossed streets and a campground. Scattered between upper Mammoth and the huge white mound of hot spring deposits to the west are various hotel and store buildings, most of which front on a large unkept field. The field was once used by the soldiers as a parade ground, but now it runs heavily to sage and badger dens. Several sinkholes, fenced off to protect the terminally careless from themselves, line the north side of the parade ground, reminders that this whole flat was once active hot springs. On subzero mornings steam climbs from these openings as from so many subterranean kitchens.

I call this headquarters, or a settlement, or home, but I have never been able to think of it as anything urban. When a tourist stops me along the street and asks, "Is there propane available in this town?" my first reaction is to look around, thinking "what town?" Somehow it's not a town, or a village, even though it has all the appurtenances of municipality: stores, chapel, clinic, hotel, even a couple of stop signs. Apparently my sense of place resisted the notion that I lived in a town. This was a wilderness, with elk, grizzly bears, and blizzards coming and going pretty much at will. Forget that two million tourists did the same thing; they were no more a part of the place than the stop signs.

No, Mammoth, for all its illusions of cityhood, was not here on those terms. The elk grazing on the lawns and the bears down along the river were proof of that. I lived, despite the stop signs, in an outpost. I couldn't believe otherwise, given the evidence.

The most imposing evidence provided the horizon: three totally dissimilar mountains. The one I knew best—my summer front door opened to a view of it—was Mount Everts. Everts was named for a hapless explorer of 1870, whose sole distinguishment was getting separated from his party and lost for thirty-seven days, providing some hardy locals with an opportunity to heroically rescue him. It is somehow fitting, in my idea of Everts as an eccentric among mountains, that the rescue took place several mountains over to the east, so that Everts (and Rescue Creek, on Everts's east side) was misnamed for an adventure the mountain did not participate in. Someone thought the rescue took place here, and named the mountain in honor of this clumsy explorer. Like most of the names we proudly bestow upon natural features, we do no harm, and probably even less good. As the old fisherman remarked after explaining the various ways to attach a frog to a hook, it's all the same to the frog. It's all the same to the mountain.

Everts dominated the whole eastern horizon from my porch. It is at first difficult to consider it visually as a mountain. It has no classic peak. It's a long north-south ridge, primarily sandstone and shale, rising steeply 1,600 feet above the north-flowing Gardner River. The whole face of this long steep ridge is deeply gullied, turning the Gardner brown after every rain. A few giant mudslide fans are fresh enough to be clean of sage, but a closer look reveals that the whole Gardner valley is an alluvial dump for the dribbling slope above it.

It is a process slow enough that the gullies are heavily vegetated in many places. I never paid it much attention until Park Biologist Don Despain aimed me toward it one day as a striking study in climatic effects. The ridges between the gullies (the gullies are probably too steep but otherwise could be called arroyos, so large are they) are heavily grown over on their north-facing slopes; he said there are about three times as many plant species on the north side as on the south side, and there is only one species common to both. The south side is three-quarters bare slope, but the north side is only one-quarter uncovered. As I did a double take, finally seeing what I'd been looking at, Don explained that the north side gets less sunlight (which I would have thought would make it less, not more, hospitable); it gets less heat and is therefore less dried out by hot weather. Plants grow there better, only yards from a less hospitable environment on the south slope of each ridge. It is a graphic display of local environmental variations, like a horizontal barber pole of earth and vegetation.

It comes into its own as a mountainous presence when the weather acts up. In the fall the snow line dusts its way down the steep face, warning and preview to us down at Mammoth's 6,200 feet. The rising sun is strained briefly through the fencerow of Douglas fir that whisker the top of the ridge, and in the evening the sun casts shadows from the western mountains, shadows that creep slowly up Everts's face like a horizontal curtain until only the mountain's hardrock cap is bathed in rose alpenglow before turning dark.

In heavy weather the top of the ridge comes and goes through ragged windows of mist, and the peaking row of trees combs passing clouds and seems black when it shows through. Once, climbing up toward Mammoth from the river, with the first heavy drops of a big storm pelting the dust as we hurried for the car, a splitting roar of lightning ignited a tree on the very lip of the mountain face. The tree glowed fiercely for an instant, then faded, leaving us awed and grateful.

Fellow ranger-naturalist Dick Follett and I spent a spring day on the east side of Everts, rambling across a dozen low ridges, each one slightly higher as they neared the top. In the uncommon and shadeless heat we sought out seeps to refill our water bottles, and had lunch on the very rim, looking into a stiff breeze at the hot spring mounds of Mammoth on the opposite slopes. The heat chased us down the ridge to the north, onto McMinn Bench, where we scared up a band of bighorn ewes and watched them race for the cover of nearby gullies. We scrambled down into the inner canyon of the Gardner, reaching the footbridge at supper time. Snowmelt from the sudden heat wave had put the river in flood, and it pushed muddily against the little log pilings of the bridge; half an hour after we crossed, the river tore the bridge loose and scattered it over a half mile of streambed.

The south end of Everts drops sharply into a small glacial valley, more a canyon, really, out of which flows Lava Creek, a small tumbling stream that joins the Gardner River at the foot of Everts's west face. The Gardner itself has just emerged from its own canyon, immediately to the south of Lava Creek Canyon. In typically muddled geological fashion, the Gardner's canyon is not glacial. It has the sharp V-shaped contours of the famous southwestern canyons, and was carved by the water coming off the higher plateau to the south. It is more than 1,500 feet deep; only the Grand Canyon of the Yellowstone is deeper among Yellowstone Park canyons.

From my front door I can see only the mouths of these canyons. Following the top of Everts's ridge from left to right (north to south), my vision dips first into the U-shaped mouth of Lava Creek Canyon, then, crossing the road that follows Lava Creek up and east, I see the V-shaped canyon of the Gardner where it emerges from the east shoulder of Bunsen Peak.

Bunsen Peak dominates the southern horizon. It was named for the German physicist who developed the famous burner; he was a pioneer of sorts in volcanic theory, and his namesake peak is appropriately the core of a long-extinct volcano. It is also a model mountain, the kind children draw, with pine-covered slopes under rocky crags that rise to a nice pointy top at 8,500 feet.

From Mammoth, or from the top of Everts, for that matter, Bunsen is most attractive for its forest. The peak itself is off center on the west end of the main sloping hulk of the mountain, most of which is uniformly green. About two-thirds the way up the lower slope there is a ragged horizontal line running across the forest. It is the Bunsen Peak fire scar, the upward limit of a forest fire that occurred in the 1880s. The trees below the line are a century's regrowth, still considerably smaller than the older forest above.

I've kicked around on Bunsen enough to acquire the favor of familiarity. From its peak, standing amid radio shacks and assorted antennae (very few peaks in the park are subjected to this; Bunsen is close to park headquarters), I've seen imponderable distances: clear into the Beartooths to the east—high hazy ridges sixty miles away; almost over the Gallatins to the west—escarpments that say more clearly than any others in the park that "the grizzly is here"; and on especially clear days, squinting across the inner park plateau to the south, I can make out the tips of a faint ridge of fantasy peaks to the south—the Tetons, ghostly and unreal through ninety miles of mountain air.

A series of small ponds nestle along the north footslopes of Bunsen; in one of them I often fished at dusk after work. It was like fishing in church, with the mountain looming gothic and monumental so near and filling the pond with its mirrored bulk. The rises of trout dimpled and pocked the image like raindrops blurring spots on a huge watercolor. Once when my parents came from Ohio to visit me—to see what had occupied my life and my soul for five years, I think—I brought them to the pond to show them the glory of a wild brook trout. They weren't at all impressed that I caught several very quickly on flies while three nearby spin fishermen caught nothing; I kept hurrying the trout back in the water, wanting to catch a brighter one with the flaming orange spawning skirt. When I finally did catch a really vivid jewel, I rushed back to where they were shivering near the car. They did what they could to act sufficiently appreciative of something that didn't excite them, and it all seemed a failure until a bull elk bugled from high on Bunsen and that wild whistling grunt rang across the pond with the force of something visible. The other fishermen stopped fishing and stood still as trout and chills were forgotten for the moment. The elk repeated his call twice more as we listened by the pond.

Bunsen's west slope drops sharply into a tight pass called Golden Gate. It's a narrow canyon of orange, sienna, and the soft limes and rusts of lichen. Glen Creek breaks free of the flats to the south here and rushes over Rustic Falls and down the rocky grade to my little ponds below and then on down to the Gardner River at the base of Bunsen. A road was pushed, blasted, and suspended through this canyon in the 1890s, the army engineer who masterminded it leaving his name on it—Kingman Pass. The rickety wooden road that hugged the west side of the gorge at its narrowest point has been replaced by a modern concrete viaduct, but the Gate still unnerves many flatlanders when they drive through.

My winter residence was in the old B.O.Q. of Fort Yellowstone—now the Albright Museum. The door opened to the west, and showed me the entire western ridge, clear from Golden Gate to the high northwest; I always thought of that ridge as a single mountain, one that climbed gradually from the Gate to a high point at the north end. Actually the ridge is not continuous, and it isn't considered one mountain. From where I stood I thought of it as one, even knowing that the southern, lower part was a crumbling limestone cliff face called Terrace Mountain and the higher ridge to my west and northwest was Sepulchre Mountain. The two join on the horizon and together seemed to participate in a single climbing ridge, and they were in fact the top side of a single drainage. Mammoth—the springs, the buildings, the campground, and the rest—sits on a sloping shoulder which one could claim is a lower extension of either Terrace or Sepulchre. The hot spring deposits are "terraces" of limestone similar to those ancient formations higher up on Terrace Mountain. The hill immediately to my right—due north of my door—blocks any distant view; it is the edge of a rolling plateau that is undeniably the foothills of Sepulchre. Streams and groundwater from both mountains cross the Mammoth area.

I think of the whole ridge as Sepulchre. I doubt that I could even stand on my porch and point to where it begins and Terrace ends. Sepulchre was named by early explorers for a cryptlike rock formation found near its peak, and the high point I see from the porch is the "false summit." The real top is behind it, out of view from Mammoth.

I use Sepulchre for weather and season. Virtually all our weather is borne to us on west winds that clamber over the Gallatins and roll down off Sepulchre's ridge upon us. When we wonder about the chances for fishing after work we automatically look above Sepulchre. One afternoon I saw a black storm beyond it, obviously dropping heavy rains on the high peaks back there before passing just to the north of Mammoth. It was late afternoon, near quitting time, and I wanted to fish south of Bunsen near Indian Creek Campground, but I knew I would have to hurry. Throwing my fishing vest into my car at 4:30, I drove up through Golden Gate and south to the creek, fishing quickly through several pools and killing a few small trout for dinner company. Within half an hour of my arrival, just as I turned back upstream toward the car, the flowing storm water reached me and the river rose slightly, darkened and cluttered with soil and vegetative flotsam. It would be unfishable until morning.

Along Sepulchre's slope, tucked into the moisture traps of various dips and ravines, are aspen groves. In eary spring they green up with delicate pastels; in late fall they shine yellow, sometimes for weeks, when the weather gets crisp and the traffic dries up. I use them as seasonal indicators; I anticipate their progress for its loveliness and for the messages it sends to the lower slopes. In winter, when the aspen stand out bare and unchanging like a smoky haze that has settled in the draws and gullies, I follow the progress of snow—downslope in the fall, upslope in the spring. On the high ridge due west, one clearing hosts an enormous snow cornice, so overhung that a long slanting snowfield lies in blue shadow below it. I watch the shadow increase into deep winter, then recede with the spring, finally vanishing as the cornice's sharp lip rots and crumbles under the warm persuasion of a March wind.

Surrounded by the three mountains, cupped in them and shaded by them, walled away from extreme weather by them, Mammoth has a milder drier climate than the rest of the park—less rain and snow, higher temperatures. During my winters there, when I felt thirty or forty degrees below zero down in the geyser basins, Mammoth's lowest temperature was minus eighteen. A thousand feet lower than most of the park, Mammoth was the natural location for the original park headquarters, even more so because most early traffic came into the park up the Yellowstone River valley from the north. Now other entrances, three of them, are more popular, and many tourists don't even visit Mammoth. They make a quick loop—Old Faithful, the Grand Canyon of the Yellowstone River, Yellowstone Lake, and out. Mammoth, even with its tremendous hot springs and history, is a minor attraction. Those of us who despair of the milling summer crowds at Old Faithful, or of the creeping auto trains that snake along the rim of the canyon, prefer it that way.

It's the same for the three mountains. None is well known or particularly challenging to climb, and there are many higher and more suitably picturesque peaks to satisfy the needs of tourists. But, living here, and getting some feel for what mountain life has to offer, sufficiency is not an issue to me. Mountains need not be shaped suitable for cigarette billboard advertising. We impose on them enough with silly names that honor men and ignore the mountains. These three, wearing our little community and its roads with no noticeable diminishing of majesty, don't disappoint me in the least. They give a solid and enduring feeling, a wild kind of grace, to the place I call home.

Elk Watch

The advantage of working late—of giving campfire programs and evening nature walks—is that the workday doesn't start until noon. I enjoy sleeping —it's something I do well—and frequently indulge in slothful mornings, dozing as the full morning sunlight warms my room. One such morning, basking by my window, I was shocked awake when the sunlight disappeared totally, as if a switch had been flipped. Even as I opened my eyes I heard the quiet tearing and crunching of a grazing elk, and the great tan flank that filled the window was no surprise. Just another late breakfast, here on Paul's lawn.

For most of the year, except in the heat of summer when they move up country to the flats south of Bunsen, elk are a daily event at Mammoth. They graze on the lawns, bed down between the houses, and generally hang around—not tame, not too familiar, just there, part of the setting. It is hard to explain how routine a part of daily life they become. For most of the year you just have them around, like so many 600-pound robins on the lawn. Seeing them daily, learning to recognize individual animals, occasionally shooing them (never without a twinge of fear) out of the way like uncorralled cattle—all this contact makes them common in the mind; appalling proof that civilized people can become blasé about absolutely anything, even huge wild elk munching the flower bed.

The elk could be African or Asian. With its darker, slightly bowed (almost camellike) neck and its grand branching rack of antlers, it is as exotic, when first seen, as an eland or a kudu. Easterners, though they have heard of elk, don't seem inclined to recognize them. When they see one for the first time they don't think "I wonder if that's an elk?" They think, instead, "What the hell is that?" And, I must admit, it doesn't look like an elk to me, either. The name has never really worked. The Indian name, wapiti, is better, but still not all I would have hoped for. It's as if such short names just can't encompass the grandness here, as if short names—Ed, Ike, Lou—are too informal to do it justice. A three-letter word doesn't measure up to what this animal displays in glory and grace, unless we call it god. We could do a lot worse than deify something as wild and mystifying as the elk.

Next to the moose, the elk is the largest member of the deer family in North America. Elk were once common in parts of the East, and a few herds have been reestablished in isolated areas in some eastern states, but now the elk is mostly a western animal and therefore a strange sight to lowland tourists. That first look at an animal almost the size of a horse, an animal with a slightly swooping neck (a neck whose hair is longer and chocolate brown in contrast to a coffee-tan springtime body) and, if it's a bull, long massive antlers, can be unnerving. When it looks up from its feeding and swings its head toward you (you notice that the long neck hair comes up to its chin, fringing and bearding it Amishly), there is something placid in its gaze, but it lacks the cowlike blankness of expression; it will not let you touch it, and it recognizes no owner.

The exotic impression does not fade easily, nor should it. Indeed, even today in Yellowstone there are times when great herds of a thousand or more elk can be seen at once, spread out as if across some mountain Serengeti, a genuine replication of the fabulous mammalian riches of pre-Columbian America. But at Mammoth it is usually one-on-one, and I don't think that either the people or the elk entirely come to terms with such intimate cohabitation.

One spring a large bull was grazing in the brush across the street from my quarters. It had been a rough winter, and his coat was ratty and faded to a dusty tan. He was in the middle of the housing area, in a patch of sage and grasses surrounded by residences; some of his buddies had settled down on a nearby lawn to snooze among the lawn furniture and swing sets. Three small neighborhood children, followed by their smaller dog, were conducting a walking romp up the street, yelling, jumping around, and generally acting childlike. As they passed my place they came nearly close enough to touch the elk, but he didn't flinch, just kept on feeding. Only a few moments later a car came up the street, driven by a tourist who had mistakenly turned in to the residence area and was now trying to find the way out. When he saw the bull (he never noticed the others, just as close), he stopped the car a couple of houses down the street and got out, camera in hand. Then, in broad daylight, he began an elaborate crouching sort of stalk straight toward the elk. As he crept and wove, occasionally ducking as if concealed behind some imaginary bushes or rocks, he held the camera near his chin, preparing for the perfect shot of the rear end of the elk. The elk was immediately edgy; noisy kids and dogs were one thing, but this was too much. While the stalker was still fifty feet away the bull moved restlessly off into the sage, never quite out of instamatic range but never close enough to satisfy the tourist, who soon got bored and drove off.

Usually it is easy enough for us—people and elk—to overlook the other's presence. The elk keep a distance that varies with their mood, and we pass each other with only mild wariness. If several are bedded down along one of the paths in the woods around Mammoth, they'll usually stay there as I pass. Like domestic stock, they're inclined to scatter if rushed, but nobody sensible about the terms of cohabitation stirs them up. Most of us have encountered less tractable elk at one time or another, one that stands her (it seems to be a cow most of the time) ground mid-path as we approach. More than once I've been walking up the path to my door and, glancing casually over at the nearest elk, have seen a restlessness in her demeanor that signified an elk in a bad mood. She must have seen alarm in my glance; she glared at me and something set her off in a quiet rush in my direction. I didn't wait to see if it was a bluff. As an early park visitor said when describing how he'd escaped from a bear, "I jest natchully faded away. I reckon that atmosphere is all het up yet with the way I come through it."

Most of the time there's no hostility, and if they never really get to trust us, they do give us the chance to learn. Having elk around through the seasons gives us the leisure to come to terms with more subtle issues of their existence than who is entitled to the sidewalk.

Take their antlers. For most people it is difficult to get beyond the wonder of an animal that grows fifteen pounds of antlers every spring and summer just to drop them in midwinter. But if you get to see them daily, and see the antlers grow, you appreciate just what the elk is adjusting to. All the time those antlers are growing, they're covered by a tender, living "skin" called velvet. It's easily bruised, and a strong enough bump can distort and deform the antler. Elk are very careful about the antlers, and how they move them, all summer.

Imagine, though, having that growth taking place all summer. Not only must you be careful about what you bump, you can't even see the problem. They grow out of the back of the skull; all you can see well are the brow tines that come down over your forehead. Worse, the dimensions and boundaries of your problem change every day. They get longer, catching on things they didn't catch on last week. They get heavier too, requiring steady readjustment of your sense of balance. Turn your head fast to the left, then imagine the momentum problems and muscular challenge of doing that with ten pounds of calcium extending a yard out behind your head. Imagine the stiff necks from sleeping on your belly with your neck stretched out and your chin flat on the ground, the antlers sticking up like dead rosebushes.

Of course it's not that unpleasant for an elk, but it must take considerable adjustment. They learn well, and know precisely where their antlers reach. Most spectacular proof of that is their sparring. Bulls frequently square off in the fall, pushing each other, squealing and grunting, across the lawns. They seem to join horns by some unseen signal, and, depending on how upset they are (bulls continue desultory sparring all winter, long after the fall rut is concluded; apparently they do so to establish a pecking order within their group), they may stop suddenly, unlock horns, and graze. I've seen these push-and-shove contests conducted three-corner, as three bulls pushed against one another, tramping and pounding on the lawn, their hooves clicking dully as they crossed a sidewalk. Their antlers scrape and crack together like dueling broomsticks, but except in the hottest fury of the rut, when mating supremacy is at stake, they do each other little damage.

Just living with the antlers, especially in heavy forest, is a challenge. When an elk throws his head back and breaks into a trot, he is pointing every possible tine back, where branches will slide off without tangling. Running head-down, he'd snag up right away. The simpler duties of the day are equally intriguing. Once from my desk by the window I watched a big bull park himself beneath a tree whose lower branches were just out of reach of his mouth. Tilting his head down slightly so that his antlers pointed straight up, he rocked his head and swished them back and forth through the lower branches, which rained loose needles onto the ground by his front feet. Then he ate the needles.

Even more impressive was a lone bull out on the parade ground. I was watching him because a magpie had landed, and was resting comfortably, on his back. The elk seemed not to mind, and after a while the magpie flew away (was it considering a nest in the antlers?). Then, in a motion of great dexterity and profound delicacy, the elk lowered his head and swung it hard around to his right side. He lifted his right rear leg, and with admirable precision he reached the utmost tine under his belly and contentedly scratched his crotch. That's control.

Antlers are occasionally a hazard in the realm of human/elk cohabitation. The residents of Mammoth, like those of any other community, like to decorate their houses at Christmas; many string lights on their walls and shrubbery. One of the local bull elk got himself tangled in a string of lights, probably while feeding on the shrubbery, and for several days afterward paraded around with his antlers festooned with lights as if he was looking for an electrical outlet. The wire trailed some feet behind him and seemed bound to cause him some trouble, so the park biologists decided to anesthetize him and remove it.

Knowing that he was a local, it was simply a matter of waiting until he made himself available. I was in the biologists' office when someone hurried in to report that the electric elk was right across from the post office. Within a few moments he had been shot with the tranquilizer gun and stripped of his ornaments.

Thus began his little adventure. As soon as the drug began to take hold but before he was overcome, he gradually started dropping his head; his neck muscles were relaxing. Unfortunately, every time his head went down he unintentionally assumed a threatening posture and one of the other bulls would respond to the challenge, hurry over and slam into him, stirring him out of the stupor for a moment. The other bulls were chased away, and before long the elk was down and resting peacefully.

It was a new drug they had used, one that gave them more latitude in dosage size (a big problem with tranquilizing a wild animal is that its metabolic state can wildly affect how great or small a dosage can be safely given), but one that also required more time to wear off. The elk was awake, but he had no muscle control. His predicament was risky, because he could not defend himself at all. Whenever one of us passed near him, his eye would follow us (I hate to think what must have been going on in that head), but he could not flee or even move his head. The problem, at that moment, was the magpies; they noticed him right away and probably would have moved in and started working on his eyes if we had not shooed them away. He was shot shortly after lunch, but showed no sign of getting up as the afternoon wore on. A couple of sympathetic people took turns keeping the magpies away, and late in the afternoon the sub-district ranger got him on his feet by rushing at him and shouting. It seemed most important to make him move around a bit, to get his system in gear again. At dusk he was moving slowly around the boulevard, but still didn't look great.

We were watching him from the other side of the street, perhaps 150 feet away, as it started to get dark. A pack of coyotes began to howl over behind the hotel, but we gave them no thought until they appeared, loping single file along the ridge above the elk. As the leader of the pack spotted the big bull, his interest was obvious. The pack, six of them, perked up and trotted quickly to the top of the ridge just above the elk, perhaps 100 feet from him. He had in the meantime bedded down, but was still awake with his head up. He did not seem to notice the coyotes, and was facing away from the ridge.

It is difficult to tell how they knew something was wrong with him. They didn't see him move, and as he sat there he looked, to us at least, like any other sitting elk. But they knew instantly that this one wasn't in full possession of his equipment. For several moments they sat on the ridge above him, in a row, like so many Indians silhouetted against the horizon in an old John Wayne movie. It was as if they were counting the points on his antlers, or were waiting for more evidence. Finally, just as we thought they might be going to move in, some silent decision was reached and the pack rose and trotted quickly down the ridge away from him. By morning he was fine.

Seeing elk daily, watching antlers grow, seeing recently abandoned calves wandering around confused and lonely (we saw a couple forlornly trailing after a cow moose one day—any port in a storm), we begin to appreciate elk life as more than a series of picturesque vignettes. What they are doing is part of their real life, not merely entertainment for tourists. One of them may be a scattered and well-gnawed carcass down along the river this time next month. They don't feel as cute as they look when they glance up with snowy noses from a sparse, tongue-freezing lunch of dead grass; pawing and kicking through crusted snow makes for a long day and a longer night. Winter really brings home the difference between a national park and a zoo.

One winter afternoon in my office I was daydreaming toward the elk on the parade ground, torn between the absorbing animal motion and my unexciting typewriter. The elk won. They were scattered, perhaps twenty-five cows and calves, across the near end of the parade ground, on both sides of the worn old asphalt road that connects the chapel with the hotel.

At once, though there was no sound or perceptible signal, they stiffened and looked to my left, where a coyote was trotting up the road toward them. He moved quickly toward the hotel, obviously only passing through, and probably hoping he would be allowed to pass in peace. No elk moved, except for twenty-five dark snouts that followed the coyote, and fifty brown eyes, flashing with suspicion. There was no simple predator-prey relationship here. Alone, hopelessly outgunned, the coyote was a vulnerable nuisance, and as he hurried through the group he glanced nervously around, ready to break into a sprint any time. As he passed from the elk to the hotel lawn and was lost to sight among the buildings, the elk relaxed and returned to lunch. Life for an elk is full of interruptions, many more distressing than that, and life for an elk goes on whether we are around to watch or not.

There are unimagined gatherings of elk in Yellowstone in the winter. Most visitors are justifiably excited if they see half a dozen in some high summer meadow, but when the snow comes the scale changes dramatically. The elk bunch up in clearings, gradually moving downhill and generally down the Yellowstone drainage as the snow deepens. As they descend into the valleys they can easily be seen from the roads. By January several hundred can be seen at once, and by March some groups exceed a thousand.

We drove out past Tower Junction one January Sunday, counting scores of elk in most clearings. In the Lamar Valley, not far past the old buffalo ranch, we almost missed a huge herd spread across the flats in the fork of the Lamar River and Soda Butte Creek. Hundreds, close to a thousand, were bedded there in the sage and scrub. The closest were at least 150 yards off, but when we stopped the car and got out, they rose as one and began to move away up the valley. Our curiosity burned up thousands of hard-earned calories as the elk trudged heavily through the snow. Crestfallen and embarrassed, we drove off as quickly as possible, wondering how much time and energy they spend each winter just keeping a comfortable distance between themselves and people.

In a rough winter followed by thaw-and-freeze-crusted spring snows, 15 percent or more of the herd might die. Fifteen percent of 20,000 elk is a lot of meat for winter-lean grizzlies, coyotes, ravens, eagles, and countless smaller scavengers, but there is more to the statistic than pounds of meat. First there is the general lesson made in so many ways in national parks, that "waste" as a concept we apply elsewhere does not apply here; waste can only occur where something is not put to use, and elk meat is cranked right back into the system by scavengers as large as grizzlies and as small as bacteria. Second, in appreciating the elk for all they are, the statistic is particularly useful. These elk are more than singular individuals, some of whom die each year. We must not forget that the individuals, for all their regal grace, are not in themselves the most poetic point being made by this herd. That point is the greater functioning of the whole population, the thousands of them that move and shift across this northern range and Yellowstone's other elk ranges like a loose-jointed amoeba, a faint million-acre organic tide that ebbs and flows with the seasons, challenging our understanding as wildlife managers and our imaginations as thinking beings.

Yellowstone's elk have been controversial, nationally, so often that they have a greater and more avid constituency than many politicians. For eighty years we have struggled with their management, trying to comprehend the dynamics of their population and generally getting it wrong. More recently, Douglas Houston's landmark study has answered many of the most difficult questions about this population and its range, but the elk still hold surprises, and Doug's study offers as many challenges as it provides answers. Yellowstone elk migrate north down the Yellowstone River drainage; when they leave the park they are hunted and are otherwise treated differently (ranchers don't like elk competition with their grazing stock). It is incredibly difficult to develop a consistent policy that satisfies the various agencies, citizens' groups, and individuals who must deal with these elk. The animals don't understand boundaries, and they don't know the hunting season. Some years they don't leave the park in any numbers until the regular season is closed, if at all. Many mystify us by staying in the high country all winter, when neighboring groups have left; the amoeba does not move evenly (Doug characterizes this uneven flow with a charming term, referring to the partial shift of animals as a "differential sieve"). In short, they don't always act like a single like-thinking population, introducing the unpredictable vagaries of exceptional or eccentric individual will here and there. But, given years of intense study, hundreds of frozen hours of airplane flight, and the penetrating vision of computerized analysis, the elk population's gross movements and rhythms have been unraveled. Their responses to cold, to snow cover, and to the other influences of their environment—including social pressures of their fellow grazers and unsocial pressures of their predators—are not yet an open book, but they are far from a mystery. We now watch the herds with a feeling of understanding that approaches our familiarity with the routines of the lawn elk at Mammoth, and we must conclude that after all, the groupness is the most important and intellectually stimulating idea each individual has to offer; that as hard as it may be for us to grasp when we are in the presence of one elk, the scientists, striving to appreciate the greater body of elk, will ultimately benefit both elk and elk-watcher far more than either can benefit the other.

Of course I don't regularly watch the elk with all this in mind. As I sit watching one, trying to understand the peculiar gumming-and-tearing process by which she pulls the grass into her mouth, I don't think of it happening thousands of times each hour all over the neighboring mountains. But I do occasionally respect the patience, or perseverance, that it takes to turn untold quantities of such grass into a sleek, dark brown masterpiece of life. It may not be patience; it may just be that a grazer's stupidity keeps her from getting bored with the endless hours of lawn-trimming. But still I don't see a cow's complacency in those eyes; perhaps it is just because the pasture has no fence, but the elk watches me with more than bland curiosity. She watches me with distrust, and with instinctive fear that is only partly calmed by my unaggressive behavior. Because she is wild, though familiar, she watches me across a far greater gulf than any cow could.

One evening in early November I was bringing my new skis back from West Yellowstone, driving too hastily up the Madison canyon. Road-clearing had stopped for the year, and we needed only a little more snow to officially close the park for the winter. The high passes were already barricaded, and occasional patches of ice made the other roads treacherous for the few last-minute travelers. That night I encountered one such patch on a sweeping left curve around the foot of a cliff. As I rounded the corner I hit the ice just as I saw that the road was crowded, for about seventy-five feet, with two dozen cow and calf elk, their eyes glinting in my headlights. The car slid into the group—no brakes, no gas—and they watched it pass with that odd blank-faced detachment elk sometimes have in the face of the unexpected: "Hmm. Here comes a car. Let's watch it slide by . . . "

I didn't feel detached, but I too had nothing better to do than watch, because the car was on its own, completely out of control, gliding quickly over the ice. I missed them all. I don't know why; I certainly didn't deserve to miss them, as stupidly as I was driving. As my car threaded its way through the unmoving elk it seemed once or twice that I would at least brush a fender against a knee cap or something, but it didn't happen. I emerged from the other side of the group, rejoined the dry pavement, and left the little crowd of them, still watching me go, still unmoving, in the dusk.

Watching elk is always like that. They may watch back, but you're never sure what they make of you.

Home River

Fishing has a reputation as an innocuous, fairly mindless pastime enjoyed most by shiftless people. Perhaps that impression would be lessened if nonfishers understood more about wild water. Calling fishing a hobby is like calling brain surgery a job. The average visitor driving through Yellowstone sees no farther than the surface of the water. At best the lakes and streams are mirrors reflecting the surrounding scenery. For the alert fisherman, especially the fly-fisherman, the surface is not a mirror but a window.

Drive through Hayden Valley, along the Yellowstone River. If you aren't a fisher you'll see many things, but the river, except where it is ridden by waterfowl or waded by moose, will rarely enter your thoughts, much less stimulate your spirit.

It's different if you fish. The surface of the water tells a story: that hump followed by a series of lessening ripples (if they were larger they would be called standing waves) is proof of a rock or a stump submerged below. Those boulders on the far shore break the current, which moves slower close to them as the rock rubs, catches, and retards it; fish and smaller creatures press themselves close to such obstructions to ease the labor of maintaining position in the current. The quiet eddies behind this log jam are home for schools of minnows and the occasional dragonfly nymph that will feed on them if it gets a chance. Soft swirls and rings on the river's surface are made by trout rising gently to inhale newly hatched mayflies floating on the surface as their wings dry. This water is a wilderness of its own, full of life we do not know and beauties we have not imagined. The fisherman is not unique in appreciating it—any good naturalist finds it absorbing—but the fisherman has found special ways of becoming involved in it.

The Gardner River is a small rocky stream born at about 9,000 feet in the Gallatin Range a few miles southwest of Mammoth. In its entire length of about twenty miles it drops over 3,500 feet to its mouth at Gardiner, Montana, where it joins the Yellowstone (because of a quirk of events, the town is spelled with an "i" and the river is not). It flows from its headwaters pond at first north, then east, then southeast, and across Swan Lake Flat to its junction with Indian Creek at Indian Creek Campground, where it crosses under its first bridge, the road from Norris to Mammoth. After this brief encounter with civilization, it runs east and then north, around what we call the "back" of Bunsen Peak, where it drops into its little-traveled canyon. Far below the vertical basaltic cliffs, the river gurgles along, pouring 150 feet in one jump over Osprey Falls and out across the eastern foot of Bunsen Peak. It passes under another bridge, the Mammoth-to-Tower road, and almost immediately is joined from the southeast by Lava Creek, which has just left its own canyon. The greater flow then follows the west foot of Mt. Everts almost due north until it dumps, rather privately, into the Yellowstone River right at the park boundary in Gardiner.

I caught my first trout from the Gardner. When my brother, a fly-fisherman of long commitment and great learning, heard that I was going to move to Yellowstone he forced into my hands a complete fishing outfit, insisting that I learn to fly-fish and initiating me in a pastime that has at times been more a way of life than a sport. That first time, however, I was so intimidated by all the new devices and techniques that I was busy fiddling with the reel when a hungry little brown trout grabbed the fly I was paying no attention to, and I landed him only after considerable discussion and with relief that I'd chosen such a private spot for my first outing.

It turned out, as I was then just discovering, that fly-fishing is genuinely unlike other types of fishing. The flies—usually small, delicate imitations of various forms of insect life, made of feathers, hair, and yarn tied to a small hook—have practically no weight. They cannot be cast with a spinning or casting rod like other lures that weigh enough to be thrown and drag the line along behind them as they go. In fly-fishing, you are casting the weight of the line, instead. Fly lines, the best of which cost thirty dollars, are thicker than other fishing lines, thick enough to be worked back and forth through the air on the same principle as a bullwhip. The fly is attached to a fine monofilament leader on the end of the line, and simply goes along for the ride. Fly lines are usually plastic-coated and tapered on the end to improve the smoothness of the cast. It takes some practice to master this kind of casting, but to watch an accomplished caster working seventy feet of line on an eight-foot rod, to see the line looping and rolling straight out behind him, then, as he pushes the rod forward, to see the line roll cleanly out in front of him and settle gently across a stream, brings to mind more artful motions—ballet, perhaps—than are normally associated with fishing.

I spent my whole first summer fishing alone, in the privacy of my own home river, until I could push out a decent trout-fishing cast of forty feet and could catch Gardner fish with some regularity (it was only later that I even realized that some people could cast three times as far with less effort, and learned how much there actually was to getting good at fly-fishing).

Learning to cast was only the beginning, and the least fun, of learning to fly-fish. Fly-fishing introduced me to the aquatic world I mentioned earlier, led me to look under countless rocks in the shallows for squiggly little marvels I never dreamed existed. It led me to learn to read water: to study a current and its behavior for what it could tell me about what lay beneath—where the insects, shelter, and fish might be found. In this it taught me to appreciate running, moving water and the constancy of its workings. For never did I visit this river without seeing something new, some slight change in the flow or in the cut of a channel or in the shape of a bank. The changes became part of the excitement for me, and each spring I eagerly awaited the passing of the snowmelt runoff, not only so that I could fish but also to see what new shapes the flow had taken in favorite spots. Over the years some pools silted in; others deepened. A dislodged log would jam in a new position, and I would investigate it as the current dug a new trout shelter beneath it.

Most of this happened very slowly. A tree might be washed from its place on the bank by a sudden flood, but more often it would be undermined gradually, as the water loosened the soil, bit by bit, finally persuading the tree to fall. If rivers were human, they would be very patient people.

Without fly-fishing I would never have gotten to know the dipper, a chubby gray bird of the West that is surely the cheeriest friend a fisherman could hope for. The dipper, or water ouzel, has puzzled many visitors; a ranger I know was once approached by a concerned visitor who reported seeing "a little gray bird commit suicide by walking right into a creek." The dipper, song-bird-shaped and a totally unaquatic-looking creature, lives on aquatic insects and small fish, chasing them down in the water without the benefit of webbed feet. Dippers build nests on low overhanging banks, right at the water, and spend their days splashing around in the shallows, frequently in very fast water (I've also seen them in lakes, where they may "fly" along right under the surface for several yards in pursuit of insects). They get their name not from their habit of taking an occasional "dip" in the water but from an enchanting mannerism. As they jump from rock to rock, or sit surveying a likely current from shore, they do little bobbing knee-bends, one after another. At first it seems like a nervous twitch— something you hope they'll get over—but soon you get used to it and the dipper's little dance and shuffle become a special part of the day. Usually there is no more than one in sight, or maybe just a quick twittering warble as one flies by, but one winter when most of the river was rimmed with ice I saw half a dozen at one time, each inspecting a different icy shelf along successive pools, a veritable platoon of bobbing, dipping, "fly"-fishers, attracted to the warm open water of the lower river. I suppose they compete with the trout for food, as they compete with me for trout, but it makes no sense to me to worry about such congenial competition. They and the trout have been living together for a long time, and I don't interfere all that much. Fishing depends a lot on such things as dippers, anyway.

But it depends as well on occasional success at catching fish. Success depends on many things, including skill, but especially luck. However, after you practice a lot you learn that more is involved than mere mechanical proficiency or good fortune, and that at times you expect to catch fish just because, well, you *feel* that you will.

For example, there are days when I feel especially in touch with the end of the line, when I feel every lift of the current, every tick of the hook on gravel, every tug of vagrant weed. Such a day was an evening in July, the most productive (of fish, anyway) I ever had on the Gardner.

I'd just read a book about "soft-hackle" flies, simple little wet flies without tails or wings: just slim bodies of fur or floss with a turn of partridge feather near the head. The partridge feather was marked with fine black lines that gave each individual barbule of fiber a segmented look; the barbules, in the water, responded to every whisp of current as the fly drifted along below the surface. Together, they flexed and wiggled like the legs on a struggling insect. Or so the author suggested: I don't know what the trout took them for, only that they took them. As more than one naturalist has pointed out, trout, having no hands, must examine curious objects with their mouths, whether they think they are food or are just amusing themselves to pass the time.

According to my stream log the water this day was "gorgeous and low," and the angler was described as "a trifle low himself," though I don't recall why; the reason is probably better forgotten and surely was while fishing on this golden evening. As the shadow of Terrace Mountain climbed the slope of Everts in front of me, the trout greeted the flies with embarrassing abandon. Each pool yielded its fish hastily; no sooner would I make my cast and begin to probe the suspected pockets and recesses of the opposite bank with the quivering fly when another rainbow would yank it, and me, from our thoughtful investigations.

By the time I reached the pool I most wanted to fish, I'd already released eight or ten small trout, up to ten inches, and was planning to throw away all my flies and replace them with hundreds of these magical soft hackles. This pool, a larger, broader version of most on the river, was about 60 feet across, and from where it was formed by a fast, bouncy riffle to where it broadened and fanned into an ankle-deep tail it was perhaps 150 feet long. Along the east bank it was three to four feet deep, and the bank itself was undercut. It was one of the few pools on the river with that ominous darkness that says "big fish." Five years earlier I'd caught a fifteen-inch brown here on a grasshopper imitation, the first respectable brown I'd ever caught.

I squeezed a couple of small split-shot onto the leader about a foot above the fly (this practice is not recommended in the book I'd been reading, and many fly-fishers are offended by such a tactic as crass and unsporting, but I needed to work the fly deeply through this run, and I am generally unhampered by delicate sensitivities at such times) and waded into the shallows at the head of the pool. Remembering a lesson from another book, I pitched the fly slightly upstream of the pool, letting it sink as it washed from the riffle into the deep quiet water. I waited until it was moving slowly through the deep water, then, with a quick upward motion of the rod, I dragged it back to the surface. This, I'd read, imitated the upward motion of an emerging caddisfly. The fish must have thought so, and in an hour I doubled my total take, keeping a thirteen-and-a-half-inch brown for a late dinner. Unlike most pools on the river, this one occasionally yielded several fish from the same spot. Never before had it yielded fifteen as it did this night, but as long as they kept coming I felt no urge to move on. Toward dark I set the hook in a less yielding mouth, and was met with firm resistance followed by a quick run that peeled a few yards of line from my reel. The fish didn't jump, but had the quickness of a rainbow (I have an unscientific approach to this; it *felt* like a rainbow). After a few minutes of short zigs and zags, parrying with the fish as I moved down to the shallow flat at the tail of the pool, I was able to pull it near enough to see. It was a big rainbow, fifteen or sixteen inches, and still quite strong. My leader was too light to simply horse the fish ashore, and I was in for several more minutes of fight when the fish turned into the current and fled downstream toward the next riffle, one of the few up here that I was honestly afraid of—a vicious little roller coaster of jagged rocks and slippery footings, nowhere more than three feet deep but a guaranteed soaking for a clumsy wader. I held tight to the line as the fish swung below me and gained weight and speed in the quickening pull of the current. As soon as the line tightened directly downstream of me he broke off, taking the fly with him into the little rapid. I retrieved an empty line, with no regrets for once, pleased to have made the acquaintance, for the first time in five years, of the king of the pool.

These good-looking pools are usually not so generous. Another one, far downstream along the road to the North Entrance, frustrated me for a year or two. It was formed where a flat riffle broke over a bank and dropped into a hole the river had dug against the road embankment. I couldn't see the bottom of this one, and so I privately christened it the "salmon hole" because several huge fish could have hidden safely in the dark shadows under its broken surface.

I couldn't even figure out how to fish it. Approach from either side was by high banks where I was visible to the fish. As I climbed down to the stream I'd see smaller fish scatter from the shallows to the hole, presumably alerting whatever big fish lurked there. One evening I started in about a quarter mile above the hole, wading back and forth across the river between the deeper spots and catching just enough small fish to keep my interest up. I arrived at the riffle above the hole just about dusk. My normal approach was the standard approved one for fly-fishermen: I would try to cast up over the pool from below with a large floating fly. This time, however, unorthodoxy struck, and I crept through the weeds to a point near the upper end of the pool. The Gardner's fish aren't too particular about fly pattern; there's usually little need to imitate the prevailing insect activity precisely, so I rarely even think about such things. I had noticed, though, that on previous nights there were a good many large heavy-bodied crane flies in the air, flying just a few inches above the surface of the water, presumably mating (crane flies are those giant mosquitolike bugs that resemble flying daddy longlegs; their immature forms are usually aquatic, and the adults lay their eggs in quiet water). I couldn't imagine any self-respecting fish not noticing these big guys, and so I rummaged through my fly boxes for a likely imitation. The one I found was a graceful monster fashioned by my brother some years earlier of elk hair on a very long hook. It was well over an inch long altogether. Still crouched in the weeds, I fastened it to my leader and, somehow avoiding the high sage that waited to grab my backcast, I laid the line clear across the pool to the shallows near the far bank. Immediately the fast water in mid-pool dragged the line downstream, and the effect on the fly, on me, and on the fish, was electrifying. The fly floated quietly for an instant in the still water, and then, as the faster water hurried the long belly of line downstream, the fly was pulled out across the deeper water, skating hurriedly along on its light hackles and looking just like those big crane flies.

Its first such skating performance was uninterrupted but not, I was sure, unobserved. With a mild case of the shakes and a quickening pulse I let the line drift completely down, then, still crouched, I lifted it into a low backcast and again tossed it across the pool.

Again the line bellied and doubled in the fast current. Again the fly rested only a second, then began its quick skittering over the deep water. But it had moved only a couple of yards when a big brown trout shot from the pool near it and took the fly in a smooth downward motion. (Too surprised at that moment to consider this attack, I later realized how rarely it happens; fish usually just stick their heads up to the surface and inhale whatever is floating there, but this fish actually jumped high and clear of the water and took the fly on his way down, as he reentered the water nose-first. Perhaps prior experience with the crane flies had taught him that they escape if approached from underneath, or perhaps he just got so excited he missed the fly on his way up and lucked out and got it on the way down.) With a power that surprised me he bulled right up into the very point of the pool directly beneath the fastest water at its head. My leader was light, so I had to play him gently, and I figured on gradually wearing him out as he fought both the current and my line. I hurried to the tail of the pool to keep well below him, but I must have pulled too hard, for he turned and raced past me into a stumbling riffle full of snags and small rocks. I somehow managed to lead him past the worst snags to a grassy bank in the quieter water below, where I foolishly dragged him up onto the shore just as the fly fell from his mouth (again, this happens often in fishing books, but of the thousands of trout I've caught this is the only time it's happened to me). He was a little over fourteen inches, a fine fat resident brown, and a fish I probably shouldn't have removed from the gene pool but did.

The salmon hole is completely gone now, replaced by a shallow silty run that developed one spring during a violent spate of snowmelt. Its trout seem to have moved at the same time to a new big run that the river created about fifty yards upstream. I fished it recently after a long absence, and in about half an hour had at least fifteen rises to large grasshopper imitations, so I apparently didn't do the gene pool any permanent harm.

The brown trout came to North America in the early 1880s from the United Kingdom and Europe. It had reached Yellowstone (and the Gardner) by about 1890, where it quickly helped other nonnative trouts replace the local cutthroat trouts and grayling. One reason this happened is that browns are a lot harder to catch than cutthroats and therefore withstand fishing pressure much better. A preliminary study done in ponds near the park showed the cutthroats are sixteen times as easy to catch as browns (brook trout, known for gullibility, were only nine times as easy to catch as browns). People who have reason to think about such things wonder if cutthroats would be as easy to catch as they are if they, like the browns, had been fished over by savvy anglers since the 1300s. What must such predation do to the genetic makeup of a fish population, having the easiest caught individuals removed from hundreds of generations?

The question is of special interest in Yellowstone, where in recent years sportfishing has become primarily a matter of fun rather than of meat acquisition. Because there are too many visitors to feed each a wild trout, park regulations and modern sportfishing fashions have combined to promote "catch-and-release" fishing—fishing for fun, not meat. Under proper lure restrictions, practically all the released fish will live to be caught again and again.

But the browns, as hard as they are to catch that first time, are harder than hell to catch again. I learned that on my home river. A tiny step-across tributary ran past my quarters, bordering the lawn and then dipping into a sage field for maybe fifty yards before swinging behind a neighbor's lawn, where it widened into a small weed-filled pond. The water was partly runoff from the hot springs, so it was mineral-rich and supported heavy vegetation and lots of insect life. Brown trout were there, apparently remnants from hatchery ponds that had once sat nearby and had been fed by the creek. The pond was fished only by a couple of neighborhood kids who rarely caught anything, and the neighborhood osprey, who rarely put anything back. And me, for a few weeks one summer.

There was a narrow channel about three feet wide through the weeds, then the pond itself, about 40 feet wide and three feet deep at the most. The whole stretch ran no more than 120 feet, the length of one backyard. The trout rose easily to insects in the quiet water of the channel and the pond, and I could see them clearly, holding there within short casting distance. On hot bright days they all settled into a slightly deeper depression in the middle of the pond. From a hillock that bordered the yard I could see them holding there, in two rows. There seemed to be about fifteen of them.

I started fishing this stretch one evening after work. It was very civilized, standing on the comfortable lawn and dropping a wiggly little wet fly in front of each trout and snaking them out across the weedbeds as soon as they were hooked. I quickly measured each fish, clipped off a portion of the adipose fin (a harmless if insulting operation), and slid them back into the water. The first evening I caught five, measuring four to thirteen inches. The next night I caught five more, four to ten inches, and again clipped them all. The next night, two more. Five nights later, seven more. The afternoon after that I caught five more. The twenty-first fish I caught had a clipped fin; it was the thirteen-incher I'd caught the first day, a couple of weeks earlier. Over the next few weeks I caught a few more with clipped fins, but I'd learned a new respect for the brown trout. As informal as my little study had been, it had shown me what tough teachers the brown trout can be. I preferred easier.

A friend from Iowa, an enthusiastic outdoorsman, visited me one September. Because of an eccentric graduate chairman we had once taught under, we had adopted a formal manner of addressing each other, after our chairman's manner.

"Mr. Palmer, you must learn about fly-fishing. This isn't the Big Muddy, you know. We have trout here, not those disgusting mudfish you're so fond of catching."

"Mr. Schullery, if you can suppress your elitism about the Mississippi, I would *like* to learn about fly-fishing."

His first lesson was on the Lamar, near Calfee Creek. The upper Lamar contains many quick, unschooled cutthroat trout, easily caught most of the time. When we walked down to the river in front of the patrol cabin it was late afternoon but the sun was still bright on the water. It would not have looked, to an Iowa angler, like a very promising time to catch a fish.

"You sit down here on this rock, Mr. Palmer. I must find a grasshopper." I kicked through some nearby brush and quickly sorted an inch-long hopper from the leaves.

"Watch this closely, Mr. Palmer. It's important." I tossed the hopper into the stream about six feet from shore. It landed kicking, stirring up little ripples as it was washed along. It had floated only a few feet when it disappeared in a splashy blur of trout mouth, a small explosion of water that left Mr. Palmer wide-eyed. He was hooked. Within a few minutes I had him slapping a few feet of line out over the water, giving these unruly little cutthroats a chance at a bushy dry fly. One after another they poked their noses up under it, inhaled it, mouthed it thoughtfully for a second, then spit it out and sank back to shelter. Each time Mr. Palmer watched the whole rise, take, and rejection with a slack jaw and a slack line, never once trying to hook the fish.

"Mr. Palmer, you have to set the hook when they take the fly. Weren't you paying attention to the lecture?"

"Yes, Mr. Schullery, I understand. I saw you do it." He was earnest in the face of my exasperation.

"Well, then, Mr. Palmer, why didn't you set the damn hook?!"

"I never think of it at the time, Mr. Schullery. It's all so interesting to watch."

A few days later I took him to the upper Gardner. I led him to the bank and rigged up the rod as I continued my instruction.

"Now, Mr. Palmer, you should learn about where trout hold in the current." As I spoke I worked about thirty-five feet of line into the air, keeping it airborne above me, casting back and forth, ready to deliver. This was one of the few stretches of river I know of where what I was about to do was not the worst kind of reckless arrogance.

"They like water at the edges of the current, Mr. Palmer. See that rock there with the little eddy behind it, where the water is sort of still?" He was attentive, if skeptical, as I dropped a small dry fly into the spot, where it was instantly drowned but not eaten by one of the suicidal brook trout that inhabited this precious run. Mr. Palmer choked quietly as I whipped the fly back with a triumphant "Aha!" Then, as I dried it with some false casts, I remarked casually, "Look for calmer breaks in the current, Mr. Palmer, even if you can't see a rock or anything, like this one up here." I laid the fly onto a little slick in midstream, immediately grabbing it back from another splashy rise. This was not instruction; this was performance. Again and again I brought trout up, hooking a couple, missing most, reveling in the show they and I were putting on. And each time I'd raise a fish, Mr. Palmer, his voice a mixture of envy, respect, and disdain, would mumble, "Mr. Schullery, you bastard," or "This can't be..." I don't know how many fish I showed him in fifteen minutes, but it was many more than I'd imagined I would. The Gardner and its trout performed royally in beginning the education of yet another fly-fisherman.

A home river is that rarest of friends, the one who frequently surprises you with new elements of personality without ever seeming a stranger. The revelations are gifts, not shocks. Like Mr. Palmer, I seemed always to be discovering new secrets of the river; they weren't really secrets at all, just places waiting for me to become smart enough to notice them. It might be a new trout lie, hidden under a log and invisible from the trail I usually walked; a beaver dam that must be fished this season because it will be silted shallow by next; a deer bed in the willows behind a favorite pool; a deep pocket I never noticed until I walked the bank opposite the trail. What makes this so precious, like so many other meaningful pastimes, is the anticipation of revelations yet to come, or discoveries not fully understood, like the dark pool swarming with diptera that I discovered one day while searching for a drowning victim and never later returned to, off duty. Like the stretches of canyon water I never fished, that pool is a mystery and a promise, probably worth more in anticipation than it will be in actual sport.

Some revelations are bigger. Recently, in an isolated stretch of the upper river, where only brook trout were thought to reside, a pocket of rainbows was found, survivors of some long-forgotten stocking mission of several decades ago. They lived, unknown and unfished, in one short stretch of river, neither expanding their range into better traveled waters nor shrinking into oblivion. Further study may prove them to be of considerable scientific value. Like the other nonnative trouts in Yellowstone— brook, brown, and lake—they were placed here in the early days of fisheries science, before distinct strains of each species were hopelessly crossed and mixed in the great trout factories of modern hatcheries and in countless rivers where thoughtless and well-intentioned fisheries crews dumped new strains of trout on top of existing native populations. Yellowstone has waters, including my home river, that were stocked before that energetic "management" chaos mutilated our western trout taxonomy and were not stocked since; waters that now may give more than sport—they may yield museum-pure strains of trout that we thought we'd lost. It may not be easy for the nonfisherman to comprehend why such knowledge makes the fishing more exciting than it otherwise would be, but it is immensely satisfying to know such a thing. Fishing is a quest for knowledge and wonder as much as a pursuit of fish; it is as much an acquaintance with beavers, dippers, and other fishermen as it is the challenge of catching a trout. My home river does not always give me her fish, but the blessings of her company are always worth the trip.

The Bear Doesn't Know

There is no trail to the pond. It lies, unnamed as far as I know, in a flat alpine saddle between Gray and Little Quadrant peaks, a perfect mountain meadow. There are a few whitebark pine trees, and the whole little plain, a few acres, is quite level. The pond is toward the north end; it may be a spring, or it may get its water during spring melt from the surrounding mountain walls. The elevation is near 9,000 feet. I doubt that the place is as warmly hospitable most of the year as we found it that day in early September.

We'd been told that we could leave the Fawn Pass Trail, to the south, and ride over the saddle by following animal trails and meadows. It's not possible to get lost, with the surrounding mountains serving as such unmistakable landmarks, but I was still a little edgy about such an extended bushwhack. Horses need a lot more space than hikers, and this was steep country.

The pond has a tiny overflow on its east end. The trickle goes a few yards and turns northward, dropping into a forested ravine. The ravine was our recommended avenue north, but it was mostly trailless. We soon were hopping back and forth over the stream, seeking the easiest course for the horses. Too often to suit us, we could only travel in the little streambed itself; steep banks and deadfall kept us pinned there, and the horses slipped and lurched along the wet rocky streambed.

31

We didn't notice tributaries, but they were there. Within a mile of the pond the rivulet was a genuine creek, tumbling and twisting over logs and rocks and making passage even more difficult for the horses.

Once, seeking safer trails for the horses, we climbed the east slope of the ravine for some distance above the stream, so far that its noise was inaudible. While moving through fairly open timber on a gentler slope, we heard a large animal crashing through the brush and deadfall ahead of us. My companion, riding ahead of me, got a glimpse of the animal. "I think we scared up a bear."

I was skeptical. We'd been jumping elk for two days, and one large animal can sound pretty much like another when it's running frightened.

Traditional wisdom has it that a surprised bear will often flee until it locates a good spot from which to check out what frightened it. About 150 yards farther along my companion pointed up the slope to our right. "There's the bear."

She stopped her horse, and as I caught up I saw an adequately large grizzly, about fifty yards off, standing on his hind legs. He was watching us from the edge of a tight stand of lodgepole pines.

My companion asked, "Should we take his picture?" just as the bear seemed to decide something; he came down on all fours and took a step down the hill toward us.

"No, the horses haven't seen him yet and I think we'd better just keep going."

We rode quickly out of his sight, but within a few minutes we were rimrocked by a sharp side ravine off the main creek, and we had to retrace our steps back to the bear. He was gone, and we moved on down to the stream and continued north.

The horses amazed us that way. On this trip they plodded past any number of elk and coyotes, and one moose we encountered at about thirty feet, without any sign of noticing. We heard but did not see bighorn sheep; their tenor baaing at least got Midget to perk up his ears. On several occasions, bull elk, getting in voice for later recreations, bugled hoarsely from the slopes above us. The horses plodded on.

But of all that trip—the echoes of elk bugles ringing across the stone walls, the stark lawnlike alpine meadows, the midnight mountains half lost in starshadow, a golden eagle soaring off the point of Gray Peak, and all the rest—that moment near the bear lingers most persistently in my memory. I've relived that encounter hundreds of times, chasing it around in my mind, picking at it for detail or depth and often finding them; running those frames through the projector, editing, enhancing, and embellishing them without wanting or needing to. The bear came down on all fours. He (we both made him male in our minds) watched us until he knew we saw him. He decided something. He came down on all fours and took a step forward. He decided something, he came down on all fours and took a step forward down the hill and into my soul.

That, I had often been told, is the way to see your grizzly—a chance meeting on his doorstep. Whether in a moment's glance or through a morning of distant observations, you must see him at home. The time it takes to see a grizzly, the waiting involved, makes it an event long before it happens. Anticipation and romance crowd into your consciousness so that you may worry, while you're "getting ready," that the bear will somehow disappoint (which isn't possible), or that you will somehow be inadequate and will fail to enjoy, or comprehend, or be adequately enriched by the encounter. That is probably not possible either, if only because once you have realized just how special the event is your subconscious will take care of making the experience memorable. Like your first kiss or shaking hands with the President, it is memorable even if it went wrong.

And, appropriately, the bear doesn't know; it all means so much to you, but the bear forgets it almost right away.

Since the 1890s, until recently, you could see your grizzly a lot more easily, and a lot less appropriately, at a garbage dump. In the 1960s those few people who knew somebody who could get them into the Trout Creek dump (not near public roads, and off limits except to researchers and park officials) were likely to see anywhere from twenty to a hundred grizzlies at once, a visual overload I have trouble imagining, and am just as glad I can't share, because these dozens of bears were all up to their appetites in garbage.

Feeding Yellowstone's grizzlies at dumps was just as much an institution as feeding the black bears along the roads, and feeding the black bears was the most desired of all visitor experiences for millions of people. I remember the black bears myself. In the early 1960s my parents brought me to Yellowstone and a small black bear tried to eat my sister's camera (or my sister; we never were sure). What I've seen in Yellowstone has convinced me that feeding wild bears, in dumps or along roads, is a stupid, ugly, typically human thing to do. What bothers me most is not so much the people who get hurt but what it does to the bears. Hundreds of people were clawed or scratched in those days (the black bears did some mean work on a few, but most were just scratched and scared; four people have been killed by bears in Yellowstone since 1872, out of seventy million visitors), but look what they were doing: ignoring all sorts of warnings; smearing jelly on a child's face so they could photograph the bear licking the child; placing children on the bear's back for a picture; feeding bears film wrappers, cigarette butts, ice cubes, cherry bombs, and even food; running over an occasional cub . . . in short, doing everything to test the forebearance of an incredibly patient providence. Providence frequently took the form of a mama black bear who finally had had too much and took a swat at the hundredth citizen of Poughkeepsie to make a grab at her cubs that day. Then the rangers would be called to destroy the "dangerous bear." The rangers, who were in on the problem and yet preferred the company of bears most of the time, ended up destroying dozens of bears. Life is not simple, even for idyllic types like rangers and bears.

The rangers knew the bears shouldn't be fed. It had been illegal since 1902. The people did, too; a survey conducted in 1953, when the great Yellowstone "bear-jams" were beginning to reach their mile-long boiling-radiator peak, revealed that 95 percent of the people knew they were breaking the law when they fed bears. Only the bears didn't know. Being bears, extraordinarily adaptive omnivores, they were simply cashing in on an obvious good thing. The Rocky Mountain Free Lunch. Dill pickles, twinkies, ham on rye . . . the wilderness was never like *this*.

The only difference at the dumps was that servers and served were more select groups. Park employees, researchers, and a chosen few dignitary-gawkers were privy audience to lunchtime for one of North America's most spectacular evolutionary achievements, the grizzly bear. But, I am happy to say, this culinary camelot was doomed.

In the early 1970s Yellowstone officials cut off the gravy train. They stopped roadside feeding and they closed the open-pit garbage dumps. The dumps had been frequented by grizzlies for more than eighty years, and their closing (with the bears thus deprived of trash food) caused a monstrous national controversy, with political influence, scientific careers, outrageous egos, and, perhaps, the bears' welfare all at stake. By 1977 only one garbage dump remained open, a small scar near the north entrance, used by the town of Gardiner. Through a long-standing agreement between the park service and the town, this dump was a part of the community's way of life. For all the usual political and practical reasons, it was more difficult to close this dump, which serviced a private community, than it was to close the others, which serviced only park facilities. In every case, something else had to be done with the garbage, and it was harder to convince a small border town to spend the extra money than it was to organize better garbage disposal in the park.

Everyone knew the dump would have to be closed eventually. Not only was it unnaturally influencing the movements of the neighborhood bears, not only was it a flagrant violation of E.P.A. standards, it was a fabulously disgusting sight, even as dumps go.

Someone in the park decided that it would be useful, both scientifically and politically, to know more about the bears who used this dump. It was common knowledge that on most nights there were a few grizzlies at the dump, only a mile or so from town. Kids shot at them with .22's. Grown-ups (ha!) drove around the locked gate at the main road and went down the old service road to the dump so they could sit in their cars and watch the bears. But nobody could say how many bears there were, or how many of them were grizzlies, or if any had radio collars or ear tags from the Interagency Grizzly Study Team. Bears move pretty far sometimes, and knowing how many use what areas is important information when figuring out population levels and such.

A few rangers began taking turns monitoring the dump. Some time after 10:00 P.M., they'd unlock the gate, drive in, lock it behind them and drive the dirt road to where it passed behind a rise and ended at the dump. They'd sit there an hour or so, trying to identify individuals by their size, colors, markings, and other features (bears are as individual as people in appearance, but very few people get to see them enough to get to know what to look for; I never got any good at it).

I'd only been to the dump once before, in daylight, so I didn't have a very good fix on the setting. The Gallatin Mountains, specifically Sepulchre and Electric, slope quickly into the Yellowstone River valley on the park boundary. Between the river and the mountains is a narrow shelf, actually a rolling flat, mostly bare of trees, about half a mile wide. In a hollow, between a low ridge and the base of the mountains, sat the dump. Well, it didn't really sit; it sort of festered. It was perfectly accessible to the grizzlies who roamed the extremely rough country in the north Gallatins.

That evening, as we rounded the rise and bounced along into the dump, Les played the spotlight across the footslopes of the mountain to our left, locking onto four or five brown bear bottoms as they galloped over the ridge into a gulch.

"The engine scares them away. They come back in twenty minutes or so."

We parked at the very end of the road, engine and lights off, with garbage dump on three sides and a small hill immediately to our right. The car sat on a little earth ramp that pointed out over the portion of the dump then in use, but off to our left and behind us stretched several acres of American Fantasia: washing machines and couches, cellophane and freezer wrapper, detergent boxes and tin cans—the broken, the rusty, and the disposable.

"They usually come in through that draw." Les pointed straight ahead to the far side of the clutter, where the hillside split into two humps with a gap between them. "Sometimes they come right over that hill," he continued, pointing to my right, "and right past your side of the car." I voted for the draw.

Fifteen minutes later, our eyes now fully accustomed to the weak moonlight and our ears searching the night for sounds (a rat scrambling over a pile of tin cans sounds a lot like a bear when you're expecting a bear), Les pointed at the draw. "There's one."

Later, I had time to realize that my brief daytime visit to the dump had left me with a poor notion of its size. In the flat moonlight my eyes had misplaced the draw about twice as far away as it really was. So, laboring under this significant misimpression, I saw a bear twice as large as a bear should be. "God, lookit how big!" Eloquence under pressure is natural to the experienced woodsman.

Les didn't answer. I assumed he was as agog as I was, but when I looked over he wasn't even watching. He was calmly taking notes— his clipboard resting on the steering wheel—about the bear's arrival. I squirmed and gaped. The bear lumbered silently down the draw toward the dump (and us), casting a moonshadow like the Astrodome. This bear wasn't large; this bear was *vast*.

Before long, he placed himself in a helpful context. He wandered past an old ice box and didn't dwarf it quite as much as I would have expected. I then realized that I'd been seeing wrong, and that he was a reasonable grizzly bear after all, maybe 300 or 350 pounds. A boar, a little lean, a little ratty; he looked as if he'd slept in his clothes.

Most of the others we saw, on that and subsequent nights, were sleek and fat. Strictly speaking, it isn't true that a partial diet of garbage makes bears sick, but it may increase the risk of natural sickness as essentially solitary animals get together in big groups where diseases that might normally be restricted to one can be transmitted to many.

Before long the boar was joined by a few others, a family group of sow with two young of the year. A coyote skirted the place nervously, almost seeming to need the company more than the food.

I'm sure that the scientists who spent years studying the dump bears in the 1960s got to the point where every moment of watching wasn't a thrill, but I didn't spend years at it, and the excitement didn't wear off. Even after an hour or so of watching them, there was always a gut-tightening surge of adrenalin when a new one wandered close, or when a giant head suddenly loomed up directly in front of the car (one ranger who made his first trip with me later couldn't get over the size of the heads; whenever I'd pick up the clipboard he'd tell me to "make sure you say that they have really large heads").

And watching them, just sitting there watching them feed, was enchanting. Sorting through the junk (one imagines the bear casually pitching a refrigerator over his shoulder, but most of the sorting was of a more delicate type), poking a claw through some wet paper (did I miss any lettuce here last night?), or strolling along swaying that big head back and forth, the bear is just like any other open-minded shopper. Is this detergent good in cold water? Are the tomatoes fresh? Do the coupons apply to the day-old bread? No, you can't have that, I saw it first. There is so much curiosity, so much of the small boy picking up pretty rocks, that you quickly begin to see personhood in the bear. Or you begin to see bearhood in yourself. It's all the same.

They can get used to the same things, too: cans with sharp edges, rubbery vegetables, a table too close to the kitchen, fire . . . Fire? Yes, fire, the great Bad Guy of all children's animal stories (along with Nasty Hunters and Wolves, of course). It seemed that some of the stuff the dump received every day was burnable, and desultory efforts to light it usually left a couple of hot spots at night. The bears pawed all around the flames, their noses so close they'd reflect orange. I understand that this happens at other bear dumps, and occasionally a bear gets too close and gets burned or singed. Adaptive omnivores indeed.

One night a supervisor asked us to satisfy his curiosity about a popular product then being touted in magazines as good defense against wild animals. It was an air horn, one of those little cannisters that otherwise sensible people blast into your ear at football games. People were apparently being suckered into buying them as protection against grizzly bears. If a bear charges you, just toot this thing at him and he'll run away. Sounds great, I'll take two.

People who believe that a good loud noise was sure to scare a grizzly bear away certainly couldn't be people who have ever heard grizzly bears making loud noises at one another. A loud noise, especially if the grizzly hasn't been having a good day or is just in the mood to match loud noises with someone, doesn't sound like a good way to protect yourself from a grizzly bear. Who knows what the bear will think about it? There's a lot to be said for loud noises when you're hiking; if you make them as you walk along you're much less likely to surprise some animal that's sleeping in the middle of the trail; most animals move off a ways if they hear you coming. But once you've surprised one, and it's checking you out on its hind legs or rolling toward you for a closer look (or worse), you might as well count on divine intervention as make a loud noise at it. Either might work, but I bet that if God does intervene he won't use an air horn.

Anyway, Les and I waited until there was a sow, about 250 pounds or so, with a big yearling, about half her size, right in front of the car. They were just getting involved in a huge pile of radishes (I can't imagine how anyone could come to have so many radishes as this to throw away at once), no more than thirty feet from the steering wheel. It was dark, and I wondered aloud at how *I* would react if someone cut loose behind my back with one of those horns at a time and place like this. The bears were chowing down with some enthusiasm when Les, in the driver's seat, stuck the can out the window and gave it a short, piercing toot. Both bears gave a start, then resumed eating.

"Hmm. Not much response." We were whispering.

"No. Maybe you should try a longer blast." Les nodded, held the can out the window, and pressed the button for several seconds. At this point the patrol car windshield seemed to be as much protection as my Audubon Society membership. Les, a calm, sensible man, had his revolver in his other hand, just in case the air horn said something horribly insulting in bear talk, but the revolver didn't look up to stopping a grizzly bear if one decided to come through the windshield.

Luckily, bears are patient, and though they don't know that rangers are their friends, they don't know how much damage they can do, either. The second blast definitely disturbed them, because they stopped eating. They both looked around at the dark car. I was never sure what the bears thought of the car, or if they could see us well through the windshield, or if they knew that cars usually have people in them (I don't know as much as bears don't know). These two, after a minute of checking us out, wandered away. Either they were restless, or annoyed, or tired of the radishes, or something else. I couldn't say, for sure, but the air horn wasn't very convincing.

Outdoor writers, who have little to lose, get a lot of mileage out of talking about bear repellents that have been proven in some hunting camp or other. Paradichlorobenzene (moth balls) is mentioned frequently as a good bear repellent. Yellowstone grizzly bears have been observed *eating* paradichlorobenzene. I know of a number of scientists who are working very hard to come up with effective "aversive agents" that might lessen the risk of harm when humans and bears encounter one another. Studies of this kind are necessary, I know; with so many people insisting on using bear country, there has to be a way to keep the injury rate as low as possible if only so the bears won't get a lot of bad publicity and end up being killed off. But I regret that it's necessary. Hiking in grizzly country without risk is like kissing your sister. One of the most important parts of the grizzly country experience, besides its rareness, is that hackle-raising humility that comes from knowing one is in the presence of a superior predator. Of knowing that one is, for once, a potential prey species. I hope we never reach the point where we are not allowed to have that feeling, but, given the gloomy outlook for the grizzly bear in the lower forty-eight, we may not have to worry about the feeling in the first place before long.

Though I learned a lot at the dump, watching those grizzlies feed, search, nap, and occasionally square off for a few therapeutic loud noises, my basic convictions about the bear were only strengthened. Most basic of all is my belief that even though grizzly bears are capable of explosive devastation, they can be lived with in places like Yellowstone. Look at the facts. Here is an animal that can bite through your skillet, or dismantle your recreational vehicle (removing the side nearest the refrigerator), or kill an elk with a good swat (ask yourself how many times you'd have to hit an elk with your hand to kill it), or reduce a dead tree to sawdust to get some ants, and it hardly ever *kills* anybody. Grizzlies can kill people, and we give them plenty of chances, the way we crowd into their country; in recent years grizzlies have been killing more people, a sign that we've reached some limit of their tolerance and the capacity of their country. But they continue to show a restraint that amazes me, and that we hardly deserve.

I don't underestimate them, and I've had my share of memorable dreams involving me, a grizzly bear or two, and small crowded places; being mauled by a grizzly bear has always struck me as one of those wilderness experiences where the novelty wears off almost right away. But look at what the bears put up with: all the thousands of sweet- or sour-smelling, careless, bacon-frying hikers who intrude on them for every one "incident" (an unfortunate euphemism that probably can't be avoided) that results in tragedy. Like a nuclear reactor, or a heart, we take the grizzly bear for granted until it does something we weren't expecting. I think, in the bear's case at least, that the problem is in our expectations, not in the bear's behavior.

We certainly make too much of the viciousness of the bear. Any species that survives by eating its neighbors is bound to make the community jumpy, but keep in mind that most of the time bears do no more than eat their neighbor's lawn, or dig up his flower bed.

Partly because in modern America being killed and eaten by a wild animal is incredibly rare, and partly because such an event is great press, we have a distorted view of the ferocity of grizzly bears. Every precaution must be taken—I always carry some honest fear into grizzly country—but let's be realistic about what the grizzly bear is and isn't.

The grizzly *isn't* a man-eater in the traditional sense. Unlike the famous lions and leopards of Africa or the tigers of India, the grizzly doesn't make its living eating people (a population of brown bears once got reasonably good at it in an isolated part of Russia, but even then relatively few people were killed). Some of the big cats have killed over a hundred people *each*. Fifty years ago, when Jim Corbett was hunting down man-eaters in the Kumaon Hills of India, he wasn't just some rich white hunter off on a sporting jaunt. He was a national hero. Those people were being dragged from large settled villages, nightly, by tigers that lived in good part on human flesh.

Rare is the grizzly bear that has killed more than one person. Many became famous as stock killers, back before 1900, but even then some profitable exaggeration occurred to the advantage of aggrieved stockmen and glory-seeking hunters. Unlike the cats, the grizzly is primarily a vegetarian. Both grizzlies and blacks can and do kill people, and once in a while eat them, and even less once in a while kill them *to* eat them, but not as a matter of habit.

A friend of mine once outbluffed a young grizzly. She was hiking alone when the bear rushed toward her, apparently interested in dinner. She waved her arms, growled all manner of foul insults, and informed the bear in her biggest voice that he must understand that she was larger and meaner than he, and was in no way to be considered dinner. Each of his charges was met and stopped by a louder and more blustery one by her. Each time the bear backed off, just unsure enough of himself to chicken out. She doesn't remember how many charges there were, but knowing her normal calm I wish I could have been there. She's gifted with language, and I would have loved to hear her when *really* inspired. The bear finally went away.

Friends have seen bison, or elk, or their own horses, grazing in the same meadow with a bear. There are times of truce, apparently, as there seem to be times that the predator only preys when the prey "acts like dinner," that is, runs or panics. A ranger I know once saw a grizzly charge an unsuspecting elk. The elk continued grazing, even after the grizzly was clearly in view. The bear stopped, probably puzzled at this imperturbable ungulate. After studying the elk from a short distance for a moment, the bear wandered away (perhaps thinking, "Gee, I could have sworn that was dinner").

Now I don't recommend charging or bluffing grizzly bears, or even ignoring them. I find the whole thing delightfully confusing. Grizzly bear authorities tell us that if we are confronted by a grizzly bear and cannot escape by climbing a tree, we should play dead. It seems that the most damaging grizzly-hiker encounters (statistically speaking; there are exceptions) are unexpected, when a hiker surprises a bear on a kill or with a mate or young. In those circumstances the bear's response may be instinctive and quick defense, and a grizzly's defense puts most good offenses to shame. The idea behind playing dead is that an inert reclining being is not threatening. Though not a sure thing, playing dead has proven itself, statistically again, the best choice. Sometimes the bear will come over and roll the "body" around a little, or munch thoughtfully on an elbow (imagine lying quietly during this), but unless the hiker panics and struggles (acts like dinner?), the odds are good that the bear will go away.

What puzzles me is that grizzlies eat lots of dead bodies, feeding heavily on winter-killed elk in those springs when carrion is available. How is it that *this* dead body, a frightened hiker, doesn't get the same treatment? I suppose part of the answer is that at the moment of the encounter the bear wasn't looking for carrion, though I'd hate even more to be in that hiker's shoes in early spring, when elk carcasses are most available.

Like almost everything else about grizzlies (or many other things worth knowing about), we can't be sure we understand. We have to admit that their food habits surprise us. A few years ago scientists observed a Yellowstone grizzly passing up easily available dead meat to hunt and kill elk of its own. Even the carcass feeders are still teaching us. The prevailing attitude about bear food makes them "foul feeders." Any old-time hunter will tell you that "them bears don't get really worked up about a carcass until it's good and ripe." Actually, no one has proved that bears have a taste preference for rotten meat over fresh meat, but it has to be a lot easier for them to sniff out a rank carcass than a new one. For that reason they may feed more on the rank ones. They may also prefer a rank carcass because it will contain more maggots, a bear delicacy. What bears need and what people find disgusting tell us more about people than it does about bears. As the beggar and dump bears most dishearteningly demonstrated, willingness to try new foods is the bear's special blessing; even were the animal able to do so, it could not afford to worry that its diet causes people to suspect a character deficiency. Maggots, escargot; rancid elk meat, buttermilk; who's really deficient here? No one, I think, but I figure we're more suspect than the bears; at least bears never make judgments about people.

A 600-pound grizzly bear, a nearly black boar, was being held for helicopter relocation at the Fire Cache. His culvert trap, a circular metal tube about twelve feet long and four feet across (made from corrugated metal culvert tubing) mounted on a pair of wheels for towing, was parked in one of the long garage stalls. It was a cool dark tunnel, away from the prying eyes of tourists and most employees, a quiet and rather dank spot that I imagined might even be to the bear's liking were he not caged up in the trap.

I shuffled self-consciously the length of the passageway to the culvert at the far end—not sure whom I was afraid of disturbing—and took a seat on an upended bucket about a yard from the metal grill at the front end of the trap, the end the bear faced.

There was enough light from small high windows to see him well. He was resting on his belly, his paws drawn up near his chin, his nose a few inches behind the grill. He didn't move as I seated myself, or during the fifteen or so minutes that we sat staring at each other in that damp corner.

Bears don't have big eyes, so they are lost in that infinity of fur and fat and ripplingly smooth motion, two small dark sparks evolved to deal primarily in the nearby because what else need a 600-pound grizzly bear worry about? Like the Union officer who threw the auxiliary sails overboard shortly after his huge ironclad battleship was launched because nobody was going to make *him* hurry, this bear needed better eyes nowhere near so much as his neighbors did. If I'm too far away for him to see me, it's my responsibility to keep it that way. I try to look him over, but I keep coming back to the eyes. I have big hands, and his claws seem as big as my fingers; I am darkly amused that he could probably hook his claws into the grate that separates us and rip it from its welded frame. In this case, what the bear doesn't know won't hurt me. But from the claws I am drawn back to the eyes, steady, unblinking, either dull beyond my comprehension or perceptive beyond my imagination, staring with evident but unlikely calm back at me. His ears are reduced by the bulk of their surroundings—a massive round skull over heavily muscled jaws—to unimportance, like some anatomical afterthought stapled indecisively to the finished animal after it left the factory. Bears hear well, but, as with their eyesight, from my bucket in front of this one I figure that they don't really need to. I wouldn't insult *this* one if he was stone deaf.

When I'm not held accountable to human reason or scholarly accuracy, which is to say when I'm alone, I lapse into a rather personal approach to what interests me; I talk to things, trying to calm a squirming fish as I struggle to free a hook and release it, reasoning vainly with a horse that is more interested in trailside clover than in getting to the corral by dark (then cussing him as I rein him in), or greeting the elk, bedded in the snow by my door, with a mixture of joy, respect, and fear. So I want to talk to this bear. I sit there wanting to *understand*, wanting to see something in those eyes besides my reflection (and not being seduced by the rhetorical opportunities of seeing oneself reflected in grizzly eyes), something in his passive stillness besides brute patience. But I don't know how to start. What to say? I know that the trout doesn't understand my reassurances, I know the horse recognizes impatience in my voice and figures he can get one more mouthful of clover before the reins pull him away, and I never have figured out what those elk think of my silly greetings, but the talking is useful, at least for me. It's a kind of reaching out. But the bear is too much. I would ask questions if I thought the bear had answers, or if I thought that by asking them, out loud, I might sense an answer of my own. I most feel a need to express regret or apology for the circumstances of our meeting, to apologize for the idiot who baited the bear into a settled area where he had to be trapped before someone was hurt; again the bear would have no answer. I would express admiration for his size and power, or for his wildness... admiration, at last, for his utter independence of my admiration, or of anything else I think or want.

That is probably why he is so important to me; it's a one-way street of fascination, I caring most for his detachment and nearly alien disregard for me, caring that he can exist without caring about me. This bear is at my mercy, vulnerable to the moronic growth of commerce, the mindless pressures of human population, and the mechanical finality of a good rifle, and he doesn't even know it. He'll die some day, and all like him, never having grasped where he stood in relation to humans, never having sat on a bucket and studied one.

This is good, I decide, and it's also a little spooky. The bear in the trap suddenly seems a lot farther away, not just a yard but uncrossable distances, and I am chilled and uncomfortable on my bucket in the presence of so untouchable a spirit. I must stir uneasily, for suddenly the audience is over. From somewhere deep in the cavernous innards of the bear, like a train still far away in a mountain tunnel, a rumbling hum begins. Impatience. The menace in the sound is palpable, though the actual animal, eyes unblinking, claws at rest on the culvert floor, has not moved at all. I still can't talk to the bear, not even an "Okay, okay, I'm going," as I right the bucket, return it to its place by the wall, and with one last wishful look at those incredible eyes, hurry from the building and into the bright morning sun.

Jumping Water

The soft inner walls of the lower Gardner River, as often dried mudflow as sandstone, are constantly sloughing off, like some patient earthen glacier pouring slowly from the mountain above. Like the whole west face of Mt. Everts, the walls of the inner canyon are a cavalcade of gullies, gravel slides, and dirt piles. The jumble is so confusing that you can best appreciate what's happening—how the river keeps clearing the slipping debris from its path—from a distance. When seen from high on the slopes of Sepulchre, across from Everts, the Gardner's course makes more sense; the great ridged face of Everts is pantomimed in miniature by the Gardner canyon walls at its feet.

Here and there in the inner canyon, harder crests of stone have been left jutting free from the receding dirt walls. One such prominence, Eagle Nest Rock, used to host an osprey pair; what is left of their nest, weathered silver and battered apart, still tops the tower like an unruly wig. One day while fishing in the canyon I saw an osprey alight there as if checking out the neighborhood. For a moment I had hope that they'd return to the rock after many years of absence, but the bird rested only briefly, then flew away. I don't know why they don't return—I've heard they left years ago after a wrecked tank truck poisoned the fish in that stretch of river—but it could be heavier traffic than in earlier days, or too many photographers. For whatever reason, the big nest remains an empty home.

Bighorn sheep move into the canyon in late fall, spending part of their time grazing up above in the open on McMinn Bench and the rest along the steep walls of the canyon. They stay there until early spring, some of the ewes not leaving until after lambing time.

So close to the road, so easily approached, these sheep seem almost unreal, and even disappointing. More than any other North American grazer except the mountain goat, bighorns have a reputation for living in places only they can go. Hunters have been writing about the extraordinary challenge of sheep-hunting for more than a century. Having a band of bighorns walk in front of your car is great, but it also seems too easy. I want to object that sheep, like bears, should be earned.

The canyon—indeed, the whole north end of the park in winter—attracts wildlife photographers in greater numbers than sheep. Stunning photographs with rugged, breathtaking backdrops can be had from a car window or, at best, an easy climb. I've seen any number of such photographs in magazines, recognizing the familiar background of north Yellowstone's scenery. The magazine's readers admire what difficulties must have been overcome to reach such a magnificent subject in such a wonderful setting. I've taken similar pictures, getting so close that through my zoom lens the nervously alert brown eyes of a restless ewe shamed me for disturbing these harassed gentle creatures.

Perhaps it's because the big animals are so easy to see when I live here, or maybe it's because I actually have become as open-minded about wildlife appreciation as I want to, but there are other, less glamorous animals that usually distract me from the sheep. For me, the center ring for the wildlife show in the canyon is down in the river, and hardly anyone knows it. While the tourists and professional photographers line the roads watching the sheep, deer, and elk, I take myself to the slick rocks below a dark pool I know, lone witness to a silent miracle in the river.

The Gardner serves the Yellowstone River as a major nursery stream. Each fall Yellowstone River browns migrate up the Gardner and other feeders to spawn. Like so many miniature imitations of their salmon cousins, they crowd nervously from the depth, space, and security of the big river into the Gardner's shallow pools and riffles, returning, as near as we know, to the natal ground—to the very gravel beds from which they themselves were hatched years before.

I first encountered this spawning run on the closing day of trout season the first year I stayed in the park through the winter. I was fishing about a mile above the Gardner's mouth at the Yellowstone, working a weighted imitation stonefly nymph through a deep trough of slow water below a small cascade. The water was full of unhookable fish; they would strike savagely, but quickly slip from the hook before I could even identify them. I didn't know larger fish were in the river, had not imagined that the pool was any different from the week before, and hadn't yet noticed the faded clipping in the storehouse at Mammoth that showed the nine-pounder that Ed Wolfe had caught a few years earlier upstream from where I was.

So I was totally unprepared when on a long downstream swing my fly came to a stop in midcurrent. I had sense enough to set the hook, but there my involvement in the action ceased. A brown trout larger than any I had ever seen immediately had my attention.

Mark Twain once observed that a man who carries a cat home by the tail will learn a hundred times as much as a man who carries it otherwise. During my brief attachment to this trout I learned much of practical value about the vigor, energy, and fabulous acrobatic abandon that the adult brown trout brings to its mating bed. Within ten seconds the fish was airborne—high arcing leaps—at least six times. It still seems impossible, as if it bounced from the surface of the water as from a trampoline rather than submerging and getting a good purchase on the water between each leap. It was not a true giant trout by local standards. I reckon it now, with the cooler eye of experience, at upwards of twenty inches, hardly three pounds. But in the confines of this small pool, the fish jumping insanely almost within reach of my rod tip, it was paralyzingly large. I was stunned, and just watched.

Actually, even had I been clearheaded and prepared, there would have been nothing for me to do. According to the books, I should have been ready to "give line" from the reel, to fight the fish with the forgiving bend of the rod, to wear the fish out. None of this seemed to apply. The fish wanted no line; the thirty or so feet he had gave him ample freedom, especially as he chose to jump and run upstream, toward me. With him spending more time in the air than in the water, and hardly any time at all in any given place, it would have taken a much better angler than I to organize anything resembling a fight.

It didn't matter. On the last jump he threw the fly. The shattered surface of the pool ran out into the next run, washing my line ashore and leaving me giggling quietly.

A little checking around brought uneven information. Yes, this happens every year, but the run usually doesn't come in until after the season is closed, and some years there don't seem to be very many fish. No, it hasn't been studied much by the biologists but we do know that the Gardner is a damned important nursery for the Yellowstone browns. Yes, people catch big ones off the mouth of the Gardner, in the Yellowstone itself—look at those monsters hanging behind the bar down at the Town Cafe. Yes, locals do poach the devil out of the run sometimes. No, it isn't reliable enough to attract fishermen the way the runs on the Madison do; the fish aren't big or numerous enough even when the run does occur before the season closes. But it is kind of fun to go watch them jump in the cartwheel.

The cartwheel?

Yeah, you know, that chute of white water below that turn in the road in the canyon that gets bad when it's icy?

Yes?

Well, the trout have a hard time getting through that up to the spawning beds at Chinaman's Garden. They gather in that pool below the chute, everybody calls it the cartwheel, and every so often one will take a running start and pitch itself ass over teakettle into the fast water. Big long jumps.

I'm on my way.

In recent years the stretch of river containing the cartwheel has been closed to fishing well before the rest of the river, to protect early spawners and to foil meat fishermen who use sport gear to snag the vulnerable trout. By the time the fish start coming in, the river is without human visitors and I usually have the cartwheel to myself.

I drive by and pull over to where I can look down the bank to the white water. If I see no jumpers in five minutes or so I don't hang around. At peak times there may be a jumper every twenty seconds, and if I see one or two jump fairly quickly I'll stop the engine and climb down to the rocks.

At low water, in late fall, the cartwheel is mostly confined to a rock chute about twelve feet wide with large flat shelves right up to its edge. The shelves have an inch or two of water flowing across them, but practically the whole river is gathered above the chute in a rocky defile and pushed wildly into the narrow cut, where it churns and foams down, more a torrent than a current. The chute empties into a tight, deep hole of the darkest water on the river, stirs there momentarily, then plunges on down through a series of stair-step rapids. The Gardner in its canyon is a high-energy river.

The dark pool serves as a staging area for upstream migrants. When the run is on, they gather in this swirling little cauldron of rock, taking turns at the cartwheel. Sometimes, standing right at the brink of the rock ledge,

I've looked down and seen a big roiling ball of brown trout—dozens, at least, ten to sixteen inches—being churned around like a tangled wad of earthworms in the quieter side of the pool. The ball seemed to drift in and out from the ledge, sometimes partly obscured by the bubbles and foam from the cartwheel, sometimes sinking deeper until it was lost to sight. From it came the jumpers.

On the West Coast I've seen big salmon jumping; it's fast, but the size of the fish makes the process observably graceful. A thirty-pounder emerges from the water in a smooth arc, shedding water from its sides as it climbs into the air. Some jumps seem almost ponderous. Not so with the trout here in the cartwheel; all is flashing speed. One at a time, the trout get a short running start below the chute and emerge from the foam somewhere near the lower end. As they shoot clear of the water, their tails often flutter, too fast to see, as if they seek a hold on the air to match the one they used to launch themselves from the water. More disconcerting than the frenetically kicking tail is their seeming abandonment of normal orientation. They do go ass over teakettle, as if they were being thrown by someone. Here comes one sideways, spinning slowly, nose-over. Here's one upside down, followed by one curled like a horseshoe. Then, a traditionalist, in a classic headfirst leap as good as any fishing magazine cover artwork.

Obviously, considering their flight plans, they land with varying fortunes. The chute is fierce, and most seem to be washed back down the instant they hit the upper end of it. In all my watching I never saw a fish make it, though I know some do. Some smack wetly, still buzzing their tails, onto the rocks at the edge of the chute (a biologist friend tells me that migrating trout in other places have been known to throw themselves against unpassable dams until their heads split open). Others land in the shallow, racing little sheets of water that cover some of the ledge. When one finds this water, truly furious swimming can carry the day, for the ledge leads along the side of the chute clear up to calmer water. Once, watching with a friend, we found ourselves cheering these ledge-swimmers on. We stood on dry rock only a couple of feet away, crouched over, yelling absurdly at a trout as it swam frantically in three inches of water (like a swimming coach running alongside the pool to exhort an athlete to keep pushing). When the trout gave up and was washed limply back into the chute, we would let out an "awww . . ." like fans watching a golf ball come to rest on the lip of the cup.

The admiration I'd gained from hooking one of these trout was nothing compared to what I came to feel at the jumping water. If I ever in my life show such intense single-minded devotion to a goal, even one as simple as procreation, I will die satisfied. The trout simply *had* to move up. They had to get through the cartwheel.

What makes this most wondrous is where they were going: the very gravel bed they, each individual to its own, had hatched from years before. In early winter I'd make my way to two or three favored spots on the river, choosing a fairly windless day if I could (it's hard to see through a ruffled surface). Watching some of the larger gravel bars, where the water was only a foot or two deep, I might count thirty fish finning quietly or jockeying for position: osprey heaven. Light spots would appear on the gravel—oblongs two feet in length—where females had dug shallow depressions by turning sideways and rapidly fanning the dirt and stones out with their tails. Eventually, with one or more males in attendance, the female laid her eggs into the depression, the male ejecting his milt in a fine settling fog at the same time. The process would be repeated until the females were out of eggs, and after a while (later in the winter, I think) the trout would drift back down to the bigger river, leaving behind only the resident trout who would dine heartily on the hatchlings (their own included) a few weeks later.

A friend and I wrote a book called *Freshwater Wilderness*, devoted to Yellowstone's fish. The book was a kind of equal-rights statement for fish, in which we tried to get people to think of fish as wild animals—as wildlife. Our point was that it's too bad that more people don't open up to the excitement of the aquatic wilderness; it's a great show and you don't have to fish to enjoy it. Even in hard winter, with no thoughts of fishing, I often find myself drawn to the river.

In fact, even when the spawners have left the beds and only an occasional fish is to be seen, and when the cliffs are crawling with bighorns and the willow with deer, my attention keeps coming back to those dark currents whose ephemeral inhabitants overcome objects like none I can imagine facing. I drive down to a parking place I know and walk the paths a little more, and as I head back to the car, kicking through drifts where in summer I would be hip-deep in sage, and as I drive back up to Mammoth, I watch the water at every opportunity. Over the years I've learned every spot on the road that gives me a glimpse of the river, and how long I dare take my eyes from the road at each one. Like the satisfaction of looking at a mountain range that you know has grizzly bears, there is much to be said for a good look at a wild river, and I always look with special joy at the jumping water, even when the foam is empty of trout.

As the Eagle Flies

As the eagle flies it is more than 150 miles west from Yellowstone to the Sweetwater basin in Southwestern Montana. It is ranch country, where the only people wearing cowboy hats are cowboys. There are a number of sheep ranches in the area, though fewer than there once were, including several within an hour of Dillon. In the early seventies the ranchers over there complained loudly that golden eagles were killing their sheep. Specifically, they claimed that they were losing many new lambs and young-of-the-year.

Now some nature magazines—and many right-thinking bird-watchers —will insist that eagles do not kill sheep; that ranchers who make these claims are only looking for a way to get somebody, preferably the government, to take blame for (and thereupon subsidize) losses due to winterkill, disease, or coyote depredation. But there's no doubt about it: eagles kill lambs. The evidence, everything from autopsy to photographs to eyewitnesses, is simply concrete.

And why not? Eagles eat small animals, and they hunt them from the sky. One small animal must seem as edible as another, and the sheep are generally too stupid to even run away. Why chase squirrels and rockchucks when nice fat lambs just stand there waiting to be served up? Eagles are too practical to avoid such easy food just because some writer with a whale on his T-shirt says they don't like mutton.

Of course the ranchers wanted to shoot some eagles, but they were thoughtful enough to ask permission first, which is more than many people have done. They didn't get it, but the U.S. Fish and Wildlife Service people in Montana came up with an idea. They wondered if maybe the eagles could be caught and moved somewhere else.

The eagles in question were young ones, full size but not mated. The sheep country didn't have many good nesting sites, so there weren't any resident eagles to kick the newcomers out. The country did have some great coulees, though, and these generated just the kind of thermals that the eagles could stretch out across and ride with ease as they selected a tasty lamb from the flocks below.

Transplanting seemed like a good idea for a number of reasons. For one, killing an eagle is a legal nightmare, and killing several dozen would have been tough even for the agency that protects them to justify. People are really touchy about eagles.

For another, there was reason to hope that transplanted eagles might not come back; that if they were dumped into some reasonably good game country they might "bend" their migration route in subsequent years and not bother with the sheep any more.

For another, after trying a few other places that didn't work well for one reason or another, they discovered that Yellowstone Park actually wanted eagles. Park records suggested that there used to be more eagles here than there are now; perhaps they stopped frequenting the area when the park service was keeping the elk population down by killing a certain number each year, thereby reducing carrion levels for scavengers like the eagles.

Norton Miner, Montana State Supervisor for Animal Damage Control, U.S. Fish and Wildlife Service, was in charge of the transplants. Norton, a veteran of many years' experience in assorted wildlife management assignments, is a large, rugged, permanently tanned man with a ready smile and obvious professionalism. He is one of the very few men I've met who look as if they deserve to wear their cowboy hats.

Every few weeks Norton and his wife would load up their horse trailer with eagles (anywhere from seven to twenty-five or more), each in a large wooden crate, and drive over to Yellowstone, where park biologists met them and helped attach wing tags (temporary, for short-term sightings) and leg bands (permanent, to trace movements from year to year of recaptured birds) to the birds as they were being uncrated and released.

The project went on for the rest of the seventies; it wasn't terribly successful, but it didn't hurt, and it provided a lot of useful information (both on handling eagles and on eagle movements) for other studies. At the same time it was enormously appreciated by a few of us who managed to convince someone that we should come along to help out at the releases.

What struck me most about the eagles was their calm. They were trapped with old coyote traps whose jaws were heavily padded. Four traps were placed under or near a sheep or marmot carcass, and the birds walked into them with little suspicion. Then, when you would expect any wild animal to struggle violently, the eagle would quietly look down at the trap like a man who has discovered something unpleasant on his shoe. They might clump around a bit (like a kid with a loose roller skate), but remained quiet when the trapper arrived, walked up, and picked them up by the feet to release the trap. The eagles were taken to a holding shed, a log eagle coop, where they were fed and watered until enough had been collected to justify a trip to the park.

I am sure there are logical reasons for the eagles' taking it so calmly, something in their makeup that gave them the sense not to struggle, but to me it was a powerful expression of their wildness. I turned it into a lesson for myself about how wild an animal can be, and decided that the eagles were simply so wild—so far beyond our capacity to affect their sense of independence, even if we domesticated them—that captivity wasn't that big an issue with them. They seemed ready to wait for whatever happened next. After watching a few of them be handled and released, my respect for this spiritual freedom that I had hypothesized deepened. When you get up close to an eagle, and he looks right through you with those magnificent dark eyes, it's easy to imagine a wildness so fiercely remote that it can only be native to a dimension you have not visited.

Several release sites were tried in Yellowstone, usually on some large open flat. Most were not really suitable for the birds, who are accustomed to landing and taking off from elevated perches. Being tossed into the air by a ranger isn't the same thing. Quite often the bird would fly only a few feet, then land and look back as if to say, "Do you feel as silly about that as I do?" Others would whip those huge wings as strongly as they could, beating a head-high course across the flats, wing tips grazing the sagebrush until there was speed enough to climb. At Panther Creek one poor unfortunate did a hard left as he was tossed, and glided hopelessly into the little creek. He floated, wings spread across the water and flopping weakly, until he washed ashore on the far bank. He climbed up the bank to a low rock perch where he sat, wings spread to dry, now and then glaring over at us with obvious disappointment. "The releases went well," we reported later, "except that Ted threw one into the river."

Eventually a better location was found, right above the confluence of the Lamar River and Soda Butte Creek. Soda Butte Creek runs west through a small flat-bottomed valley with high peaks rising on both sides. On the north side there is a considerable shoulder, a flat shelf a couple of hundred feet above the stream. Wind currents come up the valley from the Lamar valley to the west, and they eddy and climb this shoulder, providing a convenient series of updrafts into which eagles can be successfully launched.

One June afternoon Norton pulled in with nineteen eagles in his trailer. Several other cars, containing staff biologists and rangers, were close behind, and soon Norton and the others were unpacking the birds. Each was removed from its plywood box and carried by the feet to a makeshift bench, where tags were attached. Most were calm, even when tilted (like people, an eagle will react by grabbing something if it is suddenly thrown sideways, so it is wise to keep the talons out of range if you decide to turn the bird over), but one panicked while being removed from its crate and clamped a talon onto the wooden frame. Norton had to use vise grips to unlock the talon from its frozen hold.

When they're being worked on at the bench, the eagles usually lie quiet; one pecked at a nearby arm, and a cowboy hat was put over its head to quiet it. Even lying on their backs they retain the dignity of their kind. The eyes keep that impenetrable distance and return your gaze almost without seeming to notice you.

The releases moved quickly that day. At one point I walked over to Doug Houston, who was looking out over the valley at the eagle circus; there were eagles in the trees, eagles down along the river, eagles on the cliffs, and eagles in the air. We stood watching for a moment, then, as if he'd been working on the speculation for some time, he said, "You know, I wonder what the ground squirrels must be thinking right now?"

I made sure I took a turn or two with the eagles. Taking one from his crate, Norton handed it to me. "Hold onto his legs up high, on the feathers, with your right hand. Put your left hand up here, under his chest."

My right fist closed easily around the eagle's upper legs, and his talons hung loosely below. As his weight settled onto the flat of my left hand— that buoyant firmness only birds seem to have—the rapid tapping of his heart was passed from flesh to feather to flesh. The beat seemed frightened and fast, but birds, even big ones, have much higher gearing than people. He seemed calm enough otherwise, certainly calmer than I.

I was holding him about waist high, with a dusky wing draped over each of my sleeves and his head facing away from me. "Keep those talons out from your belly," cautioned Norton, reminding me of the vise grips as I carried the eagle to the crest of the ridge.

I held him higher then, out from me, with the white-banded tail brushing my right shoulder and the back of his head, golden-hackled and arced gently down the slope, even with my chin. As we reached the crest of the ridge the full updraft hit us, a mild cool breeze. His response was so automatic, so instinctive, that for a moment I was able to know something of his life in the air. Facing into the upwelling current (never did he even try to look around at my face), he automatically opened his wings against it. I held him higher and felt the lift and pull as he arched and banked his wings, canting them first this way, then that, as he tested the possibilities. The faintest movement of a wing tip translated itself into a gentle lift of his weight from my hand; an opposing turn brought his weight back full. The subtlety of those pressures, the potential for sculpting the air with those long flexible wings, was transmitted to my hands, his momentary anchor against the breeze.

The eagle knew he was about to be released. I'm sure of it. As I pointed him into the updraft and aimed him out across the valley he knew. And when, after a few seconds of holding him high, I slowly brought him back and down to me, he moved his wings in to as near a launching crouch as my grip allowed. Then, working as one, as if we'd counted "one, two, *three*" in unison, I lowered him yet farther and in one smooth upward motion I lifted him into the wind.

Geyser Gazing

It may be apocryphal, but there's a story that in 1870, when weary members of the Washburn-Langford-Doane expedition finally rode their horses from the piney woods into the valley of the Firehole River they broke into the open at the edge of a barren gray plain. As they gaped in wonder at the steaming fissured landscape of the world's foremost geyser basin, they were greeted, with a timing born of centuries of solitary practice, by the gushing plume of a geyser they soon named "Old Faithful." The story's truth doesn't matter. It *should* be true, anthropomorphism and all. It's almost too good *not* to be true: the geyser of them all that would come to signify fidelity, that has become an American character, waiting on its brooding plateau with geologic patience at last to greet those transient beings who would give it a different kind of immortality, and then saluting them and its new life with puppy eagerness.

The expressed justifications for establishing Yellowstone were both preservations: of the Grand Canyon of the Yellowstone River and of the geothermal marvels of the region. When the boundaries were drawn, they were made generous enough to include much poorly known land that might include additional springs and geysers—a hedge against the likelihood of the explorers having missed a few.

The explorers had missed a few, and the boundaries enclosed almost all of them. There are about ten thousand assorted thermal features—hot springs, geysers, mudpots, steam vents, and the rest—in the park. Two-thirds of the world's geysers are there.

The geysers, I am embarrassed to admit, have not captured me to the extent they captured the park's founders. They entertain and amuse, they fascinate, excite, and thrill, but they don't last in my mind. Grizzly bears, dippers, and fringed gentian are frequently on my mind; forests growing, streams carving themselves new channels, wind weathering sandstone pinnacles . . . I am appreciative audience to these and many other natural events. But geysers and hot springs, as fabulous and precious as I know they are, leave me looking for something else to do.

Why is this? Are they just too awesome for my feeble perceptions? Could be, but I doubt it. I think it has to do with their rarity, the very novelty that makes them so extraordinary. Novelty is the good word here; geysers are nature's great novelty act, the two-headed calf in Mother Nature's Traveling Medicine Show. They are so rare, so alien, that we see but we do not absorb. We don't deny it happened—yes, it shot water 150 feet into the air—but we don't know what to do about it.

Watch the crowd at an Old Faithful eruption. Amid the rattle of hundreds of shutters, some people feel a need to applaud, to do some act, like a gorilla beating on his chest in displacement of flight or aggression. Many people occupy themselves with photographs to show back home. There are "ooh's" and "ah's" and other scattered sounds. But even before the water has entirely subsided many people turn to leave.

I like to think that I'm better off than most people, who are too media-hooked to handle a relatively quiet miracle like a geyser; they want full orchestra accompaniment, running commentary by prominent media celebrities, and slow motion instant replay when it's all over. An event that occurs without these trappings impresses them less than it would otherwise. Maybe that's why early park service administrators felt compelled to push big bonfires over Yosemite Falls each night, or why we once played colored lights over the cone of Old Faithful at night. It's the same old story of improving on nature when all we really need to do is improve our own judgment. We are lazy, and we want to be entertained, to be passively receptive to the show. Change the channel, have another beer.

I've tried harder than that. My interest has been stronger and my opportunity has been greater. Rather than the average tourist's hour or two at the Upper Geyser Basin, I've been there for Old Faithful and the other geysers at dawn, midnight, winter, and summer. Old Faithful is a different thing when it's just the two of you, or on those rare occasions when you are witness to a geothermal chorus of Old Faithful, Beehive, and others, all playing at once (geysers "play," like spotlights across a stage or tennis players across a court). It is different as well when you walk the basins with a serious "geyser gazer," a naturalist who knows each pool and fountain not only by name and schedule but by personality and quirk. Thus, though I've not lived for more than a few weeks at a time at Old Faithful, I've spent enough time there, alone and in the right company, to try plenty hard to get to know the hot water show. But as much as I enjoyed it all, there was always a lingering shadow of uncertainty. I kept suppressing the standard tourist response that there's something *unnatural* about this most natural of settings. I kept my bearings best when I was able to relate the hot water to the more "normal" setting of the surrounding wilderness. I did best with the geysers when I kind of angled toward them from stabler ground.

These gray plains and mineral mounds bring an immediacy to geology, a scale of occurrence more in line with our own experience. To give the title one more twist, they help bring mountain time to life. While the Yellowstone canyon looks pretty much the way it did a hundred years ago, the dynamics of hot springs and geysers are daily, even hourly.

At Mammoth the pace of change is fastest. Unlike the big geyser basins to the south at Norris and along the Firehole River, where the mineral being deposited is a silicate dissolved from hard volcanic rock, the springs at Mammoth are bubbling through thick layers of soft limestone. The water seeps deep into the upper slopes of Terrace Mountain, where it is heated and directed downhill, passing through the sedimentary limestones that have been heated by hotter rock farther down. Its flow finally runs into harder bedrock and is deflected back to the surface at Mammoth. The limestone and other substrata are too soft and crumbly to permit the pressure buildups required to maintain geysers, so the flow is steady and quiet. The water emerges with a heavy load of dissolved limestone, which it deposits around its opening and which is then called travertine. It takes a certain amount of agitation of the water for the limestone to be settled from it, and this agitation occurs when the water drops quickly over an edge. Thus, the terraces at Mammoth are often characterized by steep-walled ridges with deep still pools behind them. Where the flow is steady enough, a simple coolee-hat-shaped mound is established. If the water emerges from a lengthy fissure rather than from a single vent, a long steep ridge, such as Elephant Back Terrace, is formed. If the water emerges from a hillside, or from a very gentle pool overflow, it may deposit its load haphazardly on a slope, more a series of tiny rippled rills than a grand or even identifiable structure.

Nor is all the mineral deposited at once; some may be lost in a quick fall over a terrace while more is dropped, a little at a time, as the water flows slowly down a slope.

More unusual things occur, such as travertine ice. In some especially still pools with the slightest flow of water, the mineral may collect on the surface and form a delicate opaque skim of travertine that would barely support the weight of a bird. Even less common (I've seen it in only one or two pools), tiny mineral particles will cling to a vagrant air bubble, attracted and held by the bubble's spherical surface tension until they solidify and sink the tiny gray globe to the bottom of the pool, where it and hundreds of other dull pearlish shapes coat the terrace floor.

In an exceptional flow as much as two feet of limestone can be laid down in a year (in the Upper Geyser Basin a really cooking spring may deposit half an inch of silica). This fast deposition means that we see new things at Mammoth every day. Not only is the surface being built up, but the new deposits block and redirect the runoff flow, which in turn changes the direction of future deposition. The colorful algaes that live in the hot water move right into the new channels within a few days, so that you can always tell which terraces are "alive" by their color; the ones draped in tans and browns and greens are the freshest. Those that are sugary white but dry are just recently extinguished. Those that are gray and crumbling are long dead.

The springs are so limestone-laden that they often choke off their own vents. With several dozen of them flowing, bubbling, and steaming here and there over the many acres of activity at Mammoth, we are never quite sure where a plugged spring will send its water. One may dry up and its neighbor become more active. Or, both may dry up and another, two hundred yards away, will come to life for the first time in memory. It's all potential spring territory, though the flat plain where the hotel and park headquarters sit has been inactive for centuries.

In much of the area of present activity at Mammoth, the deposited limestone is more than 150 feet thick. This means, for one thing, that the whole underground must be a honeycomb of inactive, crumbling crevices and channels. When the army was building Fort Yellowstone their wagons occasionally broke through to open sinkholes. So little confidence did the masons have in the travertine footing that the Bachelor Officer's Quarters—the present Albright Museum—was built on a floating foundation of steel girders that extend far beyond the basement walls a few feet underground, like outriggers.

But, intriguing if unexplored, the immense limestone deposits mean something else. They mean that somewhere back up the mountain, above the springs but below where the water first soaked into the earth, there must be some enormous caverns where once all that limestone resided before the water carried it out and piled it up on the surface. I imagine these unseen, unvisited caverns, wondering at their convolutions, their insufferable heat, and the shadowy slick floors they would offer a visitor—if a visitor could breathe carbon dioxide at 170 degrees—and I have no spelunker's urge.

From a near distance the springs at Mammoth are confusing. The huge mounds are a jumble of grays and whites. The active runoff channels are richly colored in browns, ochres, and greens by the algae that has adapted to live in the hot water. The general rule is that the darker the algae the cooler the water, so that there's a linear stratification to the colors, a channel's shallower edges often being darkest. It is as if someone has painted vegetable-colored paths down the travertine slopes to guide the running water.

It's only from far off, say from the other side of the valley, on top of Mt. Everts, that it all comes into focus as something pale and soft that has oozed out of the mountain at random on the lower slope of Sepulchre. From up close it is not easy to see what you're walking through as one big event; an active spring here and there is surrounded by darker ground (gray rock and shallow gritty soil), brush, and trees. Most of the ground is "inactive" and relatively safe walking. On my nature walk I took my group across a bare flat where I told them to stamp their feet, then listened to the "ooh's" as the ground thumped hollowly beneath them. An old dry channel lay a foot or two below.

It is this sort of surficial eccentricity that has compelled the park service to fence off large areas and to unobtrusively discourage the use of others. Even at Mammoth, cooler than the other major thermal areas, there are springs in the 160–170 degree range, and a bad accident can easily happen. Tourists are notoriously carefree people about such hazards, and so are many park employees.

One night during my first summer in Yellowstone, two young fellows who worked on the park's road crews got a few gourds of corn aboard and decided to explore one of the fenced-off spring holes on the parade ground. Around midnight. The less lucid of the two ran up and vaulted, one hand on the railing, over the fence, presumably expecting to land on his feet just inside the railing. Jumping better than he knew, he cleared the edge and bounced on down the cavern (a hole about fifteen feet across at the opening and angling slightly as it descended). He lit here and there against the crumbly limestone walls, finally coming to rest on a ledge about seventy-five feet below the surface. From there he moaned, irregularly, as his frantic buddy called to him from above.

Getting no response, the buddy raced across the street and into the bunkhouse, which was almost empty, it being Friday night. I, typically, was there, and so was, untypically, a friend named Big Al. The chattering survivor got us to understand the problem, and as we looked for our shoes Big Al wondered grumpily why these boys hadn't been out doing something sensible, like chasing girls somewhere.

We hurried out to the hole, and stood, leaning against the railing and helping the panicky fellow look down into the darkness. Finally Big Al and I agreed that there was nothing left to do but call some rangers. With reluctance our much-sobered explorer agreed; he couldn't even *imagine* how he would explain to them what his friend was doing down there.

An hour or so later, using suitable climbing gear and with enough first-aid backup on hand to accommodate the Union wounded at Vicksburg, the patrol ranger reached the fellow, looked him over, and called up, "He's awright." Later the ranger observed that, when he discovered there were no broken bones—the victim had yelled up that his leg was broken—he considered breaking a couple, just to justify the work. The loose drunkenness that kept the kid from breaking anything on the way down also kept him from realizing he was okay. As he was hoisted out by ropes, still groggy and confused, he was suddenly confronted with what he had caused: government vehicles in all directions, spotlights everywhere, and a formidable crowd of off-duty uniforms stowing expensive gear. Supported on each side by a ranger, he gaped in wide-eyed dismay at this crowd of freshly awakened officials and groaned, "Aww, my mother's going to kill me." That brought the only laugh of the night from the assembled group as he was helped to the privacy of some nearby bushes. His mother didn't kill him, but he wished she had by the time the superintendent finished with him.

In that case there was little danger of hot water but great danger of bad air. The springs give off immense quantities of carbon dioxide, as well as less appealing if no more breathable gasses, by-products of the limestone-dissolving process that is going on underground. They can be quite oxygen-deprived. One spring off the main trails sits in a small stone depression; it seems to boil, but it's merely bubbling with carbon dioxide, which lies in the natural bowl. Plants get along well on CO_2, so the rim of this spring is lush with them, flowering, growing, and a source of great attraction to other life forms, especially birds. They fly in, land in the snags and bushes around the pool, and, as is their habit, breathe very fast. They quickly smother. In one six-month period some years ago, more than two hundred birds of twenty-four species were found killed by this and another nearby spring. The largest was a magpie, but I've heard stories of rabbits and even larger animals also being overcome, perhaps by crawling into such a spot to take a nap and never waking up. The death of animals in such a rich and riotously lush setting is always a surprise. One large crevice at Mammoth, Devil's Kitchen, used to be open to visitors but was closed because of bad air. Some older rangers still remember climbing the ladder down into its dark tunnel.

Mammoth, for all its immensity and confusion, is a minor attraction compared to the geyser basins. At first glance the deposits in the basins seem identical to the travertine springs; there are the same bleak steaming flats, the same deep aqua pools, the same stench of hydrogen sulfide (the "rotten egg gas" everyone complains about is another by-product of the underground dissolving of rock that occasionally carries traces of sulfur), and the same delicately scalloped mineral deposits. The difference is subterranean and significant. The basins at Norris and along the Firehole rest on a plateau of volcanic rock called rhyolite; it was formed by the cataclysmic volcanic explosion that savaged this region six hundred thousand years ago. Calling this event an eruption is criminal understatement.

Yellowstone's molten basement—in some places there is molten rock only two miles down—is the top of a "magmatic plume," a massive upwelling of liquid rock from deeper in the earth. This unusual heat source conducts a slow fry on the thin crust above it. Geologists now know that every six hundred thousand years or so for the past several million this area has become unstable enough to release staggering amounts of energy, heat, and lava onto the earth's surface. The last such event, six hundred thousand years ago (yes, in geologic terms we are about due for another performance; studies of some old benchmarks in Yellowstone suggest they may be a few feet higher than they were a century ago), created the vast depression that now cradles Yellowstone Lake. The depression was caused when enormous amounts of molten rock were forced from under the edges of this great ellipse of ground, causing the center of the ellipse to collapse into the space vacated by the rock. The phenomenon is called a caldera, and the caldera's edges inscribe a great oval across Yellowstone's middle. The rhyolite under the geyser basins is part of the flow from the western edge of the caldera.

After such an event the plume quiets down and goes back to easier work, like simmering groundwater. It does this better in the geyser basins than up at Mammoth, often superheating the water; even at the surface the water may be full boiling (water boils at about 93 degrees Centigrade at Old Faithful's altitude, enough of a reduction from sea-level boiling to cause many residents to resort to high-altitude cookbooks).

A geyser works because of the heat, but it requires other conditions. It requires a good supply of water, and it requires a place to hold it. The unstable fissured rhyolite strata of central Yellowstone are cratered and cracked with opportunities. Water, either from other springs (the channels are so convoluted that two neighboring springs may be radically dissimilar in chemistry and temperature) or from precipitation, seeps and drains into an appropriate set of subterranean openings, where it is heated by the hot rocks a few hundred feet down. It may sit there, showing itself only as a steaming vent or a quiet sky-blue pool with its tight vent yawning darkly at the bottom (do not desecrate this beauty with a coin and a wish). In a few cases—two hundred places in Yellowstone—circumstances are right to establish a less stable system; some peculiar set of restrictions in the throat of the feature gives us a geyser. The deepest water is held down and pressurized by the cooler water that piles up on top of it. The heat at the bottom is fierce, but, as in a pressure cooker, the boiling point is not reached. The deep water reaches 300 degrees. 400 degrees. 450. The cooler lid of this aquatic pressure cooker begins to weaken and roil. Finally, a shot of the hot water manages to rise through the colder water to a lower pressure area where it can flash into steam, forcing a little of the cooler lid out of the geyser's surface vent (many geysers have this preliminary burp, either from the main vent or from a smaller "indicator" vent). The loss of some water lightens the entire cool lid, lowering its pressure (the technical term is hydrostatic head) on the water below and setting off a reaction; more and more of the superheated water rises far enough to flash into steam, and the lid bursts into an eruption until the deeper water has exhausted its energy. Then the water seeps back down or runs to the river. Some geysers do it every few minutes, some every month or so. Old Faithful is neither the largest nor the most constant, and the average interval between its eruptions has lengthened several minutes in recent years. Everything from earthquakes (Yellowstone experiences thousands every year, but only a few of those are strong enough to be felt by residents; most register as bumped needles on seismographs) to earth tides to barometric pressure affects the rate and behavior of the geysers, and none of them performs with perfect predictability, even after years of study and computer evaluation. They are natural phenomena, not clocks.

Our obsession with time interferes here. People approach me at the visitor center wanting to know the time of the next eruption so they can plan their day to arrive at Old Faithful just right. ("When does the geezer spout?" "When does the, uh, the . . . the old geezer blow?" "Can we see the geezer before dinner?") There is evidently something endearing about a natural event that has the decency to follow a human schedule.

In enjoy it all best in winter. The basins are virtually empty; frozen spray and deep snow make the boardwalks hazardous on foot and genuinely unnerving on skis. But the show is incredible. The dominating feature is no longer grayness. All is white. The snow has covered everything but the hot spots, and I see mostly steam, a tower of animation above every heat source, big or little. On a still morning, with the air almost painfully clear, the valley has grown a forest of pillars of climbing steam, each signifying by its diameter the size and power of its source. On a windy gray afternoon, with lowering snow-fat clouds crowding the ridges, the steam billows and rolls, sliding across the basin to settle in a hollow or swirl into a misty rooster tail. In the lower slanting light of the winter sun shadows streak the land and the steam upon it. I cover my camera lens as a tongue of mist and spray passes, to protect it from being coated with the traces of minerals in the geyser steam. Eyeglasses are a constant annoyance, alternately steamed and frosted.

I shuffle cautiously to the edge of an icy, snow-piled boardwalk and kneel clumsily to study a runoff channel. Between gusts of steam I search the mats of green algae for . . . aha, here they are—some tiny orange dots. They are eggs, and nearby I find their parents, the brine flies. These flies, smaller but roughly similar to houseflies in appearance, live on the algae, grazing, mating, and dying (there's a little spider that preys on them along with the local killdeer) on the shallow margins of this bizarre geyser world. The water heats the air only a trifle above the surface of the algae, and the flies live in that fraction of warmth. They don't fly, simply, forward. They seem to sort of lift and hover, so to move without sticking anything into the freezing zone right above them. As I watch, they buzz here and there, from one egg cluster to another, across the tiny creeks and ridges of their algal landscape. Beyond the algae, under the open water—an ocean to them—I see the lace-and-china lip of deposition framing a hot pool. The color of faintest rose, like the fading stripe on a dying trout, this delicately formed lip of minerals is as much supported by the water as vice versa. Many pools have these thin crust lips, extending out for a foot or more from their edges and making them seem smaller and less dangerous than they are. Crouching awkwardly there, I can imagine the lip not mineral at all, but ice sculpture by the same master who built the "ghost trees," coated with spray and snow, that rim the basin in lumpy improbable postures. As usual my attention has been diverted, first by the flies and then by the trees, from the hot water show I'm here to enjoy.

I don't know why I find it easier to enjoy in winter; physically it's a lot more work. Perhaps the snow gives it a familiar or welcoming softness and enables my archivist's mind to locate and catalog the hot spots more satisfactorily. The alien feel of the place is actually heightened by the drifting steam; I walk knee-deep in it one moment, crouch below it the next, and squint and dodge as it thickens and fades. It's an old struggle I'm having, really, one we face with every new landscape. On a much grander scale the explorers of the southwest's plateau province—Powell, Dutton, and the rest—faced the same challenge when they were mapping that country in the 1870s and 1880s. They (especially Dutton) struggled consciously with defining the scenic and aesthetic possibilities—the conceptual parameters—of that vast and spectacular landscape. It was so unlike any geography of their prior cultural experience that they were compelled to define a new perspective to fit the new world.

Maybe that's it, here in the basins. As I crouch in the fog I share Joseph Krutch's feelings about strange country:

> There is a kind of beauty—and it is presumably the kind prevailing throughout most of the universe—of which man gets thrilling glimpses but which is fundamentally alien to him. It is well for him to glance occasionally at the stars or to think for a moment about eternity. But it is not well to be too continuously aware of such things, and we must take refuge from them with the small and the familiar.

When I divert my attention from the surroundings to watch the flies, I am taking just such a refuge. When I sit by a spring finding faces in the steam I again seek the familiar. I seek to relate the basins to easier places and easier times. Thus, I hope, I succeed in relating them to me.

When I see a little spring slowly creeping up on a sprig of silky phacelia, or choking the life from a ragged and forlorn old juniper, it's geology at a pace I can understand. When a butterfly falls into a quiet backwater pool and we find it only a few hours later, it is a fast sculpture in lime, an incredibly delicate casting from life that shows every faint veination of the wings, every waist and thickening of the body. I can understand that, as well.

But when again this whole country—this vast network of ranges on which the geyser basins are only a small thermal blemish—lifts and buckles over its magmatic foundation, and life and landscape for hundreds of miles are twisted, seared, and obliterated; when this happens, and Yellowstone is again reborn in fire, if anybody is standing back far enough (perhaps an astronaut) to watch and yet survive the show, that fortunate observer will get an appreciation for the pace of mountain time that has so far eluded me.

PART TWO

A REASONABLE
ILLUSION

The Resource Is Wildness

It's no secret that the national parks are in trouble. Yellowstone is in trouble. The immensity of the threats and already active destroyers is staggering: geothermal energy exploration up against the west boundary; ever larger recreational vehicles and ever larger crowds; reckless, whole-sale, and shortsighted development (what I have elsewhere called the "creeping chamber of commercism that infects all beautiful land") in surrounding national forests; water-, mineral-, and energy-starved cities hundreds of miles away; an avowedly antiwilderness—antinature, really—government administration; and, most dangerous of all, a diffident and parsimonious citizenry. Few believe there's much hope in the long run. Parks will go on, no matter what we do, but they will be lessened and cheapened. The tragedy may occur so gradually that at no one point will defenders be able to generate alarm enough to stop it. Each year a little more grizzly habitat is chewed away, whored off, or simply paved dead, and the elusive and hard-to-count bear population diminishes (one? two? five fewer bears each year? Who knows? We only know it's happening). In thirty (twenty? forty?) years they will be gone.

When politicians and developers challenge grizzly-bear defenders to prove that each new intrusion is actually a threat to the bears, they adeptly subvert attention from obvious truths: grizzlies don't live in most of the West any more; they used to before we got here; we're settling their habitat on all sides of Yellowstone, one of their last refuges. Any moron can see we're wiping them out. When, on the other hand, the endangered species laws challenge developers to prove that their latest plans won't hurt the grizzly population, they circumvent these same basic truths by complaining that the bear population is not yet adequately studied, and the scientists don't yet agree on how many bears there are so how can we innocent entrepreneurs know what is wrong, and so on.

No single intrusion is the point. It is the cumulative erosion of habitat that must cease if the bear is to survive. There is no question that it must cease immediately. Now.

The grizzly is only the most spectacular indicator of Yellowstone's health. Everything else, from carbon-monoxide-sensitive lichens on roadside rocks to worn and eroded backcountry trails to easily neglected ideals, is just as vulnerable and nearly as important, even if it hasn't sufficient glamor to appear on T-shirts and calendars. It is difficult to discuss the threats in a calm voice, and I think that even those who care are becoming numbed to the urgency of it all. Like the television viewers of the nineteen-sixties who became accustomed to the gore and nightmare of Vietnam because it was presented to them in a calm professional voice nightly on the news (between the Dow Jones averages and the weather report), we are deadened by the flood of bad news. Perhaps it would help briefly if the most outrageous violations of the earth's dignity were printed in bold, or red, in the press.

So there you are, reading yet another gloomy report on the parks, wondering how, now that I have written off Yellowstone's hopes, I expect to keep your attention for the rest of the book. I have no sunny, upbeat wrap-up in mind. I can't talk Yellowstone out of its doom. What I can do, though, is assess the damage so far. For all our talk about the health of the parks, we've done a pretty poor job of considering just how we measure that health.

Some provocative and insightful work has been done recently by popular writers and scholars who have explored what we call the "national park idea." Actually it's not an idea but a rolling cluster of concepts, laws, and impressions. As it rolls along, some things fall off and others are picked up. Some, like feeding park animals for public display, fell off some years ago. Others, such as legislative exclusion of motorized vehicles from wilderness portions of parks, were picked up not all that long ago.

The studies that have been done have evaluated public attitudes, habits, and enjoyments in parks. They have traced administrative and legislative attempts to quantify what constitutes an appropriate direction for Yellowstone's organic act, which left an infinity unsaid when setting the park aside "for the benefit and enjoyment of the people." But for the most part, what we are hearing about is the people. The people, as important as they insist they are, are only half the story. The other half of the story is the source of their benefit and enjoyment, the park and its parts. The park is the resource upon which their recreation depends, but the real character of that resource—not only its ecological elements but its philosophical definitions—is lost on them. The resource is not what they think it is.

Plant ecologist Don Despain was lecturing a group of ranger trainees. He wanted them to understand that Yellowstone's natural world has a value as a whole. Unlike a zoo or an art gallery, its worth depends almost totally upon its wholeness:

> In Yellowstone, the resource is not 20,000 elk, or a million lodgepole pines, or a grizzly bear. The resource is *wildness*. The interplay of all the parts of the wilderness—weather, animals, plants, earthquakes—acting upon each other to create the wild setting, creates a state of existence, a wildness, that is the product and the resource for which Yellowstone is being preserved.

A state of existence as fragile as Yellowstone's is difficult to visualize, much less quantify in scholarly, economic, or legislative terms. It is most difficult when we must quantify it in terms that will accommodate the presence, activities, and appetites of two or three million tourists. We risk losing sight of the resource's need for wholeness when we attempt to define what constitutes an appropriate use. For example, Joseph Sax, in his provocative study *Mountains Without Handrails*, attempts to distinguish between rewarding individual recreational experiences that can best be had in wilderness and those that can be had as easily elsewhere. He places motorized pastimes such as snowmobiling and trailbiking in the latter group for their obvious disruptive influences. He places fishing in the former, largely because it has generated a literature that speaks eloquently to the joys of fishing as a solitary communing with the natural world. As we will see in the following chapters, these lines cannot be so easily drawn; snowmobiling, properly controlled in Yellowstone, is doing less harm to some important parts of the resource than are other, simpler, and less technological pursuits. Worse, Sax seems utterly unaware of the appalling damage that sportfishing has done to the Yellowstone ecosystem. Workable definitions are hard to come by, and they get harder the better we appreciate the complexity of the resource we are responsible for.

I will not suggest in the following ruminations that the purity of the resource should always have primacy in our decisions; that would lead to a dead end as pointless as always giving preference to the baser wants of the crowds. I will, however, try to keep the resource's primary need—reasonably good health and a close approximation of the primitive state—foremost in my attention. If this is history at all, it is informal history of how the resource has fared. Other threats to the park, be they political, commercial, or philosophical, are outside the scope of these discussions. I seek, by representative example, to test our fidelity to the goals we have set ourselves as we learned to manage the Yellowstone wilderness.

I warn you also that the national park idea is a philosophical rat's nest, a self-contradictory, ironic, incurably anomalous, and socially anachronistic bundle of challenges and frustrations, as well as one of the most stimulating projects our society has come up with. I hope nothing I offer sounds like a simple answer, for there are none. I wince, or flare, when I hear yet another park defender begin a diatribe with that most arrogant of confidences, "What the national parks really need is . . ."

The national parks need many things, including much more money, many more friends, and quite a lot of understanding. I offer here some words for the resource, which is so often the least-understood part of the national park idea. I'm concerned mostly with the wholeness of it. I will introduce many of the parts, but only to illuminate the thing they together constitute: the wilderness they inhabit and the wildness they represent.

A Reasonable Illusion

The American public has never received an adequate introduction to the national park idea. To them, or to most of them, the parks are little more than grassy Disneylands, and the name park has no more meaning to them than forest or monument or any of the other titles the federal government has bestowed upon its holdings. It may have less because the other parks they are familiar with are amusement parks and city parks. National parks, forests, monuments, and other federal reservations, as well as similar state areas, are all viewed, simply, as public places of recreation.

The basic premise that has long distinguished parks from other federal lands is that of preservation versus conservation. Most federal lands, such as national forests (Department of Agriculture) are managed for a variety of purposes, including timber, minerals, water, power, and recreation, with a vaguely recognized goal of the greatest good for the greatest number of people (thereby guaranteeing that they truly satisfy no element of their constituency). National park lands, which constitute a tiny fraction of the public domain, are set aside to preserve a few undisturbed samples of primitive natural America so that we can enjoy them and learn from them. The product is much less tangible—and less economically quantifiable—than the products of the multiple-use lands.

In its purest form this is a lovely notion—the resource is wildness. Wildness, or naturalness, implies all the natural functions of wild country working without inhibition to maintain the primitive scene. The concept has troubled many harvest-oriented managers because it can only succeed if they don't interfere: what kind of manager does not manage? No other major agency has quite this mandate. Other agencies administer wilderness, but they administer it for certain uses, and their primary goal is not wildness.

But it's never that simple. Parks are not ecological islands, even the largest of them. Exotic flora and fauna move into the park, and native flora and fauna move out onto lands with other legislative mandates. Too, the park service mandate requires that *human* fauna be able to move about in the parks as well, and their migration routes become paved and clustered about with habitations. Very quickly the challenge to use and yet preserve grows imponderable.

Americans have radically altered their attitudes toward wild country in the past three hundred years. As Roderick Nash and other historians have pointed out, the colonial American viewed wilderness as an unqualified evil. By the early 1800s, as the country came to control its unsettled regions, Americans had begun to romanticize some elements of wilderness (the noble savage; the hardy woodsman), and by the time of the Civil War we were well along into idyllic pastorals about an idealized natural life (*Walden* and the Transcendentalists; George Catlin's suggestion that everything west of the Mississippi be set aside as a great "nation's park") that no one lived but that many admired abstractly. Against that gradual increase in respect, the preservation of Yellowstone in 1872 would seem a logical, if surprisingly grand, step; philosophically, setting aside two million acres of wild mountain country was not that remote from Catlin's original suggestion, though greatly reduced in scale.

Politically, of course, anything resembling such foresight or federal altruism was improbable. It was a time of magnificent dreams, fabulous growth, and stupendous profligacy of the public domain. Recent scholars have reminded us that proponents of Yellowstone were compelled to convince skeptical legislators that the land in question had no other value, commercially or politically, before they would agree to set it aside. Western land was being parceled out in a frenzy that would only really burn out when the land proved that it could not live up to its boosters' absurd hopes; when the arid West forced us to accept at least a few of its geographical limitations.

For Yellowstone, being "reserved and withdrawn from settlement, occupancy, or sale under the laws of the United States, and dedicated and set apart as a public park or pleasureing [*sic*] ground for the benefit and enjoyment of the people," the worst of the pillaging would be avoided. Often it has been grievously threatened—by railroads in the 1880s and 1890s, by dam builders in the 1920s, by timber interests in both world wars—but the whole has not been grossly violated. In that respect, despite numerous disagreements over specific issues, Yellowstone has remained more or less true to its organic act.

But the act was quite vague; it did not distinguish between necessary administrative and commercial "occupancy" on the one hand and excessive occupancy on the other; it did not define what constitutes a "pleasureing ground," and, perhaps most critical as far as the resource was concerned, it did not suggest what constituted appropriate "benefit and enjoyment."

It did not do these things partly because that job was someone else's— presumably the Secretary of the Interior, who was given charge of the new reservation, would attend to such details—and partly because no one really understood the questions posed by those distinctions and definitions. Like many significant statements, the organic act dealt only in main principles.

One thing the act clearly did not do, however: it did not create a wilderness reserve as we understand that term today. The park was set aside primarily to protect its extraordinary geological and geothermal wonders from commercial monopoly and despoliation. On the final fate of much of what we now value Yellowstone for, including its wildlife (both animal and vegetable) and its primitiveness, the jury was still out. Today we look upon most principles by which we manage the parks as obvious truths; it is hard to grasp the extent to which such truths did not exist one hundred years ago.

Yellowstone Park was virtually uninhabited in 1872. A small band of Shoshone sheepeaters occasionally occupied the park (they were moved to a reservation) and a few shacks squatted near or on Mammoth Hot Springs, one of them practicing the shameful self-delusion of calling itself a hotel. A few people came to partake of Mammoth's "healing waters," which were channeled from the formations in crudely dug trenches into rude bathhouses (the less modest patrons just tromped out onto the formations and slipped into a handy pool whose temperature they favored).

With no services, visitors—fewer than ten thousand in the first ten years—were totally on their own. There were virtually no decent roads, much less any stores and restaurants. Many modern park enthusiasts might prefer it that way, but in those days of slow travel the lack of such conveniences was hard on the resource. To visit this wilderness one had either to pack in necessary provisions or live off the land. The result was more or less random destruction: tree-cutting, hot-spring diversion and destruction, runaway campfires, and so on. Another result was hunting. Sport hunting is now anathema to almost all national parks (and the rare exception stirs well-banked fires of controversy), but early visitors shot, ate, and wasted elk, bison, deer, bear, and anything else they could find. Some found the hunting so good in this little-disturbed sanctuary that they considered establishing hunting-guide services.

Yellowstone had not been perceived by its founders as a game reserve. The act directed the Secretary only to establish such "rules and regulations as he may deem necessary or proper" to "provide against the wanton destruction of the fish and game found within said Park, and against their capture or destruction for the purposes of merchandise or profit." Hunting was okay. Commercial abuse of hunting was not. (Commercial *fishing* continued, supplying hotel restaurants; this uneven treatment of different types of wildlife will be examined later.) Presumably the founders did not want the game wiped out, but wildlife management science was barely born in this country in 1872, and game was being destroyed thoughtlessly, with little notion of any population's long-term prospects, almost everywhere. Yellowstone could not have expected much better at first, and didn't do all that bad. As historians of American wildlife law have observed, federal control of wildlife protection is often more restrictive than the more common (at that time) state or local control.

By 1883 the indiscretion of public hunting in Yellowstone was manifesting itself in waste that appalled even the Gilded Age mind. Urged by a few leading sportsmen and naturalists, the Secretary outlawed hunting that year; three years later, when the U.S. Cavalry was assigned to protect the park, all but a few bold poachers ceased to shoot the elk and bison.

In those days not all animals were deemed equally deserving of such protection. Predators, such as coyotes, wolves, and cougars (bears were usually safe after 1886, but hawks and other smaller predators were not entirely safe until the 1920s) were "bad" because they ate the "good" animals. In order to protect the elk, deer, sheep, and so on, the predators were subjected to increasing persecution. The predator-control program began under the army and was continued by the park service. Between 1904 and 1935, 121 cougars, 132 wolves, and 4,352 coyotes were trapped, poisoned, or shot in the park. The cougars and wolves were virtually wiped out, and the coyotes, remarkably resilient animals, thrived.

Within a few years of the hunting prohibition, say by 1890, the animals became less wary and were frequently seen by visitors. Yellowstone soon became a wildlife showcase of unprecedented size, with visitors expecting to see an assortment of animals almost daily. This quickly became an important visitor attraction, successfully developed as such by the hotel company and other companies; it then became an additional reason for maintaining the hunting prohibition, because hunted animals do not pose for camera-wielding tourists. As new parks were added to the system, no-hunting rules became standard in most of them. Today, from Hurricane Ridge in the Olympics to the Anhinga Trail in the Everglades, animal-watching is an important part of the national park experience.

By the time the cavalry arrived Yellowstone had an established annual patronage of thousands. They were appreciative of the park's wonders, but typically short-sighted. Tourists do not change. Then, as now, they were careless with their campfires. It did not occur to them that if they loaded their wagons with chunks of hot-spring deposits to take home that others could not enjoy them (nowadays they load their trunks). It did not occur to them that the rest of the world did not care to read their names inscribed in the delicate film of algae that grew across the travertine formations, or to see the hot pools filled with coins, garments, and rubbish. It did not occur to them that the resource here was wildness, and no one could have expected them to understand that. The people in charge of the place were only dimly aware of it themselves. A great many value judgments had to be discarded before the resource could come into its own. What is probably most remarkable about the process is that it happened as well as it did; it may be that the really significant foresight exercised by Yellowstone's early champions was not so much in setting it aside as in defining it so carefully.

The U.S. Army Corps of Engineers, now the nemesis of most environmentalists, was placed in charge of road construction and maintenance, and several corps officers displayed exceptional sensitivity to the land, trying always to follow slope contours and in other ways make the roadways as unobtrusive yet functional as possible. They did not always succeed, but they understood the mission and did their best. Of course, landscape architecture and related crafts were well developed in other parts of the country; many modern park enthusiasts would object that the park has as many roads as it does, to hell with where they are. The roads could be a lot worse, though, and there could be (and almost were) many more of them. We owe these officers something for relying on the best value judgments they had to work with.

The army did more than suppress random vandalism and promote aesthetic construction. They took on the greater task of protecting the entire forest. There was considerable confusion in government circles about trees in federal reserves. The first national forests, established a few years after Yellowstone, were actually pure outholdings that could not be harvested. Only the intervention of both foresters and politicians brought those greater reserves into public use. But Yellowstone was never seriously considered, in those first days, as a source of wood. The mandate of the act seemed clear enough on the point: no commercial use of the forests was permitted. However, the forests were put to other uses, including providing timber for any number of park buildings, firewood for park residents, and similar local projects. Today we think of park forests as sacrosanct, but early managers had to be practical; if you know where to walk you can still find the stump fields, just as you can easily enough find the small dams and impoundments that provide the larger park developments with water, or the scars at the foot of Mt. Everts where the army mined the coal to warm Fort Yellowstone during the long winters. The difference, again, was local use. In most cases building the little dam or carving into the local coal vein was the cheapest, most efficient way for a perpetually underfunded administration to solve its basic problems of supply. In that sense, though we may now regret these early violations of the park's purity (the dams still exist), they are not really important. The act provided for them by its very vagueness.

The act also stressed protection, and the U.S. Army has always had a very positive and energetic notion of what constituted protection. In Yellowstone they immediately busied themselves protecting the park from vandals and other minor destroyers, but they also concentrated on bigger problems, especially fire. They spent much of their time putting out runaway campfires, but they also put out any naturally caused fires, starting an eighty-year period of fire suppression in the park. Like the predator-control program, it seemed like a good idea at the time.

Once these basic needs—human supplies and park protection—had been satisfied, the army undertook more creative management. With an energy that showed why so many early military men in this country were sportsmen-conservationists, the cavalry looked for even more to do, and they found plenty in helping the good animals. Starting about 1900, some of the elk, deer, and other grazers were fed, from hay wagons, to help them through the winter. Thus was created the potential for short-circuiting the natural culling process winter had been conducting on the animals for thousands of years, and thus was assured an even larger population of animals to be fed the following year, and the following, and the following.

Thus also was established an unnatural and ecologically damaging concentration of animals in the immediate area of the feeding grounds. The removal of the wolf probably didn't have much effect on the elk or deer, because in Yellowstone wolves seem never to have served the function of controlling population; winter's weeding out of weak animals was (and is) much more important. (The same is true in other areas, where biologists are now discovering that the removal of predators was blamed for population irruptions that were actually caused by other factors.) But the feeding of animals in winter was the kickoff of a seventy-year preoccupation with wildlife population control in Yellowstone.

Basing their premises on poorly understood and often erroneous information, the army and the park service lived in dread of an elk population irruption. Such an event was even announced to have happened in the early 1920s, when an actual count of elk revealed only about half as many elk as had been reported in earlier years in the northern herd. During the final army years, before 1918, the elk population was reported in excess of thirty thousand. Finding only half that many was a shock and resulted in an official report of a massive die-off the previous winter. An acute shortage of actual elk carcasses did not deter managers in their announcements. What seems to have happened, according to an exhaustive review of historical records by recent researchers, is that earlier accounts were grossly inflated. A careful review of the thousands of pages of records the army kept revealed, among other things, immense duplications that resulted in many elk being counted more than once. It seems that the counters conducted their censuses in the spring as the elk were moving up country; the counters would work an area, then return the next day to another area a little way up the valley, sometimes moving along at the same pace as the elk. I personally suspect there was more to it than that. It was politically good to report expanding animal populations in those days, just as many modern deer-herd managers must worry about having a large enough harvest during hunting season, and I wouldn't be surprised if the army officers in the park puffed up the totals. Or, as a friend of mine put it, "The Major probably called his scouts and non-coms into the office and said, 'Boys, I want you to go out there and count the 30,000 elk,' and a couple weeks later they'd march back in and tell him, 'By golly you were right, sir, there are 30,000 of them out there.' "

However it happened, the effort to have lots of elk turned into an effort to have a "safe" number, to avoid the dread starving winter that had regulated the population for so long.

Nature keeps things controlled, but rarely keeps anything constant;

witness the cyclic population dynamics of many small animals, from rabbits to grouse to lemmings. Elk in Yellowstone, left alone, would have lean and fat years; they would have winters of high losses and easy winters. The population existed not on a balance but on a swinging pendulum, in dynamic response to the environment. It was this ebb and flow that park managers sought to smooth out.

Zoos are stable, constant places. So are most game parks. With little experience to suggest alternatives, Yellowstone's managers were forced by their ignorance and the fashions of the times to adopt the zoo mold for Yellowstone. The idea of letting the elk population take care of itself in the park, as it had done for thousands of years, simply wasn't *human*, and Yellowstone was in many ways managed for humans first. It was still a great outdoor zoo, and the animals needed keepers, as in any other zoo.

One quiet winter afternoon I took some time from typing and cataloguing in the archives to lug a projector over from the radio shop to my office to view and index a stack of home movies we had recently received. They were made by a park employee in the 1930s and 1940s. The projector thrummed smoothly, and with the shades drawn I was soon lost in a flickering black-and-gray world of Christmas parties, ski outings, and familiar local streets where the trees were all peculiarly short. I was about to take a break before I dozed off when the scene changed. I saw the corner of a high wood corral, with an agitated young elk backed against it. He was prancing and wild-eyed, watching something near the camera. The ground was oddly black beneath him, though there was deep snow along the corral wall. A bulky figure appeared, approached the terrified elk, and with a well-practiced stroke smacked its head with a hammer, cutting its throat as soon as it hit the ground. As the blood squirted out I realized why the ground was black. This was one of the slaughtering operations that went on in an effort to hold the population down. Elk were herded into corrals and either shipped to other areas alive (Yellowstone elk have repopulated ranges all over North America) or butchered and given to other agencies such as Indian reservations. Elk control went on into the sixties, when rangers shot hundreds at a time and generated such a giant public outcry that management had to change direction. As the film rolled on, with huge cartloads of stiffened carcasses sliding over the darkened snow, I was again reminded of how much we have learned here and how difficult the lessons have been.

Not that they're getting any easier. As I mentioned a moment ago, Yellowstone's elk (to say nothing of the bison, grizzly bears, and other animals) leave the park in good numbers in the fall and winter. Once outside the park they are under the administration of other agencies with other mandates. Most of them are hunted. Thus, by leaving the park the elk guarantee that the park's mandate to preserve naturalness will not ever be purely honored, because other agency mandates must also be satisfied. Though cooperation between the various state and federal agencies that deal with these roving elk will help everybody at least *sort of* honor their mandates, it is pretty much impossible that all parties will ever be satisfied, or that they will ever stop scowling at each other across the boundaries, as they often do now. The boundaries the elk cross are as much philosophical as geographical, and while the park service has a commitment to preserving a natural setting, state fish and game departments have equally heartfelt commitments to reasonable harvests of big game (*in* the park elk are wildlife; *outside* the park they're game).

But all of this jumps ahead of the story I was telling, about Yellowstone's days as a zoo. Attracting a few hundred elk in to feed them hay was nothing compared to what was done with the bears.

They started showing up at the hotel dumps about 1890. At first just a few blacks, then an occasional grizzly, would come in at dusk to sort through the day's leavings. Tourists discovered them and the dump show was on. By the 1930s, when there were large grandstands (seating hundreds every night) at the Canyon dump, watching Yellowstone's bears chow down on trash was a well-established tradition at the outdoor zoo. The bears were wildly affected by the unnatural food source, and the visitors got an exciting if regrettably inaccurate impression of wild animals.

Even more unnatural settings occurred in the park. Possibly most unnatural, even more so than the eradication of the predators, was Yellowstone's buffalo ranch. Park bison, the last free-roaming herd in the lower forty-eight, were down to a few dozen head by the late 1890s, and a single effective poacher could have put them beyond restoration. The army brought in additional animals from captive herds elsewhere, and trapped a few of the wild ones to interbreed. At first a small corral at Mammoth held them, but after about 1905 they were herded out to the Lamar Valley in the northwestern part of the park, where what amounted to a ranch operation was established. For fifty years after that a semi-domestic herd (the few remaining wild bison hung on, then gradually increased, so that Yellowstone remains the only place in the lower forty-eight that has had a continually wild herd) was grown much like any other mammal crop, with culling, feeding, roundups, and all the rest (bison are not as easily herded as cattle,

but it was done). Movie companies and publicity-conscious park superintendents staged stampedes that appeared in popular westerns of the
day—hundreds of shaggy bison thundering up and down the valley for the
edification of the cameras or visiting dignitaries. If not for the elephant-size
corrals, one would have thought one was at a normal cattle ranch.

Eventually, in the 1950s, the herd was weaned from the ranch care;
gradually Yellowstone's several bison herds were restored to some sem-
blance of their prehistoric state, but, like the elk and the bears, they had
been thoroughly used to satisfy their protector's notions of what a National
Park should be.

Change in treatment of park wildlife came slowly through this
century. By 1916, when the National Park Service was created to centralize
management of the growing family of parks and monuments, there had
developed a body of thought that more or less answered the many questions
left unsettled by the Yellowstone Park Act of 1872. The National Park
Service was given a legislative mandate of greater sophistication and balance than Yellowstone had had before:

> The Service thus established shall promote and regulate the
> use of the Federal areas known as national parks, monuments,
> and reservations... by such means and measures as conform to
> the fundamental purpose of said reservations, which purpose is to
> conserve the scenery and natural and historic objects and the
> wildlife therein and to provide for the enjoyment of the same in
> such manner and by such means as will leave them unimpaired for
> the enjoyment of future generations.

The mandate contained an internal conflict that is an eternal challenge: to use and enjoy, yet protect and preserve. As one contemporary
ecologist put it not long after, "Countless times it has been pointed out that
here was an inconsistency in a first premise; that a lion and a fawn were
being expected to share the same bed in amnesty; that ice and fire were
expected to consort together without change of complexion, in short, that
the vast American public should be brought to the parks for a vacation
without disturbance of the pristine loveliness of these sacred areas."

In the 1920s the National Park Service had the opposite problem it has
now: there were not enough visitors. From 1905 to 1915 Yellowstone
averaged fewer than twenty-five thousand visitors a year (in the 1980s it
sometimes has that many in a single day). The park service embarked on a

fabulously successful publicity campaign, because the only way to increase their paltry budget was to swell the ranks of their friends. The park managers, though more thoughtful and enlightened than in the 1890s, still treated wildlife as a convenience. It could be argued that Yellowstone stopped killing wolves and cougars as much because they had wiped them out as because they became more reasonable about the predator's place in the park, and that they stopped killing coyotes because they were wasting time trying to destroy an animal more indomitable than they. The extent of human preference over wildlife was still great; in Yosemite National Park, noisy woodpeckers were shot if hotel guests complained about them. There was still much of the friendly innkeeper in the way the park service did its job; make the people comfortable, keep the animals in line.

At the same time, though, there was a growing park constituency, both scientific and popular, that saw new directions in the National Park Service Act.

Many saw Yellowstone's policies as drifting from a greater, higher purpose into more pedestrian paths: treating wildlife as convenient entertainment and altering wildlife behavior to suit shallow whims and preconceptions; aborting and diverting hot springs to fill swimming pools, thus destroying many depositions and formations. A vacation resort atmosphere prevailed where something else was more suitable, and where a rare opportunity for providing that something else was being wasted.

It is rather too easy to fault the park service for these shortcomings. Most federal agencies must respond to public demands, and few are given the sort of mandate that the park service has always struggled with. More important, faulting the park service for mistakes made in wildlife management, or park philosophical directions, is treading on thin historical ground because such judgments are often made out of context. Most vacation resorts, except for the lavish ones only the wealthy could afford, were far tackier than Yellowstone's campgrounds and hotels were in those days. There were enormous public and political pressures to manipulate the natural setting for the convenience of visitors. Not nearly so much was known then as now about wildlife ecology. Yellowstone was one of the most important classrooms for providing some of the lessons we have since learned.

A few years after the National Park Service was created, influential scientific organizations, including the Ecological Society of America and the American Association for the Advancement of Science, began to look harder at park policies. They resolved to oppose all future introductions of nonnative life forms to the parks, in an attempt to protect what remained of the pristine state of being in some parks. They were as concerned about fishes and plants as about mammals, and were reinforcing decisions Yellowstone's managers had made even back in the army days; after about 1907, the park's cavalry administrators had resisted efforts to dilute or confuse the wildlife setting any further. Specifically they had withstood considerable pressures to introduce more nonnative fishes, reindeer, chamois, mountain goats, and several game birds, thus showing an impressive devotion to the natural integrity of the park.

In the 1920s and 1930s, especially after New Deal legislation provided additional funding, the National Park Service generated its own staff of biologists and naturalists and had the assistance of those from other agencies, especially the U.S. Fish and Wildlife Service. Some of these scientists were superb, and they eloquently pointed out the flaws in traditional thinking about the parks. They helped stop predator control, and initiated some of the most important studies of wildlife yet undertaken in the parks.

World War II provided the parks with a respite from heavy visitation, and Yellowstone took advantage of it to close the public bear-feeding grounds at Canyon, meeting with relatively little public objection because visitation was so low; again, the park service showed both the vision and the guts needed to go against a popular trend. Bears still fed at dumps, and were still fed along the roads, but the formality had been reduced in the face of overwhelming popular enjoyment of the dump show. Progress as significant as that should not be slighted simply because it was not enough to solve the problem; the bear problem was not yet fully understood anyway. There was increasing awareness in the service of the ideal of wildness, an awareness that required great effort on the part of managers and rangers who had received their training in a simpler world of good and bad animals and black and white issues. Many people believed, for example, that Yellowstone had so many bears only because the dumps were there; that only a few could survive without garbage. Many more believed (and still do) that predators commonly wipe out prey species; that elk and deer populations can expand infinitely to the greater pleasure of the public.

Progress was halting, though, and it stopped just as it started. The same respite that permitted the park to close the dump show cut their budgets way back to help fund the war. When the war was over paltry budgets were not increased to handle the massive tourist boom that occurred. Visitor facilities, outdated by 1940, were hopelessly wrecked by the 1950s.

But by 1950 an element in the conservation community—scientists, naturalists, interested bystanders, journalists, and the rest—realized that the goal of the parks was not being done justice, and that many of the traditional "problems" with the animals were in truth people problems, caused by human selfishness or ignorance. It was tough to go against popular will when popular will had been allowed to exercise itself so freely for so long; most bureaucrats are not conditioned to make the kind of waves required. It became illegal for visitors to feed bears in the park in 1902, but bear-feeding was perhaps the most popular visitor pastime for more than sixty years after that. Hundreds of people were injured, hundreds of bears were destroyed (and hundreds more ingested all manner of glass, cellophane, and cardboard), but no one tried to stop it. Nothing the park service could do seemed to keep the northern elk herd down. Laboring under appalling illusions, they were trying to keep the elk numbers to five thousand in a herd that naturally "wanted" to number fifteen thousand or more. Helplessness in the face of growing ecological problems was only a minor annoyance compared with the despair of facing ever-growing crowds of humans who seemed bent on consuming, feeding, or fouling everything in sight.

There were two major turning points. One occurred in 1955 with the initiation of Mission 66, a major federal program to upgrade facilities in all parks by 1966. Mission 66 is now seen as a mixed blessing, if a blessing at all. It did indeed make huge improvements in visitor facilities, but some feel that it did so at considerable sacrifice to wilderness goals; that the park did not need the additional commercial development. Others answer that objection by pointing out that the park would be much worse off had the debatable "improvements" not occurred. As usual the question comes down to just how much use, or occupancy, or enjoyment, is appropriate. Given only the choices of adding the new developments or doing nothing, I would have to say that Yellowstone's resources might be in much worse shape today than they are had the Mission 66 developments, which at least helped control and manage the growing crowds, not been built.

As an aside it is worth pointing out that Yellowstone's system of hotels and other services largely developed during the stagecoach era; automobiles don't need nearly as many overnight stops as do stagecoaches, and on those terms the park could get along with many fewer such developments. But moving all the hotels and other services to just outside the park is, like most easy answers, not all good. Wherever those facilities are, either in or adjacent to the park, they are going to consume grizzly bear habitat. They are going to concentrate people in great numbers where commerce can

have its way with them. The same people who complain about developments in the park complain even more loudly about the unruly, ill-planned
way "threshold areas" around national parks grow. At least within the park
the National Park Service can strictly control the ugliness and dirtiness of
each facility.

The effects of the park's developments are considerable. They were,
mostly, designed and established long before there was sufficient ecological awareness to know if they were being placed where they might do grave
harm to the natural resources of the park. The Fishing Bridge development, for example, sits next to the outlet of Yellowstone Lake, in the
middle of a crossroads of life forms and energy flows unlike any other in the
park. Now that the park service knows that this development must be
removed for the welfare of the park (particularly the grizzly bear), the
campgrounds there have a tradition of use and a constituency with considerable political power. It is extremely difficult for the park service to fight
pro-development powers even when they have the guts to try. In recent
years many grand futures have been envisioned for parks of Yellowstone's
size, with mass transit replacing cars, planned threshold developments
replacing overnight accommodations within the park, and other progressive ideas, but until the park service and its friends have a lot more clout
than they do now, these plans will remain just that—plans. In the meantime, the park's resource will have to live with what it has, and take its
chances in the political present in the hope that it can survive until some
perfect future. We can hope.

The second turning point was scientific, and of several parts. The park
service was widely criticized, by conservation groups and private citizens,
for not devoting proper attention to its ecological needs. Like any small
underfunded agency, it is always at the mercy of people who want it to
spend money it doesn't have, but there had been a decent research program
in the service up until World War II. The agency never recovered from the
budget cuts of the war, and never got its research program up to speed again
until the 1960s.

In 1963 the Advisory Committee to the National Park Service on
Research, while studying the parks' ecological research, was "shocked to
learn that the research staff (including the Chief Naturalist and field men in
natural history) was limited to 10 people and that the Service budget for
natural history research was $28,000—the cost of one campground comfort
station." That's $28,000 for the entire national park system, not just for
Yellowstone. That same year the Secretary's Advisory Board on Wildlife

Management completed a report entitled "Wildlife Management in the National Parks" (known as the "Leopold Report," after the committee's chairman, A. Starker Leopold). It was later adopted as park service policy, and it formalized even further the mandate of the National Park Service Act of 1916, giving most attention to the needs of the resource:

> As a primary goal, we would recommend that the biotic associations within each park be maintained, or where necessary recreated, as nearly as possible in the condition that prevailed when the area was first visited by white man. A national park should represent a vignette of primitive America.

The committee, while recognizing that perfect primitiveness was not achievable, knew that a high level of authentic primitive setting could be attained:

> If the goal cannot be fully achieved it can be approached. A reasonable illusion of primitive America could be recreated.

As with previous significant statements on park management, these two dealt with main principles. Their interpretation has varied because of certain questions arising out of them: What is the actual goal of the parks? Is it to preserve a static natural representation of how the area looked when first seen by whites, or is it to preserve an ongoing natural system that may alter itself but that we may not alter? The Leopold Report maintained (and A. Starker Leopold continued to maintain, until his death in 1983) that the goal was to "preserve, or where necessary to recreate, the ecologic scene as first viewed by human visitors." The Leopold Report recommended such things as habitat manipulation and ungulate population regulation, where necessary, to maintain those essential elements of the setting "as viewed by the first European visitors." There was no question, in the firm statement of the Leopold Report, of a completely unhindered system doing what it wished to do to itself; the native species that were first seen by whites were to be kept in reasonable abundance. Nor was there any question that the writers of the Leopold Report hoped to keep such managerial intrusions to a minimum. But the commitment was to protecting the native species, not to protecting the wholeness or unhindered integrity of the natural system.

Since then there has been an internal tension, often not even a conscious one, in management decisions that must resolve just how far from the "discovery condition" the park may be allowed to wander. It is complicated by how little we know of just what condition the park was in when it was discovered, by how often the countless elements of the natural setting vary without being measured, by how little managers can actually do to control many of those variations, and by a growing feeling among many park enthusiasts that the dynamics of change are more interesting and fulfilling to watch unhindered than suppressed. If there has been a trend, it has been toward letting the natural setting express itself at some cost to the maintaining the condition of the park as it was when discovered, but managers continue to be aware of their option to interfere if some part of the setting appears to be in danger.

Most disagreements over this policy seem to be disagreements over how far to let the natural setting go. Do we permit one animal to out-compete and displace another? Do we let nonnative grasses run wild and displace rare natives? Some of Yellowstone's hottest controversies in recent years, such as over whether or not the grizzly bears should be supplemen-tally fed in an attempt to increase their numbers, have revolved around just such disagreements. The future promises to be the same. Managing the natural setting—determining just how wild the wildness can be—will continue to be a series of philosophical compromises.

But in the early 1960s, when the Leopold Report was issued, there was still much to be learned, not only about these philosophical compromises but about the practical politics of getting *anything* done in the park.

With the impetus of growing attention from the political and scientific worlds, and the steadily heightening public dissatisfaction over several policies (elk control flared brightly in the early 1960s, with major national news coverage of rangers shooting the animals; the controversy was of several parts, including people who wanted the elk fed instead, people who wanted to hunt in the park, and people who just wanted to criticize the park service about something), Yellowstone began to receive the money needed for an adequate scientific staff. By the late 1960s the park had several full-time biologists with a number of summer assistants and students, and the U.S. Fish and Wildlife Service was maintaining a staff of researchers in the park as well. Rather than intermittent and catch-as-catch-can studies, the biggest ecological problems were now receiving professional attention.

The results are still being sorted out, and are, predictably, controver-sial. Douglas Houston's monumental study of the northern Yellowstone elk herd ran for more than a decade and straightened out many of the historical tangles and discrepancies of past management. Based on his conviction that the herd will indeed level out at some naturally occurring size (one that varies with the hospitality of the climate from year to year), this major elk herd has been permitted to grow or decrease as it will within the park. Hunting of it, when it migrates outside the park, continues to have an influence on the number of elk. There have been no elk reductions in the park for more than fifteen years, and therefore no public outcries over rangers shooting elk. But other controversies have arisen. Some still worry that the population will outgrow its food supply and overgraze its range, thus hurting everything that lives there and leading to some massive die-off of animals. Much of the time it is this feared die-off that stirs people up. Houston's work is based in part on the premise that winter will regulate the herd, which means that elk will die every winter. He does not deny— indeed he assumes—that in an especially harsh winter some large percent-age of the elk, say 20 percent or more, could die. Indeed, that's what natural regulation is all about: nature regulating itself. Some critics of the park service don't like that kind of management, though; they either want to hunt the elk, or somehow keep them from dying, which is a philosophi-cal difference of opinion, one that will surely not go away. It seems at this point that the big test of the park's elk management *will* be the once-a-century winter that kills a fourth or even a third of the northern herd. When there are 5,000 elk carcasses lying around out there, we will learn just how true the various interest groups will permit the park service to be to its mandate of naturalness. An elk population can recover from heavy losses much faster than a federal agency can.

The bison have undergone similar study, by Mary Meagher. Her work and the general redirection of park management in the late 1960s has led to the park's several distinct bison herds being allowed to seek uncontrolled population size. What makes the bison especially interesting in the ongoing evolution of managing wildness is a disease they carry, brucellosis. Brucel-losis causes miscarriage in domestic cattle, and many bison carry it without harm to themselves. This has made ranchers near the park nervous for decades, and now that the bison are more common than at any time in a century, more and more of them are apt to wander out of the park and create ill will. It's a complicated issue (aren't they all?), because the park service is unconvinced that the bison will even transfer the disease. Also, elk and other wild animals also carry brucellosis, and they roam at will over many ranches. The park service has for some years attempted to turn back bison that appeared to be heading for the boundary, but now some Montana residents are starting to show an interest in bison hunting; once the animals leave the park they become property of the state, which then must decide how to deal with them. The state isn't too happy with the thought of having to kill several dozen bison, the hunters would like a try, some conservation groups don't want *anyone* shooting them, and once again the park's goal of a naturally regulated setting is running into trouble.

It's safe to say, though, that for all the anger and confusion generated by the elk and bison, no other aspect of modern park management—no other attempt to respect wildness as a resource—has caused as much heat and controversy as has bear management. The Yellowstone bear-management controversy of the 1970s and 1980s is easily one of the most notable wildlife management controversies in American history. At least three books have been written, including one by me, that prove the impossibility of calmly analyzing this story, so what follows is only a summary of a summary.

The bears were living the good life, black bears along the roads and grizzlies in the dumps, all happily betraying the park service's professed goal of a wild setting where the animals interact more or less naturally. In the late 1960s, when Jack Anderson became superintendent, he took on the bear problem as energetically as he approached the elk, bison, and other glaring inconsistencies between what the park service claimed it was to do and what it was actually doing.

It was relatively easy to restore the black bears to a wild existence; roadside feeding was no longer permitted, and people who fed bears were fined. Bears were chased from the road, and some that could not break the begging habit were killed, but according to the park service (and some observers disagreed) the black bear population was not significantly reduced. It was just redistributed in its natural range, with no concentrations along park roads. By the mid-seventies you could drive through the park for a couple days and not see a black bear, but when you did see one it was a wild bear, not a zoo bear. Many people objected, but when confronted with the facts of bear life along the road and with the realities of Yellowstone's higher purpose, most agreed the change was for the better.

Sanitation practices, both in developments and in camping areas and picnic areas, were gradually revamped over a few years, so that all garbage cans were bear-proofed and infractions of the new sanitation rules were subject to fine. There was no half way about this; either there were bears eating human food or there were free-roaming bears.

The grizzlies were another matter. In 1959 a team of scientists led by two distinguished naturalists, Drs. John and Frank Craighead, began a landmark study of Yellowstone's grizzlies, working primarily with the animals that frequented the dumps (dumps still existed, they were just out of sight of the public now). Over an eleven-year period they tagged, radiotracked, and researched their way into international leadership as grizzly authorities. When Superintendent Anderson decided that the dumps must be closed, the Craigheads and the park service differed in many respects. The Craigheads, while bowing graciously at the notion that park bears should be in a wild state, did not have confidence that the grizzly population was big enough to make it without help. They suggested, in 1967, that the grizzly population be treated differently, and be kept inflated if possible. They further suggested that if the dumps must be closed, they be closed gradually, to wean the bears from garbage.

Based on his experience in other parks with garbage bears, and on the Craigheads' inability to convince a special session of the Secretary's advisory board that weaning was the better approach, Anderson and his staff disagreed. They closed the big dumps abruptly in 1970 and 1971. No one thought the bears were going to starve; at least none of the serious participants in the debate did (many casual observers and journalists jumped to that conclusion). What was most feared was an uncontrollable dispersal of bears to developed areas, where an unusual number of bears might have to be destroyed (that is, a number greater than the customary annual control kills) and some people might be hurt.

The books that have already been written review most of the important events of the next ten years of debate, bear management, acrimony, and cheap journalism. By 1980, scores of bears had been killed either in the park or in the surrounding lands, some by state or federal agencies, some by poachers, some by accident, and the grizzly had been almost totally divorced from garbage. The park service was calling the program a success; they believed that the grizzly bear had been restored to a wild state, and that if an awful lot of bears had been killed in the process the population would soon recover. The Craigheads were still maintaining that the population wasn't big enough to be abused much in the first place, and that ten years of management had placed it in serious danger of extinction. Numerous committees, independent authorities, and organizations offered their opinions, and most people heard what they wanted to hear. I offer an example of the degree of uncertainty about the welfare of the grizzlies. In 1980, when I finished my book about the bears, there was cautious optimism among park scientists that the population of grizzlies had indeed recovered and was as high as 300 or 350. Two years later the

Interagency Grizzly Study Team, who began to study Yellowstone's bears in 1973, revised that estimate to about 200, a figure as frighteningly low as 350 was comfortably high. There are still those who think the number is high, and there are still those who think it's much lower than 200. They all point up the desperate uncertainty of keeping track of something as footloose and elusive as a grizzly bear.

Far more than the elk, the bears depend on non-park land for survival; half of their remaining range is outside the park, and that range is being whittled away steadily. Development will probably not increase much in the future inside the park, but it increases almost daily outside. Illegal killings, by sheepherders, ranchers, and market hunters (claws, teeth, and other body parts are worth a small fortune), are occurring at an unknown but probably considerable rate. Ironically, we may never know to what extent the closure of the dumps caused the decline that most scientists now agree has occurred. Perhaps the park service estimates of over 350 bears were optimistic, and there has been little decline. Perhaps the combination of illegal killings, agency killings, and accidental deaths has just been too much for a population of bears that is more crowded than it was thirty years ago. One scientist has suggested that the decline of grizzly numbers in the 1970s could be due to a drying trend in the climate in that decade; less succulent vegetation could result in fewer bear cubs each year. I think it most likely that there is no one cause, but many.

It is regrettable, though, that efforts to restore the grizzly bear population to its natural state could come to such a sorry and confused point. All the while that scientists, administrators, journalists, and others have been haggling over the number of bears, the bear's range has been disappearing under wells, condominiums, and a variety of leases. There are truly promising signs that the various agencies responsible for the grizzly bear in and around Yellowstone can learn to cooperate, and the controversy has helped generate a national constituency for the bear, but I can't yet be hopeful. A great many people who live near the park, people with a disproportionate influence on how grizzly habitat will be managed, are sick of hearing about grizzly bears, and as enthusiastic as ever about turning the lands near the park into profitable developments. If it comes down to it, there aren't many people who believe the grizzly bear can survive if it has only the park itself for habitat.

In some ways Anderson took bolder steps than his bear program. He was among the first park superintendents in the service to stand by and watch a wildfire burn itself out. After eighty years of suppressing fires, we discovered that fires, naturally caused ones, play important roles in a wilderness. Among other things, they help to maintain the vegetation mosaic so necessary to diverse wildlife habitat. The evils of uncontrolled wildfire are well known, but Yellowstone is not here as a harvestable crop. It is a primitive vignette, and fire is the consummate primitive force. In a place as big as Yellowstone fires are a patchwork process, burning small (and occasionally large) spots here and there, gradually replacing each portion of the mosaic with a new one. When white men first came to the park it was practically all green. Over a period of centuries, any portion of it might burn, but at any given time most of it will be green. It sounds simple and good, but when the smoke rose from those first few fires, sparks were ignited in quite a few federal offices; it took more guts that most "lifer" administrators have to face the heat. Now a good many fires burn in the park each year. If they threaten a development they are put out; I think that's a small concession compared with the process of letting any go in the first place.

An even more challenging extension of the "let it be" philosophy, certainly more challenging than free-ranging predators or winter-killed elk, has been the reinstatement of the tree predator to the Yellowstone wilderness. Attempts have been made in Yellowstone to suppress insect infestations for as long as the technology permitted, but again the question must be asked, "Why deny this part of the wilderness cycle its function?" Now, in Yellowstone, a stand of reddened or dying trees is not a cause for shame. Old-time foresters and other people brought up on the Smokey Bear ethic are offended, but this forest is not here to build houses or make cardboard boxes. If the resource is wildness, the wildness needs pine bark beetles and budworms to be complete.

As with so many Yellowstone issues, this one gets harder to handle as you approach the park boundaries. Like wildfire or grizzly bears, bark beetles are not especially welcome on lands outside the park, and the people who own and use those lands don't appreciate seeing the park let such expensive nuisances get up a good head of steam on park land before hitting them.

And so it has gone, ever since a few enlightened people saw the opportunity to make Yellowstone something special, to give it a "higher purpose" than most public lands. There is a controversy at every turn now, where once there was mostly disregard. The park service has a gift for generating hot topics, just as the park's assorted constituencies have a gift for confusion and anger. But how else could it be when the goal is itself only an illusion, even a reasonable one?

Some look at all these issues—elk, grizzlies, fire, and all the other controversial topics—and say it's hopeless; they say the park service is playing a silly game that it cannot win, and that the park is already so unlike its original state that there's no point pretending it's "natural" any more. I disagree. I don't see the park service pretending any such thing. Besides, considering our general propensity for screwing such things up I'd have to say Yellowstone's *real* resource—its wildness—is in better shape than it has been for nearly a century. With wildfire, elk, grizzlies, bison and all the rest actually out there wandering around relatively unhindered by park managers; with hot springs overflowing as they will rather than being piped into swimming pools; and with a far higher awareness of the concept of wildness as a resource than ever before, it looks to me as if the illusion is indeed growing more reasonable.

In an interview shortly before his death the famous writer Joseph Wood Krutch wrote Yellowstone off as a "lost cause." Those can only be the words of someone who was either fifteen years behind the times or who has never stepped from a boardwalk or a parking lot. It is easy enough to leave the crowds at Old Faithful behind, and when you do you find a wild setting that is in better shape ecologically than it has been since before 1900. Internally it is robust. It has the flaws already mentioned, and it has others: too few wolves, a lack of influence by pre-Columbian cultures (whatever those influences may have been), too many meadows growing to timothy and other domestic grasses that were imported to feed horses and bison, and, ever and always, the incurable idiots who scrawl their names on the algae beds. But the whole, the greater resource, isn't all that bad off. The machine is still running, and practically all the cogs are still there. It isn't perfect, but it never was intended to be. It *still* isn't intended to be. After all, when Yellowstone was established no one was claiming that the resource was wildness. As the national-park idea has matured—as we have continued to establish Yellowstone, so to speak—the concept of wildness as a preservable resource has solidified. But by the time it did so, we'd already lost some of it, thus guaranteeing the illusion would never become a perfect reality. It could be argued that Yellowstone had to pay the price of learning the hard way: it had to lose its wolves, or impair the health of its grizzly population, in order to realize what those things were worth. Now, as those realizations are coming home to us, we are struggling to decide just what can be saved, and what should be saved. In both cases I think that the answer is clear: we can save far more than enough to make it worth the fight.

The Other Wilderness

There is another Yellowstone wilderness. Its animals are as wild, beautiful, and fascinating as the ones we know well. Its vegetation and topography are complex, often difficult to understand. The abuses that we have visited upon it are spectacular.

By definition, or at least by virtue of the agencies in charge of them, fish are apparently not wildlife. Every state has its "Fish and Game Department," and the federal government has a "U.S. Fish and Wildlife Service." Fish, for several reasons—some subtle, some obvious—are not perceived in the same terms we use for warm-blooded creatures. They are not wildlife.

This is in part a practical consideration, because fisheries biologists and managers are often a necessarily distinct bureaucracy within a given agency, and they do deal in a very different world than do nonaquatic biologists. But ultimately all managers of wild lives are concerned with the same things: habitat relationships, population dynamics, predator-prey relations, and so on. All managers of fish, game, or what-have-you are concerned with finite populations of wild living beings. I am far from being the first to suggest that we, by our distinction between fish and wildlife, are encouraging and reinforcing a prejudice in the public mind. It may be a prejudice that needs reconsidering in many places, but it certainly needs it in Yellowstone. Such a prejudice here, where we are trying to give equal rights to all wild inhabitants, strikes deeply at our preconceptions, even more deeply than approving of predators. Fish are less like us than raccoons; fish are less likely to receive anthropomorphic sympathies from us than mammals that have big brown eyes. When was the last time you saw a children's book where the main character was a redside shiner (much less a snake or a leech)?

Our treatment of Yellowstone's aquatic wilderness diverged permanently from our treatment of the rest of the park in 1883 when sport hunting became illegal. Sportfishing would never disappear, and it is only recently that it has been seriously questioned as an appropriate use of the park.

Prohibiting hunting and restricting fishing are of course only two examples of how visitor impact is controlled in parks. As the parks became popular, it became necessary to eliminate many seemingly harmless activities, so that it is now illegal in Yellowstone to pick the flowers, collect rocks, or feed wildlife. Except when such activities are done for research purposes and under strict control, they have long ago been shown to be too destructive. Many of these policies were formulated fifty or more years ago, but as visitation to the parks changed from thousands to millions they have been more strictly enforced. Most are not challenged by serious students of park management; they were proven necessary even before the parks became crowded.

The national parks were young at the same time that fisheries management was young. To enhance public enjoyment, many "improvements" were made for the sake of fishing. That mostly meant stocking. A great variety of nonnative species were stocked, first in Yellowstone and the California parks, and later in newer reservations such as the Great Smoky Mountains. Fishing was quick to become an important part of the park experience. Commercial interests, including hotels, boat liveries, guide services, and tackle shops, developed around each fishing attraction. Fishing became a park tradition, and both angler and businessman clamored for more fish.

Because of its volcanic history, the Yellowstone region is characterized by topographic uncertainty; the Continental Divide runs for many miles through the park, so that waters flow from Yellowstone to both oceans (Glacier National Park is even more generous, sending waters to both oceans and Hudson Bay). There are numerous waterfalls and cataracts that create natural barriers to the upstream movement of life-forms in many streams. A full 40 percent of Yellowstone's waters was originally barren of fish life. This included almost the entire length of the now world-famous

Firehole River. It also included two of the park's largest lakes and countless smaller lakes and streams.

These barren waters were stocked shortly before 1900 with rainbow, brown, lake, and brook trout plus other fish. Stocking was often casual, with little attention paid to what fish may already have been in a given stream. Many stockings did not take hold, but enough did to radically change the fish populations of many waters. The Madison River, for example, originally contained westslope cutthroat trout, Montana grayling, and whitefish. Today's fish population in the Madison in the park is almost exclusively rainbow and brown trout and whitefish. Similar changes occurred in other waters, quite often at the expense or to the elimination of the native fish. This has been of little consequence to the average visitor, who cares only that there be plenty of fish to catch. But in the aquatic ecosystems of the park it was the ecological equivalent of replacing major portions of the park's elk herd with reindeer, Barbary sheep, and axis deer. The native resource has been disastrously altered.

Like other park animals, fish were managed primarily for the convenience of the visitors. This was often a matter of state-of-the-art recreational management's being no more advanced than the ecological sciences, but sometimes the offenses were less forgivable. In the 1920s, for example, it was discovered that the white pelicans on Yellowstone Lake were alternate host for a trout parasite; there was active enthusiasm among park managers for an egg-stomping campaign on the pelican nesting islands. The enthusiasm was further fueled by resentment over how many fish those pelicans ate, thereby depriving tourists of just that much good sport. The campaign was actually initiated—eggs were stomped—before a few private citizens got wind of the plan and forced the park service to desist.

As early as the 1920s a few ecologists and park planners began to wonder about fishing as a proper use of national parks. As ecologists grew to understand their legal obligations in parks—to preserve the natural setting—they were horrified to discover how much damage had been done. The introduction of nonnative fishes was bad enough, but native stocks were mixed in hatcheries and pumped back into park waters at random, hopelessly mixing many museum-pure subtypes (this was especially bad at Yellowstone Lake, where various portions of that huge body of water had their own separate runs of fish that may have been in the first stages of developing into distinct subtypes). Widespread baitfishing resulted in many incidental and regrettable introductions, as fishermen commonly dump their bait buckets at the end of the day, even if they purchased the bait seventy-five miles away in another drainage on the other side of the Continental Divide. Private citizens, such as outfitters and anglers, sometimes stocked isolated waters for their own use.

Similar introductions took place in park flora, but of all park wildlife none were subjected to such continued and thoughtless impositions as the aquatic animals. What a few people realized in the 1920s, and the realization was slow in dawning, was that the aquatic communities of the park were no less legally sacrosanct than the nonaquatic ones. There was, in other words, no legal reason to value the underwater wilderness in a national park any less than the rest. As important, ecology of wild settings had matured enough as a science to *want* those aquatic settings protected. As one scientist put it in 1924, "Some of the same persons who are very eager to maintain a wilderness for certain purposes have never recognized that others are equally interested in an untouched aquatic wilderness."

While this kind of talk was getting a little attention from the scientific community, Yellowstone's fish were getting more and more attention from anglers. As the park service's publicity campaign of the 1920s took hold, Yellowstone became an ever more popular fishing resort, a nationally famous trout-fishing center. Yellowstone's managers had established small hatcheries in the park by 1900, but they took advantage of the demand and geared up a truly monumental hatchery program. Run by the U.S. Fish and Wildlife Service, the hatcheries grew, sending millions of trout eggs to other parts of the country as well as placing fry back in Yellowstone's streams. By 1938 the park was producing over 43,000,000 eyed trout eggs. Up until World War II, Yellowstone was the world's leading cutthroat trout factory. Basing their removal of so many eggs from park waters on the widely held notion that all animal populations produce a surplus (and the less often articulated but equally prevalent notion that mankind has a moral obligation to harvest that surplus), managers cranked out as many trout as they could.

By 1960 the same thinking that had led to other changes in ecological management reached the hatchery program and shut it down. The park fish were, in one regard, being accorded equal status with other park animals: they were being put on their own, to maintain whatever population levels they could. Since then, except in rare instances where some endangered strain of native fish has been planted in a sanctuary stream to give its population a "booster shot" and increase its odds of survival, the mixed community of native and nonnative fish in Yellowstone has been on its own.

The fishery resource that attracted all the anglers had been deteriorating since at least 1900. It was noted in the 1920s and 1930s, a time that fishermen now regard as the halcyon years in Yellowstone, that fish populations were in serious trouble; halcyon was itself only a shadow of the original vigorous setting.

The deterioration was observed and was responded to over the years with increased stockings of fish and with occasional restrictions on tackle, such as fly-fishing-only waters. Such restrictions were, however, aimed only at controlling and maintaining a considerable harvest under the now-challenged "maximum sustained yield" concept that sought to take the most fish that could be taken without jeopardizing the reproductive capacity of the population. They were not designed to protect the natural balances of the aquatic wilderness.

To further complicate and mystify our destruction of the fishery, we were doing ill even where we thought we were doing good. Recent investigations show that the mineral content (upon which biological productivity in large part depends) of Yellowstone Lake has declined dramatically since the 1890s. Some have suggested that suppression of wildfire is the culprit, as minerals that are normally released into streams after a fire have remained locked up in the trees. As the lake became less mineral-rich, its capacity for supporting life—from plants to insects to fish—was reduced correspondingly. In the name of protection of the resource we thought we saw—trees—we may have damaged the resource we did not understand— wildness (I say "may have" because not all scientists agree with this theory).

Beginning with Jack Anderson's superintendency in the late 1960s, Yellowstone's fishing regulations were overhauled so that the resource was given higher priority. Sportfishing became less consumptive. The spectacular success, in terms of improved fishing, gave added impetus to similar programs in other parts of the country. Each year, it is said, the fishing in Yellowstone improves. Popular writers are now comparing it to the 1930s and 1940s, and predict it will eventually approach primitive quality.

This success was achieved by reducing the harvest, which has now become only a minor concern for many Yellowstone fishermen. Even in waters where a limited kill is permitted, the no-kill philosophy is promoted. More and more waters are regulated as catch-and-release, providing thousands of visitors with the experience of catching a wild trout without trying also to provide them with a fish dinner. The result, in time, may be a completely no-kill fishery, at least for those waters containing native fish;

the nonnative fish are still in a no-man's-land as far as their status as park creatures is concerned. (A later chapter deals with them and the threat they pose.)

Today Yellowstone has excellent sportfishing by any standards, despite millions of visitors; the fishing is better along many park roads than it is in wilderness areas in many other parts of the country. But even more important, at least from the viewpoint of ecologists, the aquatic ecosystems of the park are in better shape than they have been for decades. Fish populations that were for many years depleted have been restored to a level more closely resembling their primitive state (even if the species are now different, the "biomass" is similar), and the fish are functioning more naturally as part of the park's nutrient chain. Sportsmen proudly point to Yellowstone as an example of nonconsumptive use of a fishery, where fish and fishermen live in harmony. Yellowstone is widely used as an example of what progressive management can do to turn around a deteriorating fishery.

Success occurred in this park rather than in some others because of the political situation: Yellowstone has exclusive jurisdiction over its management. Yellowstone's superintendent has almost kingly powers. The park was established before any of the surrounding states were more than territories, and has many legal preferences. Because of the great independence the superintendent has, ambitious programs such as the present fisheries-management plan can be implemented. Most park administrators do not have so much power or freedom.

But success is not that simple. Though Yellowstone seems to be a shining light in fishing, it is not without its problems. Many people are not yet satisfied that things are as they should be, or that the park service's legislative mandate is yet being served.

By the time of the Leopold Report of 1963, ecological thought and park-service management had both matured tremendously. The park service found it increasingly important to adhere to the legislative mandate as greater and greater crowds threatened the resource. It became increasingly difficult for tourists to be consumers in parks. Rock-collecting, tree-cutting, bear-, deer-, or squirrel-feeding, and other interferences with the setting were punished. The resource, that ephemeral goal of wildness, was getting more equal treatment in all its parts. And fishing became more and more singular as a consumptive activity, a direct wilderness-to-mouth use of the national parks.

Rangers began to hear the question "Why can we fish here if we can't hunt here?" Which is to say, "Why do you allow the capture and harvest of some animals when others are completely protected?" Or, rhetorically, "What's the difference between fish and wildlife?"

The difference, despite the great improvements that have been made in recent years, including a strong trend to catch-and-release fishing, is that fish are not treated as first-class citizens of this wilderness; they are not yet wildlife.

Anglers quite naturally respond with alarm to this sort of talk: "Why, that's absurd! Everyone knows that you can harvest fish and still have a healthy population!" That's true, of course, but it's also true of the mammals in the park, which by choice and law we don't harvest. That we've always done it that way is no proof it should be done now.

Management in national parks involves an endless series of trade-offs. We sacrifice wild country so that we can build access roads, hotels, and campgrounds. We sacrifice wilderness silence so that we can reach remote shores of lakes by motor launch. We sacrifice trees to telephone wires, water to drinking fountains and showers, and backcountry soil to Vibram soles. Fishing, like so many park pastimes, is viewed as such a trade-off. Few parks these days regard the sport as a way to feed visitors. Many recognize it as an important and frequently used way to involve visitors in the natural surroundings. Anglers are quite proud of their awareness of the natural setting that makes their sport so enjoyable, and fly-fishermen often become excellent amateur entomologists.

Fish, furthermore, are not so easily enjoyed as are many other types of wild animals. Trout and dace don't graze in meadows, and are not readily photographed except under some special circumstances. For most people appreciation still means direct contact.

The overall trend toward no-kill fishing in the parks has been important; it is a major step toward nonconsumptive use. By reducing the harvest, the fish populations are permitted to play their natural roles in the park's nutrient systems. A greatly reduced trout population or a trout stream crowded with wading fishermen cannot provide as much food to osprey, otters, bears, gulls, pelicans, and other animals as would be available naturally. The reduced harvest has benefited the sportfisherman, too, in terms of numbers of fish caught (and released) in Yellowstone. So it is that the interests of both anglers and people wanting the resource better served have dovetailed nicely, and both groups are happier than they have been in a long time. The park ecosystem is benefiting from the greatly reduced harvest, and at least that portion of the angling fraternity that is more concerned with sport than with meat has also benefited.

The cordiality that now exists between anglers and other park users in Yellowstone is tenuous. A growing if not yet organized or self-recognized group of people—scientists, park-service employees, and private citizens—finds the practice of sportfishing in national parks objectionable enough to wish it would cease. They are troubled by the distinctions being made between fish and other park wildlife, and they even find such conciliatory and progressive doctrines as catch-and-release fishing to be only unsatisfactory political expedients.

So far their dissatisfaction is the result of the same reasoning that led to the prohibition of hunting from the parks; hunting became visibly incompatible with developing park ideals. Their dissatisfaction is not based on a moral repugnance to sportfishing itself. It does seem almost inevitable, though, that other people, whose motivations are morally oriented, will discover this issue. Catch-and-release fishing seems especially vulnerable, even more so than meat-fishing, to moral criticism: it involves subjecting wild animals to the shock, trauma, and outright terror of being captured, merely for the fun of it (a wise old fisherman once said that if trout could scream a lot of things would be different). A popular sarcasm among skeptics runs like this: "Why not have catch-and-release elk, too? We could lasso them and let them go, just like trout. Wouldn't that be fun?" The point, a difficult one to deal with objectively, is that trout and elk are both wild animals; elk just happen to be warm-blooded and more complex morphologically, just as trout are more complex than the park mosquitoes that we swat without a second thought. What use is appropriate for park animals may ultimately be a matter of moral judgments after all; we may come full circle from the time we applied a set of moral judgments that led us to kill predators and extinguish wildfires. Animal-rights movements and other morally based phenomena will almost certainly play an increasing role in the development of the national park idea. After all, the very decision to let a park be wild is based on moral and aesthetic considerations in the first place.

For now, though, the most outspoken critics of sportfishing in the parks are confining themselves to their interpretation of the park service's mission to preserve. One of the most influential expressions of their interpretation appeared in 1967 in the important book *Man and Nature in the National Parks*, published by the Conservation Foundation. Written by two distinguished conservationists who had conducted a lengthy personal examination of the parks and their management during the early stages of the ecological overhaul that occurred in the 1960s, the book was quite blunt on the subject of fishing:

We would put the point of view at this juncture that the privilege of fishing in national parks is one that needs radical reconsideration. The privilege was given without question at the beginning of national park history; the right to fish with a rod is the almost inalienable right of every American; but again we are up against what was once a perfectly sensible decision being carried forward into a period and circumstances entirely different...

Fishing, surely, is one of those outworn privileges in a national park of the later 20th century...

Yellowstone had not yet undergone its great management overhaul when those words were written, and their authors demonstrated little appreciation for or understanding of the intangible rewards of fishing; nor were they aware of the possibilities for maintaining a near-primitive quality fishery under proper restrictive regulations. But the principles they espouse would probably not be seriously affected by the improvements that have occurred in our management of Yellowstone's aquatic wilderness since 1967. They would probably still find fishing an outworn privilege.

Fishing has been reaffirmed as an acceptable use of the parks in recent studies conducted by the U.S. Fish and Wildlife Service and the National Park Service. The reaffirmation has occurred with greater and greater emphasis on no-kill regulations and other restrictions on human consumption. But even under the best, most stringent restrictions, Yellowstone fishing is still easily criticized, and Yellowstone's aquatic wilderness has farther to go than the dry land before it is again a primitive vignette.

First, it is frequently pointed out that many park waters were originally barren of fish life. If this 40 percent of the aquatic wilderness were instead 40 percent of the dry land, our introduction of fish—a major new predator on all the smaller organisms that occurred naturally in the fishless waters—would be the equivalent of giving over 40 percent of the dry land to grazing livestock. Those aquatic ecosystems hardly represent their primitive state. The question is, were we capable of it, would we be obliged to remove the fish from the Firehole River, Shoshone and Lewis Lakes, and all the other waters that were without fish before we arrived? The very suggestion causes anglers to grow pale, then livid. The park service has not expressed any interest in such actions, but there is no doubt that the question will eventually come up; it is an inevitable consequence of committing ourselves to restoring national parks to their primitive state.

The potential for dialogue, debate, and quarrel are endless, but it must be pointed out that there is, at last, a conceptual difference between anglers and all other park users on the subject of fishless waters. To an angler, a lake without fish is simply barren. To a naturalist that same lake is only barren of fish life; it hosts a horde of fascinating creatures and plants. Anglers, for all their enthusiasm for aquatic natural history, are basically uninterested in any setting that lacks fish, and sport fish at that; pity the poor dace and suckers that don't have pretty spots or rise to a dry fly—most fishermen write them off as "trash fish," of no interest except as bait. The broader view of the naturalist who appreciates each aquatic setting's life-forms for their own sake, rather than as objects of sport, is more defensible in modern national park thinking, but fishermen and nonfishermen alike are unaware that this issue exists. When they become aware of it, we can assume that angling societies will exert considerable influence in the future direction of park management.

Second, as wonderfully improved as fishing is, and as greatly restored as the fish populations are, the present arrangement still has major flaws. It has been proven, through numerous studies, that fly- and lure-caught fish have a very high survival rate when released. A recent study of the cutthroat trout in Yellowstone showed that only about 2 percent of the fish died when released (bait-caught fish commonly swallow the hook deeply, so that half or more die in the process of getting the hook out; this is why baitfishing is prohibited in the park, though prohibiting it also avoids the chance introductions that occur when fishermen empty their bait buckets at the end of the day). In some seasons the water is warmer and the mortality rate may be higher for a time. Two percent is negligible when considering the health of the population, but it is still 2 percent. Visitors would not be allowed to kill 2 percent of the elk or ground squirrels.

Third, and most important in principle, fishing in Yellowstone remains an interference with and manipulation of a wild-animal population. If these fish were somehow transformed into eagles or cougars, we would immediately afford them full protection and would jail anyone caught trying to snare one. The basic dilemma—an inconsistency of treatment—remains.

Ironically, public education—the elevation of public taste we would like to see the park accomplish—provides one of the best justifications for continuing sportfishing in Yellowstone. In 1978, the park service issued 218,000 fishing permits in Yellowstone. There are at least twelve states that have fewer total licensed anglers than that, and those 218,000 come from all fifty states and many foreign countries. I issued hundreds of permits to Yellowstone visitors, and I saw every imaginable response to the progressive management policies there: everything from outright disbelief ("You mean we gotta throw'em back? What's the sense of that?") to abject ecstasy ("Finally, the government is doing something right!"). People whose only acquaintance with fish is as something to eat are bound to take home some new ideas, both about sport and about the natural world and how we respect it, when they encounter Yellowstone's fishing regulations. The fishing in the park is so good compared to most parts of the country that there is little chance the visitor will be disappointed.

Another justification for fishing in the park will probably by itself ensure the sport's future for several decades yet. Fishing is an industry here. Anglers annually spend about four million dollars in and near the park, so that the local economy depends in part on their trade. The many implications of this financial stake in the park will be obvious to anyone who considers changing the order of things. But the future will not be easy. The late John Townsley, superintendent of Yellowstone until his death in 1982, would say publicly that fishing will be eliminated in fifty years. Privately, to me, he said thirty. John was a fisherman himself, a third-generation park service employee, and he did not personally advocate or favor the elimination of fishing; he believed it was coming, based on the directions he saw the national park idea taking.

It is both encouraging and illuminating to know that fishermen—and I am a devoted one, so I speak here from that perspective as well as from others—are no longer the only users of Yellowstone's aquatic wilderness. Closures of some key areas of streams and lakes to fishing have resulted in increased opportunities for "fish-watching," a new and measurably significant visitor activity. There are several good fish-watching locations, but the most popular by far is the old "Fishing Bridge" across the Yellowstone River where it leaves Yellowstone Lake. Some years ago the bridge was closed to fishing to protect cutthroat trout spawning runs (serious fishermen avoided the place anyway—it was a circus of tangled lines, minor wounds, and unleashed adolescence). Since then, watching trout from the bridge has become a major activity, and the trout population has responded to the protection by regaining some of its primitive vigor. You can now stand on the bridge and see hundreds of trout, twelve to twenty inches, feeding, fighting, and mating in total naturalness below. In 1981, 148,000 visitors parked, got out of their cars, and walked out onto the bridge just to watch the fish. That's more than two-thirds of the total number of park fishermen that year, and though it's impossible to equate levels of interest or duration of activity, we have to admit that Yellowstone has again, as when it first became a wildlife sanctuary where animals could be easily seen, added a new purpose to its definition. The national park idea has taken a small but significant step on Fishing Bridge.

I love to fish. I love the places it leads me, and I love the intensity of concentration and tranquility of spirit it somehow simultaneously provides. I rarely kill a trout any more, though. I lived for five years in New England near a famous stream that I had fished frequently for three years before I even realized I had not yet taken a trout home, and after five I still hadn't. I don't mind killing one now and then, but I never seem to get around to it any more. I can't rationalize the sport in a way that will convince the nonparticipant to take it up, any more than I can explain away the moral objections I forced myself to elucidate a moment ago. But I have come to terms with my place in the trout's world. I enjoy the skills involved in fooling a fish into being hooked, and I enjoy the struggle that ensues. I don't especially need the kill, but I don't object to it, in moderation. I'm comfortable enough with my physical identity to recognize the animal joys involved in fishing, as well as to respect the aesthetic and spiritual fulfillment it can bring when practiced thoughtfully. I suppose I could lean on the old saw about it being every person's responsibility to understand and personally participate in the food-gathering process once in a while, just to keep in touch with the earth. I do doubt the logic of the beef- and chicken-fed urbanites who don't think *wild* animals should be killed; an animal's domestic state has no effect whatsoever on the terror and pain it feels at death, nor on the moral compromises we undergo when we kill it. But participation in the food-gathering process, or recognizing that all animals have an equal right to life, does not begin to justify the pleasure I find in fishing. I could be smug knowing that I, a fisherman, know more about the fish's world and do more to conserve and protect it than do most nonfishermen, but again, if fishing be wrong in some ultimate sense, my good work does not justify fishing.

For me, at last, it's all simpler than the philosophical struggle would seem to allow. Because I have fished, and because I have fished both thoughtfully and well, I am closer to the trout than I was before, and I am closer to the world the trout inhabits. The damage I have done is the price I pay for that closeness, and it's a price I respect. Perhaps some day I'll put the trout and its world so completely above my own needs that I'll quit fishing. But not now, not yet. I'm willing to put my needs above the trout's the way the trout puts its needs above the needs of thousands of insects it eats. If, as a "higher animal form" (a term I suspect is not only irrelevant but also insulting), I am obligated to behave more "humanely" (an equally suspect term given humankind's destructive nature), I'm willing to fail that obligation. If I am criticized, I'll then refer my critic to the good work I've done for trout conservation; I don't expect it to satisfy him, but it will get him off my back long enough for me to go fishing.

I care about fishing in Yellowstone very much. I learned to fish there, and only someone who has learned to fish in the fullest sense of the word can know what gratitude the experience can bring. I am grateful to Yellowstone for teaching me to fish while teaching me so many things about fish and the other wilderness. If fishing becomes illegal in Yellowstone, I will be saddened but I think I will understand. To me, Yellowstone, this extraordinary place with its resource-that-is-not-a-crop, does not have to have fishing. Many of my friends will disagree with this, I am sure, but I know there are other ways the fish can be enjoyed, and I know plenty of other places to fish.

That redoubtable volume *The Hitchhiker's Guide to the Galaxy* tells us about the planet Bethselamin, a fabulously beautiful place that was threatened by the tremendous numbers of people who came from all over the galaxy to enjoy it. The residents of the planet, though they liked the tourist trade, became "so worried about the cumulative erosion by ten billion visiting tourists that any net imbalance between the amount you eat and the amount you excrete while on the planet is surgically removed from your body weight when you leave: so every time you go to the lavatory it is vitally important to get a receipt."

Yellowstone is a little like Bethselamin. The more of us who go there, the graver the risk of damage. For the unusual purposes of Yellowstone we've learned to treat predators with respect, to approve of wildfire, and to treat fish like other animals. We come, expecting our pound of flesh ("shed thou no blood . . ."), but also expecting the park to go on unchanged by our visit. We crave the illusion of primitiveness, but in order to enjoy it we must affect it. And each time we further reduce our effects—each time we get a receipt at the lavatory, so to speak—we step nearer the ideal, the illusion fades slightly, and is replaced more clearly by the wildness we seek.

Trimming the Yardstick

One summer day in 1977 as I was leaving the Visitor Center at Mammoth I ran into Aubrey Haines. Aubrey, Yellowstone's premier historian, lives in Bozeman, Montana, having left Yellowstone in 1969. His visits to Yellowstone were all too infrequent to suit me, but before I could express pleasure at seeing him he confronted me with the tall, yellow-blossomed stalk of a plant he'd obviously just picked from the parade ground.

As if we'd been sitting in the same room all day, instead of having just encountered each other for the first time in months, he demanded information. "Paul, what's this?" There was the endearing insistence of the naturalist who has been surprised by an unfamiliar and unexpected species of anything.

"Hi, Aubrey... uh, it's dalmation toadflax. They call it butter and eggs, but I think that's really the common name of some other flower. Dalmation toadflax is the formal name. It's all over around here." I vaguely waved at the parade ground, bright yellow with the stuff. "It's an exotic."

Aubrey continued to stare at the plant in his hand with the look of a man whose umbrella has suddenly spoken to him, and it occurred to me that this pretty little flower that decorated the flats all over my sub-district was so strange to him because only eight years earlier, when he left the park, it hadn't been here at all.

Yellowstone's experiences with exotic, or nonnative, wildlife defy

summary. The native fishes, as I've suggested, have suffered most grievously from introductions of new species, but plants and mammals have
faced intrusions almost as serious. Dozens of new plants, some intentionally added and some just hitchhikers in stock feed or on the wind, have
entered the park.

Or consider for a moment the case of the moose. When the park was
established, and in its earliest years, there were probably a few moose
roaming the southernmost portions of the new reservation. It was, therefore, native to the park. But since that time it has greatly expanded its use
of the park, so that now moose are commonly seen throughout the park,
with a range and in numbers quite unlike their presence when the region
first became known to whites.

Such are the fluid conditions under which we try to define and separate
the native and the nonnative. People use the terms "exotic" and "nonnative" interchangeably, but technically speaking, exotic means "from
another continent." For example, most of Yellowstone's introduced
species of sport fish—lake, brook, and rainbow trout—are from North
America; the brown trout, on the other hand, is from Europe and is,
therefore, a true exotic. Generally the rule holds that native species are
those that predate white settlement of the area, but sometimes the rule
seems pretty arbitrary.

For example, it requires contradictory compulsions of us. On the one
hand we obligate ourselves to preserve the wild setting as it was when first
discovered, and on the other hand the wild setting may not want to stay as it
was. It was not static in its primitive state. The last glaciers vacated
Yellowstone only a few thousand years ago. In geological or ecological
terms that's not much time, and the park's vacancy sign is still attracting
passing species. After a few hundred generations of a life regime of colonist
plants (ones that don't need much help to grow), the soil starts to build up
so that it can accommodate a broader assortment of plants, which in turn
can provide food and shelter for a broader assortment of animals. They
don't read boundary signs, much less the *Federal Register*. Like the pre-
Columbian Indian tribes whose territories drifted on the tides of war and
migration, so are the wild residents of the Rockies inclined to greater
transience than we might expect. Yellowstone has very few life-forms for an
area so large. It can accommodate a good many more, and if white men had
never come here it would have received them, slowly and naturally.

It's a problem common to all national parks. A waterfall breaks down,
allowing a pair of dace to pioneer upstream across a park boundary. They

flourish, compete with and then replace a native chub that happens to be on the endangered list. Biologists express interest, conservation groups express concern, administrators express alarm, and nature has, again, expressed herself. Action, interaction, and reaction, the latter often by humans and ill-considered. In a case like this one, which could happen in many parks, the dace might get poisoned out so that the stream could be maintained as a refuge for the rare chub. This is less likely than it used to be, and would only happen anyway if the chub was in really big danger of extinction. The dace got there naturally, and it comes down to a question of which rule is more important: preserving naturalness or preserving an endangered species.

What scares me most is not a minor holding action of the sort that might poison a stream to protect a rare species of fish. That doesn't scare me at all, really, because it demonstrates a real devotion to important principles, even if the principles don't always agree. I'm not even terribly bothered when I see the park service mowing meadows in Shenandoah National Park to keep the forest from encroaching naturally on them. That sort of finger-in-the-dike fight with a very patient mother nature is more amusing than anything else. What really scares me is the possibility that in our desperation to appear successful in dealing with the impossibly complex problem of nonnative species we may lose sight of the reason we care at all.

A great many exotics are irremovably established in parks. We simply don't have the technology or talent to get rid of them. A prominent ecologist who has honored me with his friendship and patience for several years recently summarized the lament heard from many conscientious park biologists:

> Let's take the example of an exotic grass such as the ubiquitous cheat grass. Most of the western parks are overrun with this exotic and all of us wish it wasn't there. But clearly it is not in the realm of practicality to ever eliminate it. The question then is should we manage the vegetation in such a way as to minimize the extent of cheat grass or should we announce to the world that we are against cheat grass and that we are setting out to exterminate it, knowing damn well we'll never succeed. There are shades of interpretation, I'll fully admit, but nevertheless they characterize the two viewpoints that might be taken toward exotics. I am all for the principle of purity and motherhood and so on but at the same

time I am keenly aware of the practicality of administering an area like a park and the hypocrisy of saying that we are going to do something that we know we cannot do.

It is the peculiar lot of the park service to be placed in this position of seeming hypocrisy.

But let's dream a minute, just for argument's sake. Another biologist I know tells me that some day poisons will exist that are so selective that we could treat a huge body of water, like Shoshone Lake in Yellowstone Park, and then row around and pick up the body of every lake trout in the place—no crustaceans, no invertebrates, no redside shiners, no plants—just that one species of trout. Maybe in some future world that will even be possible with the plants; one pass with a crop duster, and no more cheat grass. For reasons I'll get to in a minute, I think it's important to keep that dream filed somewhere in the back of the park service's administrative mind (or soul, if it survives). And, for reasons I'll get to right now, there's cause to worry that by the time we do have such awesome technology we will have lost the discretion needed to apply it.

In February of 1980 the Department of the Interior, acting on the recommendations of an Ad Hoc Fisheries Task Force (a panel of authorities appointed by the director of the U.S. Fish and Wildlife Service to "review and evaluate the effectiveness of the National Park Service's fisheries policies and practices"), published various proposed revisions in the fisheries-management policies of the park service. They appeared in the *Federal Register*, a publication more people should see more often. These revisions were generally directed at refining the park service's legal commitment to preservation of native conditions, pointing out that "the existing National Park Service fishing policy deals generally with the act of fishing (as authorized by law) and not with the conservation of fish resources." We've been here before, but I have a different kind of news this time.

The news is a troubling element in the proposals, a strange suggestion reminiscent of the Big Lie, or an ostrich. It was suggested in these proposals (listen close) that "where appropriate and after careful analysis the Director, National Park Service, should be empowered to declare certain introduced species 'naturalized' and managed as natural components of the ecosystem."

The alarm sounds, and I reach for my shoes as I jump from bed.

Admitting we can't get rid of them is one thing. Pretending they're something they're not is dangerous. Very dangerous.

As I have said, the expressed ideal of a national park is to preserve a primitive portion of the American scene in its natural state. The ultimate goal would be to have a natural scene exactly like primitive America—a setting with only its original life-forms and environmental conditions. Obviously this is impossible, mostly because the park service Act requires the service to make the area available for human use. Practical management realities do not permit us to achieve the goal.

It is one thing to accept that we cannot achieve total primitiveness in an area; we are willing to accept this in all the parks. It is quite another thing to weaken, legally, our commitment to the goal of primitiveness. The countless compromises we make in order to accommodate visitors are undeniably necessary. We do, however, recognize them as compromises, and also recognize that they are potentially hazardous to the ideal goal of primitiveness. By acknowledging the need to compromise, we are serving the public without doing any harm to the primitive ideal. On the other hand, once we start tampering with the ideal itself—once we start redefining the park goal—the central notion upon which the National Park Service is based becomes weakened. Once the ideal has been undermined, we no longer have any absolute quantity against which to measure subsequent compromises. The ideal, though unachievable in practice, is absolutely essential if the park service is to maintain its identity. Once the service's ideal has been compromised, as it would be by "naturalized" species, and once our commitment to the absolutely untainted natural scene has been softened, the integrity of the whole arrangement is shot.

There has long been a healthy and dynamic tension between the two conflicting mandates of preservation and use. Preservation is the only one of the two that has an imaginable absolute, that being the complete exclusion of all nonnative life-forms from the park. While we deal with human use as a matter of degree (it can be regulated, increased, or decreased), we cannot similarly deal with the concept of preservation. Preservation can only mean what it says it means. We cannot redefine what is natural, any more than we can change what the park was when white men first visited it. If we try to redefine an area's natural character by announcing a new "native" species, we are only fooling ourselves. The area, in its unique and elaborate ecological character, "knows" that we are not telling the truth. The result of creating "naturalized" natives will be a transient paper construct that will never become more than self-delusion.

It cannot, therefore, be "appropriate" for the director to designate any species as "naturalized." Such an action by the director would be a violent assault on the guiding principles of the National Park Service.

Moreover, such designations aren't necessary. Future managers can deal with exotics as have past managers. They can recognize them as unfortunate facts of life. They can dream about crop dusters. They can, most importantly, go ahead and accept that the exotics are there to stay. They can do all these things without losing sight of the ideal, and without compromising the ideal. There is a profound and timeless lesson for both managers and visitors in the admission that we have caused irrevocable change in a natural scene. That lesson alone is valuable enough to compel us to hold onto the traditional ideal.

The designation "naturalized" serves no good purpose that I can see. All it does is allow some administrators to trim the yardstick; to run a four-minute mile by shortening the mile. It would allow them to relax and admit defeat where defeat is not one of their alternatives. It would allow them to stop worrying about some particularly annoying exotic. It would short-circuit the park service's institutional conscience. Once that had been done, and once a few weak people in the right positions had tasted the sweet relief of a problem deftly ignored, it would be hard to stop further encroachments on the remaining principles the parks live by.

Thus I have preached myself into a contradiction, for earlier I promised that I would have no simple answers to offer you. Here is one after all, though it's not so much an answer as a sort of rule: If we're going to make the most of Yellowstone, and if our ongoing "establishment" of the park is to continue fruitfully, we must not lose our guideposts. As unattainable as the absolutes are—both perfect purity and total public use—we dare not circumvent the principles they represent. Our success is not measured simply by how close we come to an ideal but by how honestly we recognize the importance of that ideal in guiding us through the maze of practical realities that are the real challenge of Yellowstone.

A Percentage of Fools

During my first summer in Yellowstone the park service initiated a backcountry permit system. A dramatic increase in overnight camping in the backcountry made such a system necessary in many parks in the 1970s; backpacking became enormously fashionable then. The system involved a simple non-fee permit that all overnight hikers were required to obtain. A network of clearly marked backcountry campsites was established along the major trails, and hikers planned their trips at a ranger station, consulting topographic maps and reserving a specific campsite for each night. Once the campsites were all reserved—one party to each, no more—no additional permits were issued for that area. On the one hand, this system relieved backcountry hiking of much of its spontaneity because it required people to end up in a specific predetermined spot every night. On the other hand it kept use of fragile areas down to an acceptable level, it gave us a good idea of how much use each part of the park was getting, and it gave us a chance to talk to the uneven and unpredictable assortment of people who were going back there.

That first summer the system was new to all of us, and the service wasn't what it would be in a few years. One day when I was on duty at the Visitor Center information desk a stack of permits was plopped down in front of me with very little explanation, and I was left to assume I could handle the job of issuing permits.

I issued only one that day, to a party of hikers who planned an extended trip up on the Buffalo Plateau along the north boundary. There are very few footbridges in the backcountry (for the same reason there aren't sidewalks), so I got out a map to show these people—two young men and a woman—where the fords were on the streams they'd have to cross. I'd never been near the area, but I could read a map with the best of them. They thanked me, we wished one another well, and off they went.

Five days later the ranger office got a call from the Tower sub-district ranger. Seems he'd just fished a couple of hikers out of Slough Creek after they'd tried to ford it when it was in full flood, and he wanted to know what "damn fool" had told them to try such a thing so early in the year.

The hikers (and I) were lucky; they suffered no permanent damage and, when they stopped in at the station several days later, told me they thought it was all very exciting, being rescued and everything. But I was sick about it. I nearly quit, right then. I was furious at being given a responsibility I wasn't prepared for, and equally furious at myself for being stupid enough to accept it. I'm glad I didn't quit, for many reasons, not the least being that a few years later I was a supervisor myself, and I tried to make sure none of my people were put in a similar position.

But if one of those hikers had died, who would have been to blame? I would have judged myself guilty, I'm sure, and my boss probably would have done the same thing to himself. Perhaps the surviving hikers would have considered themselves to blame; anyone with bad enough judgment that they would attempt to ford a raging stream is not without responsibility for the consequences.

There is a more fundamental question here, one that anyone experiencing a national park ought to be asked: Must a wilderness misfortune result in blame being assigned as it always is in other more civilized settings? I wonder, and so do many others, about individual responsibility in national parks, and how the parks suffer from the erosion of such responsibility under modern law and modern thinking.

At the beginning of the century, a visitor to Yellowstone took the risks as they came. In 1904 a hotel employee who was mauled by a bear he was feeding "got simply what he deserved," according to the superintendent. Park authorities took some care to keep people out of trouble, and with so few visitors to deal with it wasn't all that hard. In 1916, when a teamster on a road crew was killed by a grizzly bear, great regret was expressed but no one put anyone at fault. The grizzly had been raiding camps for weeks, getting into food caches and scaring the daylights out of people; but even then grizzlies were so widely thought of as harmless that the only dialogue resulting from the death of the teamster was over how unusual such an attack was.

In the 1920s and 1930s, as more visitors crowded in, more incidents occurred. Some years dozens of people were hurt, some seriously, by begging black bears. Though in those days and earlier people complained about the bears (or even recommended that the bears be killed of), there was little talk of blame, much less of recovering damages or making someone legally at fault for the actions of the bears. This was partly because society was not yet caught up in the fashion of suing itself silly, but it was also because damages were difficult to recover. Until 1947 the only way a private citizen could recover damages was through a petition to Congress for a "redress of civil wrongs committed by the government or its agents." Payment was approved, or enacted, when the petitioner's representative, usually their congressman, managed to attach a rider to some unrelated bill, specifying an amount to be paid to the wronged party.

Of course the grizzly bear or the hot spring is not the "agent." The agent is the manager who stands accused, often just implicitly, of not properly managing the wild setting to protect the people. This actually happened in Yellowstone in 1942. Miss Martha Hansen, a forty-five-year-old Idaho resident, was fatally mauled one night at the Old Faithful campground, and two years later President Roosevelt signed a bill, rider attached, awarding her family $1,894.95 in damages. In his report that year, the superintendent noted that "this is the first relief bill of record due to an injury to a park visitor by a bear."

This incident is as good as any at illustrating the dilemma of responsibility for wilderness misfortunes. Park rules forbade bear feeding (and had since 1902), but it was so popular that it was commonly allowed. Bears were also fed daily at open pit dumps around the park, including one quite close to Old Faithful. Visitors watched the bears at the dumps, seated at huge grandstands or held back a "safe" distance by rope fences, up until the 1940s, when the dump show was recognized for the travesty it was. People came to see bears, yet they didn't want to be hurt by them. We now know that bear management in those days was trying to achieve the impossible. Fed bears are certain to cause problems, just as zoo-minded visitors are. In 1941 and later, ranger staffs were greatly reduced because of the war. Maintenance crews were reduced, and already casual sanitary procedures worsened. As visitation dropped off, there was less garbage to eat in the dumps. Some bears seem to have moved to campgrounds looking for easy food. Natural food shortages, caused by a dry spell, further affected bear movements that summer. The issue isn't a particular bear and a particular person. The issue is a broad circumstance wherein a mauling is either more or less likely to happen, and blame is pretty difficult to assign, even back in the days when Yellowstone's wilderness was being run for the comfort and enjoyment of the visitors at the wholesale sacrifice of the resource's welfare. Looking back, knowing that bear management that sought to keep bears handy for public viewing was doomed to fail, it is hard to approve of payment; it amazes me that more people weren't killed. And it's easy to see that blame for tragedies such as Miss Hansen's death is circular. Blame the rangers for not keeping the bears out of the campground. Blame Congress for cutting park budgets so that there aren't enough rangers to do the job. Blame the public for allowing Congress to cut the park appropriation. Blame the park visitors who insist on feeding bears. Inevitably, responsibility rolls itself back on the accusers, but blame is attached only unsatisfactorily to anyone in a case like this. You might as well blame poor Miss Hansen for camping at Old Faithful, or blame the bear (its species was never determined) for developing an appetite for chopped beef and restaurant leftovers.

But blame became more easily assigned, to the government at least, in 1947, with the passage of the Federal Tort Claims Act. The act, which has undergone various revisions since then, provided a legal mechanism by which a tort ("a civil wrong, not arising from a contract relation, giving the person who suffers from the wrong a right of action for damages") can be redressed. In layman's terms, it amounts to taking the government, or some agency of the government, to court, as in a suit, and it seems like a perfectly logical legal process in a modern society.

According to current park service guidelines, tort claims against the service almost always involve blame for a damaging encounter with the wilderness:

> The Government's liability under the Federal Tort Claims Act is nearly always based on negligence, defined as a breach of the legal duty to use reasonable care for the safety of persons and their property.

The most celebrated tort claims in Yellowstone have involved injuries or deaths due to hot spring immersion or bear mauling. Huge amounts of money are demanded and sometimes received. Even when the claim is disallowed, the government spends a fortune on the case. I learned a new meaning for the expression "settle out of court" when I saw the park service agree to such a settlement, to pay a compromise sum to a complainant, even though everyone in the agency firmly believed that the complainant was utterly unjustified in his claim, because the agreed-upon settlement was considerably less expensive than the legal battle would have been even if the park service won it. As budget cuts give the agency less and less cash, this sort of demoralizing legal bullying is bound to occur more often; it's tough to tell a group of committed employees, "Sorry, we're right but we can't afford to prove it."

But again I don't think that any specific incident or case is as important as what's happening to park standards as the public becomes increasingly accustomed to compelling someone else to pay the bills when someone gets hurt. Certainly there's no excuse for stupidity of the sort I was guilty of when those hikers almost drowned. I don't claim the park service is entitled to "no-fault" protection from suit. What I do claim is that we haven't considered what we're expecting from Yellowstone these days when we get in trouble. We're expecting quite a lot.

We're expecting the park to be tame enough for the busload of senior citizens who want to walk on a reliable boardwalk out to the geyser basins. We're expecting it to be wild enough for the most confirmed "granola-cruncher" to get ten miles from the nearest human being. We're expecting it to support the traffic of two and a half million people a summer. And, in the face of these expectations, we're expecting it to contain the heart of one of the last grizzly bear populations in the lower forty-eight, thousands of free-ranging elk, deer, black bear, moose, sheep, chipmunks, and other wildlife, and the world's foremost collection of geysers and hot springs. Quite a lot indeed.

I was walking the boardwalks at Mammoth Hot Springs one day, answering questions and generally providing what's called a "uniformed presence," when I saw a small crowd gathering excitedly by some juniper trees near the parking lot. They seemed disturbed, so I hurried over, arriving just in time to see a trim middle-aged man finish pounding the head of a snake to a pulp with a softball-sized rock. It was a bull snake, a four-foot-long beauty, and I wanted to take the rock to the man for killing it, but I did my rangerly best to be calm.

"What's up?"

He turned to me as he straightened from the dead snake. "Oh, hi, ranger. I was just killing this rattlesnake."

I made a show of going over and kneeling down to look at it, as if I had to get closer to see that it wasn't a rattlesnake. As I read the group, they were pretty grateful to this guy, and I wasn't sure yet how to come down on him for killing a park animal.

"It's just a bull snake. They're harmless—kind of pretty, actually—they eat small animals. It wouldn't have hurt you." Some people wandered off, but the man's family, including several children, gathered closer. For some reason that I still don't understand, I began to worry about making him look bad in front of his family. I rose, and as I spoke to him I walked down the path, leading him a little distance from his family, who followed.

"You know it's illegal to kill animals in the park? That was just a harmless snake."

He was instantly defensive, a little defiant. "It was there on the boardwalk all at once and my kids were all around, and someone yelled it was a rattlesnake. I didn't wait around to find out. I got my family to think about. They're more important than some snake."

"See, we've never seen rattlesnakes up here, and they aren't known for jumping out and attacking groups of people." This was futile, at least to his mind; his family was more important than some snake, even if it was the wrong snake. "For God's sake don't ever try to kill a real rattlesnake that way. Even the bull snake could have bitten you. It would have gone away if you'd let it. Probably was scared silly to find itself in the middle of all those people anyway." Doubting it would do any good, I gave him a little lecture on learning park regulations and urged him to be more careful. For all I know when he got home his kids were still starry-eyed about the way their dad had saved them from the rattlesnake.

Later, back at the station, I told my friends the story. "I'd have bonded his ass, right on the spot! A nice fat fine would teach him that ignorance is no excuse," one ranger volunteered.

Maybe he's right. Maybe I should have dragged the guy down to the station and written out a ticket (if I could find the ticket book; I didn't have much practice at that sort of thing). But my uncertainty about the ticket isn't what I remember most about the incident. I remember instead the man's pride, and his family's worshipful trust. In his mind, and in his children's eyes, he was a hero. Never mind that the snake was harmless; he *believed* that it was deadly, and that's what counted. He faced up to a natural enemy and proved his personal fitness, whatever the ranger might say.

There is a mighty need in us to know that somewhere danger does exist, and that we can face it if we have to. Though we ride the buses of Rochester for forty years, when we get to Yellowstone we're ready for anything.

And that need implies a second need: a need to know that "anything" is actually out there, waiting to be a potential threat. The trouble is, we only want it there if we can be sure of mashing its head with a rock. There is an incurable dichotomy here. Some folks require the park's wildness, and yet deny its right to exercise that wildness upon them.

A few years ago a young woman was severely mauled by a bear along a trail in Yellowstone. When the superintendent's office got word of the mauling, the usual steps were taken, including notifying the media. Someone called one of the major wire services, in accordance with normal procedures, to notify them that a mauling had occurred (the park isn't into publicizing sensational incidents; they have to do this or be accused of trying to "cover up" a politically damaging incident), and that more information would follow soon. The person who took the message on behalf of the wire service (one imagines a huge air-conditioned office with rows of pale, well-dressed people answering designer phones) greeted the news with enthusiasm: "Oh, great! Chicago just loves bear maulings!"

That's sick, of course, but many of our responses to wilderness carry overtones of just such thrills. In a world where nature rarely does more than give people colds, death by grizzly bear is so sensational and bizarre that people far away savor the chill of it, finding some excitement in the tragedy. We who like to hike in grizzly country appreciate the uneasy awareness of being in the kingdom of a potential predator, and in more subtle ways we may be open to the same criticism. I think not, because we're not out there for the risk so much as to soak up the humility and stimulation of a primitive setting, and to do it with respect for the bear's dignity. What happens in Chicago is different. Without too much sociological arrogance I think I can suggest that the grizzly mauling is a little bit of the stone age, the old West, Tarzan, and Daniel Boone, all stirred up and printed on page six of the tabloids, right there with Jackie's new diet and the latest Elvis clone. News is largely unreal to many people anyway. They'll never see the bear or the person who was mauled (though they wouldn't mind a few color photographs). The whole story is just entertainment.

What fails to reach Chicago is the marvel of it all: that such a ghastly encounter between human and bear can still happen at all in this country, and that, after it happens, no one goes out and shoots the bear. And that, horribly scarred and nearly crippled, the woman neither blamed the bear nor sued the park service. Like a good many people who are hurt by bears in the backcountry, she took the blame herself, as an intruder in the bear's home, an interloper who got inside the bear's margin of insecurity and paid dearly for it. Perhaps there'd be hope for the grizzly yet if its country was used only by such people.

Ours has become, progressively and I think wisely, a consumer-oriented society. The rights of the individual citizen to reliable advertising, pure food products, safe housing and transportation, and a thousand other daily needs have been defined and protected by law. But wilderness is not a typical consumer product. By implication, if not by definition, it loses its value—its consumer interest, so to speak—if it is made safe. It is no longer able to serve its function if it is paved, fenced, labeled, and regulated into a form palatable to zoo- and television-minded visitors. It cannot stimulate if it is crippled or lessened.

But wilderness is about the only thing left that's that way, and so people don't deal with it well. They aren't accustomed to the responsibilities it requires of them because those same responsibilities were judged to be encumbrances in the rest of their world and have been engineered out of existence.

I can only be so forgiving, or tolerant, about this because the victims of the park's worst tragedies have so often been children. Between 1919 and 1970 nine people were killed in hot pools. Seven were children.

July 18, 1919—boy, age four
July 13, 1932—girl, age three
July 18, 1933—boy, age fifteen
July 14, 1955—boy, age five
September 13, 1955—girl, age four and a half
June 13, 1958—boy, age six and a half
June 28, 1970—boy, age nine

This is a litany of shame that I just can't hold the park totally responsible for. The parents of these children, like the ones who used to tell their kids to go stand by the bear for a picture, can't all be written off as victims of a "negligent" park. Adults were able to keep from falling into the springs, and adults are responsible for their children. It could be that in each case one more sign, one more railing, would have prevented the death, but parents who do not control their children are generally incurable except by tragedy. No number of restraints would be adequate protection against their type.

People react to tragedy with rage. They are confused and frustrated and need to strike out. They need to hate, or get revenge; they need to *blame*. They need, most of all, to avoid blaming themselves. Sometimes someone else is handy; sometimes that someone even deserves the blame. As a historian of Yellowstone I know better than most just how many dumb things have been done in the park by managers. Some of those things have hurt people. But occasional stupidity in park administrators, or occasional tragedy among park visitors, is not a good barometer of the health of the wilderness. When someone is hurt in the park, and the need to blame aches for fulfillment, you can almost count on the innocent resource getting stuck with part of the bill. A tragedy at a hot springs, whether the result of park negligence or parental neglect, will bring a clamor for more barricades or signs. The present trend of increasing federal responsibility for individual welfare in the parks will inevitably increase the number of tort claims. Some will probably be justified, but whether they are or not I am uncomfortable knowing that the direction of wilderness management in Yellowstone and elsewhere is going to be ever more often defined in courtrooms thousands of miles away, and that the number of railings and restraints and warning signs will be most heavily influenced by the misdeeds of that incredibly small percentage of visitors who are the lowest common denominator of personal responsibility. The result of letting urban courts and urban juries rule on what is and isn't good management practice is not likely to be wholesome. Getting mauled by a bear in a national park is *not* the legal equivalent of slipping on an icy sidewalk. Someone else owns the sidewalk; you own the bear.

In 1904 Theodore Roosevelt wrote a few paragraphs about Yellowstone's bears, remarking how harmless they seemed to be under most circumstances, even at the feeding grounds:

> Of course among the thousands of tourists there is a percentage of fools; and when fools go out in the afternoon to look at the bears feeding they occasionally bring themselves into jeopardy by some senseless act.

This percentage of fools cannot be removed from the visitation, nor can they be adequately guarded against. They will always find their chance. They, like the biblical poor, will always be with us.

They are of several types. There are the arrogant fools, like the fellow who marched into the Visitor Center one day to defiantly announce that he'd just spent three nights in a restricted area of heavy grizzly concentration. He demanded to know what we rangers were up to, keeping people out of there: *he* hadn't seen any bears. The arrogant fool is the quickest to jump to sue when something goes wrong, I think. I once encountered a young couple hiking in Glacier Park with their Irish setter. When I pointed out to them that the dog was illegal in the backcountry because of grizzly bears (dogs are known to excite or anger bears), the man answered angrily that "the rangers have killed all the bears." Three people have been killed by Glacier's non-grizzlies since then. A biologist friend, hearing that story, observed drily that "Yeah, some day they'll carry him out in a plastic bag too." The arrogant fool is characterized most often by disbelief, and by the conviction that he somehow knows more than the experts. And, for my money, the arrogant fool is the one I would vastly prefer to be involved if we must continue to amuse Chicago.

But he won't be, because of other fools, like the parents who don't control their children, or the selfish fools who leave food out at night to bait bears into their campsite for photographs, bears who arrive just as some unsuspecting person walks by on the way to the rest room. Or the silly fools, the ones who hear John Denver singing "Rocky Mountain High" and say, "That's for me!" and take off into the woods with a $14.95 backpack and street shoes.

But it's pretty easy to ridicule the foolish few, the idiot fringe. It's too easy, as well, to generalize and assume that *only* fools get hurt, which isn't true. But I think it is foolishness that results in most injuries in Yellowstone: the foolishness of a manager who neglects some obvious safety hazard; the foolishness of park concessioners who persist in using pictures of cuddly, friendly bears in promotional literature, encouraging a host of misconceptions about wild bears; the foolishness of a few scientists who advocate removing grizzlies from Yellowstone to make the park "safe" for visitors, thus encouraging the notion that a wilderness can be safe and still be a wilderness.

Safety can't be a matter of simple solutions, such as more fences or fewer bears, or anything else that will reduce Yellowstone's natural setting to some wimp wilderness just to satisfy the misplaced consumerism of urban vacationers. There must always be a tension, as long as people visit wilderness, between the needs of the visitors and those of the land. Keeping the tension in control is the challenge. Keeping the public informed of Yellowstone's dangers is a good part of the answer, but another part is not being unduly influenced by the misbehavior and misfortunes of the inevitable percentage of fools.

Existence Value

Some of my colleagues were made restless one summer when the National Park Service incorporated into its philosophical armory the assertion that "parks are for people." We began to hear the phrase at training sessions, and were encouraged to work it into our campfire programs. Little signs and posters, sure proof of official party line, appeared in supervisors' offices.

On the surface it is mystifying; of course parks are for people. They're for people, for American avocets, for bladderwort, for the eight winds, and, with a little luck, forever. As near as I could figure, this sudden attention to the obvious was a defensive reaction. People who have some gripe with national parks (who seem most often to be people for whom more visitors mean more money) commonly accuse them of elitism—of catering to the specialized wants of some exclusive group of users. Apparently it was felt necessary to respond to that criticism, and to do so with a relatively understated campaign that reminded the millions of park users that the parks they were using were indeed there to be used. Though it all seemed merely lame to me, some of my fellow rangers found it unwholesome. "Parks are for wilderness preservation, too! Aren't we supposed to tell people about that?"

As much as I admired and supported the environmental firebrands, I had to admit that they already *were* talking about that. They were talking about it so much that they said very little about people, or where people fit into this wilderness we have in Yellowstone. The approach we had been taught to use was that people fit into Yellowstone only by not disturbing it, by having as little effect as possible on things in the park. That's been the direction of management for many years, as I've pointed out already. So it seemed to me that there was some question of where the people fit.

I'm always surprised by the durability of populist rhetoric. After all the horrible things that have been done in the name of the people, everything from inquisitions to Auschwitz, you'd think the phrase would wear out and be replaced by some new, equally meaningless, cliché. But it doesn't disappear. I don't know if it still has any impact on "the people" when they hear it, but every fresh cause, clear across the political spectrum, employs it to prove their devotion to some implied but undefined Public Good.

Most recently, under the conservative Reagan administration, there has been much talk of this sort. Without bothering with even a thin veil of implication, the new administrators are talking about "opening the parks up to the people." Elitism is the certain enemy here, as if the people have somehow been denied access to the parks; as if Yellowstone's two and a half million visitors constitute an exclusive crowd who are keeping the park from the rest of us.

Just how "open" a park needs to be is a subject for great debates which, sad to say, are not occurring. In their place we have uncommunicative exercises in rhetoric, some quite eloquent but few intended to do more than inspire and reassure those already converted. Preservationists read what they want in their magazines, and developers read what they want in their magazines. If they really wanted to get somewhere, at least to start moving, they'd maybe consider guest columnists from the opposition.

Perhaps the most profound implication of the charge of elitism that is being leveled against wilderness defenders is unAmericanism; wilderness, we are told, is elitist, and therefore is a violation of everything the country stands for. Everything should be available to everybody; nothing should be held out for the favored few.

It would be interesting if the American system worked that way in the first place, but it doesn't. Free enterprise is praised by many because it ideally encourages each to achieve according to his or her own abilities. Capitalism is a competitive system. Nothing is ever for everybody.

With that thought in mind, I suggest that antiwilderness, pro-developing people try a new perspective on wilderness. It ought to appeal to the most aggressive capitalist, if he's got the guts to face the challenge of it, because I see wilderness as an example of free enterprise at its best.

The most successful businessmen I know happen to be in marketing. They get an enormous kick from convincing people to buy things. They get an even bigger kick from convincing people to buy more things from them than from anyone else. They're deeply into competition, into the *game*. Business talk is full of metaphorical athletics (team plays, end runs, outrunning competitors, playing hardball...) and violence (making a quick killing, cutting off or wiping out the competition, thrusts, parries, and shots at competitors or at the market itself), giving rhetorical excitement to what is done sitting around highly polished tables by quiet people dressed as if they were going to church as soon as the meeting is over.

They want their entertainment to be the same way, especially the organized games. They argue bitterly over football plays, and yell coach-like commands at their television sets on Monday nights. Business is called the heartbeat of American life. I often think the beat is weak or irregular or in need of some retarding, but there's no denying that the American people "the people" of our present concern—thrive or suffer as part of this aggressive system. If, indeed, free enterprise is what "the people" want, then look at how well it works in wilderness.

Wilderness is best enjoyed by the person willing to work hardest at it. Unlike the spectator sports, which require only a specialized knowledge of arcane statistics and good enough eyesight to watch, the wilderness challenges us on many levels at once, requiring of those who want to be fully tested the use of a uniquely broad variety of physical and mental resources.

The challenge is whatever sort you make it. For some it is the longest, ruggedest hike imaginable. For others it is the quest to find something, say a rare calypso orchid, to be seen but not picked. After all, any challenge you accept, either in profession or recreation, is largely a state of mind; you determine to abide by the rules, otherwise the challenge disappears. And if you don't put your heart into it, and work at it, you'll fail, whether you're seeking serenity in some quiet place or saving the known universe in front of some video game.

Winning in the wilderness, to coin a nice capitalist slogan, can take as much guts and sweat as annihilating the competition in the retail shoe business. But if you gut the wilderness with roads, or lace it up with safety railings, you no longer permit the hard worker to achieve more than the lazy one. You even out the challenge, and everybody gets more or less the same thing from the experience. If someone suggested doing that to the nation's economy, everyone would assume he was communist.

Once the antiwilderness capitalist recognizes that the wilderness can challenge him and provide him with competition, perhaps he will be a little more sympathetic to wilderness in general. And if that happened, then maybe he would be in a position to learn about all the *un*competitive ways to enjoy wilderness as well. But he has to start somewhere.

Wilderness advocates claim that the wilderness experience (which is rarely defined at all) as provided by the national parks is a higher form of recreation—a qualitatively *better* kind of recreation—than other kinds. They claim that it is more elevating to enjoy wilderness than to, say, play golf. Though I will agree that the person who spends his evenings watching roller derby is not exposed to the possibilities for spiritual enrichment available to someone who reaches the peak of Mount Washburn during a flaming sunset, it takes a zealot's arrogance to insist that one form of recreation is "better" than another, even if it is undeniably more uplifting. The parks offer a different experience from most others; there's no denying it. I'd even agree with recreation scholar Joseph Sax, who maintains that parks can and should function not only to serve public taste but to elevate it. Lord knows it could use some elevation. But that doesn't make parks unique.

I am a devotee of baseball, a game of magnificent geometry and fabulous statistical delights. Well-played baseball is, for the sport's aficionados, no less intellectually stimulating than is the study of the natural history of, say, the elk, to nature lovers (take one example, the observation by one baseball writer that baseball is the only game where the ball doesn't score the point; roll that concept around in your mind for a while, considering the infinite possibilities for variation in the action on the field, and how those actions are affected by the unpredictable behavior of the ball). The highly structured games of urban society satisfy many people's needs for diversion. I know that some find intense emotional fulfillment in watching an extraordinary athletic performance, because I have done so myself. I don't think it would be honest for someone to claim that the intensity of some wilderness experience—watching an eagle fly, or a flower grow—is finer. It is not better, or stronger, or anything of the sort. It is just different. The random wild setting can satisfy a different set of yearnings. Without foul lines or fourth quarters, it reaches to us from the opposite end of our psychological boundaries, inviting us to find wonder in a world whose rules we did not make. I've accepted that invitation as well as baseball's, and I much prefer wilderness these days, but I often savor memories of moments in more civilized recreational settings, and I intend to enjoy them again. Life is not simple. Recreationists need to be more tolerant of one another.

And so parks, like baseball games, are for people. The trouble with trying to decide how people should use a park is that almost any definition falls short of the truth or leaves out some group with a partly just claim. Wilderness recreation is composed of many imponderables and is practiced under an infinity of personal limitations. Few would try to keep score. Unless you are the rare expert climber or adventurer, you do not "win" in any socially identifiable sense. The experience does not draw applause, or appear in neatly arranged box scores in tomorrow's paper. It is this indefinable element that makes wilderness enjoyment so easy for people to write off as meaningless, or expendable, or, perhaps worst of all, mystical. The wilderness has rewards that don't translate tidily into batting averages or bowling trophies, but I tell you those rewards are as genuine as any others.

A few years ago a court case explored the rarefied atmosphere of such rewards, and gave them a legal identity I find quite satisfying. Under the National Environmental Policy Act of 1970, federal agencies are required to prepare environmental impact statements considering any "proposals for legislation and other major Federal actions significantly affecting the quality of the human environment." Notice that it says *human* environment; I figure that to be the equivalent of the environment of "the people." The N.E.P.A. has been at the center of some unusual litigation and debate as lawmakers have attempted to define the human environment and what constitutes a significant effect upon it. In 1974, in the case of *Minnesota Public Interest Research Group v. Butz*, the U.S. Forest Service (Department of Agriculture) was challenged for not preparing an environmental impact statement on proposed logging in the Boundary Waters Canoe Area. In a ruling of considerable initiative and maybe even a little poetry, the court defined the human environment at some length, pointing out that the adverse effect of logging may far exceed the simple removal of timber:

> We think the N.E.P.A. is concerned with indirect effects as well as direct effects. There has been increasing recognition that man and all other life on this earth may be significantly affected by actions which on the surface appear insignificant.

Though it's nice to hear of such talk in a courtroom, so far nothing has been said that ecologists haven't been telling us for years. But the court went on, coining a phrase that I hope some day becomes a household one—Existence Value:

Existence value refers to that feeling some people have just knowing that somewhere there remains a true wilderness untouched by human hands, such as the feeling of loss people might feel upon the extinction of the whooping crane even though they had never seen one.

Despite the commercial cliché (whose *un*human hands touched it?), this statement has a powerful eloquence, an almost revelatory freshness; of *course* whooping cranes have existence value, just as do the great cathedrals or the Pyramid of the Sun at Teotihuacán. I am better because of the existence of the Pietà, the Mona Lisa, and any number of other masterpieces. I am better for them because, being aware of their glory, I am inspirited by their beauty and enriched by their achievement. I enjoy, with many others, the enchanting puzzle of the Mona Lisa's smile. It comes to mind as I drive along, and I wonder about it as human expression and as art. I would be furious and grieved to lose it, though I don't expect to get to Paris soon to see it.

The same long-range pleasure is available from the wilderness, or from some part of it. A grizzly bear may have its most stunning effect when actually seen. If you can't see one, it helps at least to be able to stand on the edge of grizzly country looking in, your imagination stirred by the thought that they're right out *there*. But if that's not possible, they still have worth and can be deeply appreciated.

I assure you I am not a mystic. I could not keep a straight face were I compelled to mutter a mantra. In airports I am openly hostile to robed people who approach me about paying their way to Nepal or Bakersfield. But I can enjoy Yellowstone with a mystic's fervor, from any distance. Visiting my family in Ohio for Christmas I can sit back comforted by the knowledge of brown trout threshing their way through the pounding rapids of my home stream. I can imagine them, and thereby enjoy them, as they fin nervously into shallow water over exposed gravel bars along a willow-lined bend I know. The wind is snowy, and it roughens and hazes the surface over them until they cannot be seen by the osprey cruising above. Partly because I've been there, but partly because I share some feeling for the importance of what they are about there in the shallows, I am better for knowing of their travels and labors.

Existence value requires knowledge, of course, and the more the better. In January, wherever I am, I'm better for knowing that two or three hundred massive grizzly bear hearts are lumbering strongly through winter's deep hibernation, pumping only eight times a minute. I count seven and a half seconds on my watch, my own pulse keeping pace with the second hand as a sow bear's great patient heart shivers through one contraction. There is a shallow "microclimate" above and in her heavy fur; some undisciplined guard hairs extend beyond it to where the air is several degrees cooler. She nests on a bed of branches that suspend her body just inches above the cold, heat-sucking earth, so that the microclimate created by her own retarded respiratory and circulatory functions completely envelops her. The den is carved into the side of a steep slope, with its opening slightly below the chamber; the air she warms with her body cannot rise to escape. In a few days she will stir enough to give birth to a squirrel-size cub, the product of a biological short-circuit of poetic beauty. She mated last June, but the embryo ceased growth almost immediately as a microscopic blastocyst, delaying further progress until November. About the time she retired to her den, the blastocyst implanted itself in the uterine wall and resumed development. She will give birth to a cub that grew through only three months of a seven-month gestation, a cub so small that her limited resources for milk and heat will be sufficient to sustain it and her until April thaws bring her out to search for food. I know all this is happening as I know the blinding sting of the blizzard that sweeps the drifts over her den, and I am enriched by it. It is a celebration I need not attend to enjoy.

I suppose that eventually the concept of existence value could be used by some extreme thinker to suggest that we need not visit wilderness at all, that if only we can all open our minds enough to enjoy everything long distance, or by proxy through someone else's books and pictures, we can just close up places like Yellowstone and let the animals alone. That's silly for several reasons, perhaps most important because it violates the spirit of every significant legislative enactment relating to the management of the parks. But it does at least suggest how truly broad a use the parks can have. Properly understood, the parks are truly for all the people. We are a better society, a better people, for having established them, and they by their existence value are available for our enjoyment in a multitude of enjoyable ways. And here at least it may be that the latter-day Thoreaus, who would have us believe that wilderness enjoyment is "better" than other recreations, have a point. As a baseball fan I am comforted by knowing that every year, without fail, there will be a World Series, but unlike appreciating the grizzly in her den, I am not content with warm imaginings. It's not enough for me to know that the World Series happens. I have to know who won.

*　　　*　　　*

One of the most seductive criticisms of the wilderness movement is that it is not so much elitist as separatist. Wilderness enthusiasts, according to this criticism, want to preserve wilderness for enjoyment and spiritual edification, yet they bind wilderness up so tight legally that enjoyment consists primarily of standing on the edge watching it. Look at the American Indian, we are told, who saw *all* land as sacred rather than just a few parcels here and there; if we are ever to get as close to the land, and have as much attachment to its needs and health, as did native Americans, we must be able to touch it a little more firmly than we can in places like Yellowstone, where we're not even allowed to pick a flower or kill an animal. If the parks are going to be for the people, they're going to have to stop telling the people that they are "only guests here," and let them be a part of the natural system.

Like many oversimplifications, this one sounds great at first—Yeah, right, let's open'em up for the people to really *enjoy*! However, Yellowstone long ago showed us just how much it could and couldn't stand in the way of enjoyment. People showed us how much a part of it they could become, and how massively they could damage it by doing so (many wilderness defenders and writers say, in effect, that if only everyone could have their wonderful experiences in wild country, then everyone would want to protect wilderness; if everyone even tried to have those experiences, wilderness would expire under the weight). What it comes down to is that the parks are not enough, nor are the other wilderness areas. These strictly regulated and hotly contested little pieces of wild land cannot alone fulfill the function of keeping us in touch with nature, no matter how we manage them. They cannot do for 250,000,000 people what the entire North American continent once did for a few million native Americans.

Where this criticism, that the parks are too hard to enjoy because they are so withheld from practical enjoyment, most readily disassembles itself is in the broader view of nature appreciation in America. When we concentrate just on the parks, we smokescreen the bigger picture; some anti-wilderness people do it intentionally. No one should really expect the parks to serve such a purpose, because there are plenty of other places—forests, farms, city parks, lakes, backyards—where we can also get close to nature. Leveling a criticism of separatism at the parks is taking them out of their greater context as part of a large assortment of opportunities available to us as creatures who need contact with our natural surroundings. I suppose that it would be possible to argue that all traces of nature have significant existence value (the little boy, for whom a certain untamed patch of woodlot is the center of the universe, would probably agree could he only articulate it), because all nature is potentially enriching and inspiriting, but few natural places have had their purpose—and their limitations—as well defined by law as have the national parks. In order to fulfill certain of their prescribed purposes, the parks *must* be used quite gently, more gently than most other types of recreation area. Some may not approve of the prescribed purposes, but they should not try to justify circumvention of them in the name of public enjoyment. Public enjoyment is largely dependent on that gentle use.

We modern people seem unlikely to escape from our desire to codify things. As long as we look at the world as something needing regulation and control—and with our numbers I don't see another way short of total cultural overhaul—we are going to give some natural places greater respect than others. Considering this, and considering as well our determination to pretend that all of us are equally entitled to everything that is public, the parks will be for the people, but the people will find that their share of the everything we say they are entitled to is long on "existence value" and short on calories. A park that is for the people must remain a park after the people leave. Unlike the native Americans who are so often referred to in lectures on reverence for the natural world, we must take Yellowstone and its kin to our hearts without taking them to our mouths.

PART THREE

MOUNTAIN TIMES

Divide Cabin

Late in the fall of 1974 a ranger riding boundary patrol decided to explore a few unfamiliar meadows just inside the park. There were no established trails in the area, and it was one of those parts of the park rarely visited by anyone, ranger or hiker. A mile or so in from the boundary, along the edge of a large meadow but tucked well back in a protruding grove of lodgepole pines, he found the ruins of a small cabin.

There are quite a few small ruins scattered around Yellowstone's backcountry. Most served the army, before 1918, or the rangers afterward, as outposts for overnight patrols. The modern system of backcountry cabins, as basic as they are, are palatial when compared to these earlier buildings, some of which were hardly larger than the space needed for two men to stretch out with a wood stove between them.

As patrols and trails changed, some cabins were simply abandoned or replaced with new ones in better locations. All that remains of some are foundations marks under the duff of fifty years or more.

No one knew anything about this newly discovered cabin. It wasn't situated to have been of any great use; it was miles from the nearest road and even old-timers couldn't remember a patrol cabin in that area. When we heard about it, we figured it was either a forgotten patrol cabin from before 1920 or was a poacher's cabin. Before 1900 or so, elk hunters were known to have small shelters near the park boundaries (some still do), from which forays could be made into the poorly protected park for a quick kill. A hasty drag would get the elk back out to national forest land with no one the wiser. What was most intriguing was the ranger's report that the cabin was undisturbed. So well had its builder concealed it that no one had visited it for a long, long time.

The November snows were already several inches deep when Park Curator Thea Nordling and I topped the long ridge that sloped into the big meadows. Our instructions were kind of vague—the ranger put a mark on the map that covered a lot of woods—so when we reached the meadow we split up, each following one edge, looking for the ruin. After an hour of stumbling over buried deadfall in the wet snow I rejoined her along a narrow isthmus of open snow between the meadow we'd just circled and its nearest neighbor. The sky was threatening more snow and we were near giving up when she yelled that she'd found it.

It was farther back into the trees than I'd imagined, at least a hundred feet from the open, and it was far more "ruined" than I'd expected. The sod roof had long ago caved in, leaving log walls less than four feet high and a sawed board door frame that stood a little higher. A large pine tree, about eighteen inches thick, had fallen almost squarely across the middle, further reducing one wall and slipping some logs loose from their crude corner notches. Four or five young pine trees, eight feet high, had sprouted from the dirt floor, growing up through the rotting collapsed roof poles. It *had* been a long time.

We made some quick measurements. The cabin was fourteen feet across the front and seventeen feet on the sides. The front doorway was three feet wide, and the door itself, a rough-cut iron-hinged affair hanging skewed against the inside wall, was sixty-four inches high.

There was nothing unusual in the size or construction of the cabin, though we knew that a trip in the summer, when the roof timbers weren't frozen hard over the floor, would be more revealing. What surprised us was what the cabin held; as near as we could tell, everything was there. All the appurtenances of housekeeping lay, undisturbed, probably as their last user left them. An axe and mattock leaned against one wall (these certainly would have left with the first hiker to discover the place). Scattered about the dirt floor, and stacked against the walls, were a host of smaller items. Decades of freezes, thaws, rains, and rust had fused much of this into one twisted brown mess, but we easily identified skillets, lard cans, metal plates, cups, and brittle old crates that presumably once held more of the same. Countless tin cans, both in the cabin and a few yards away in what was evidently the dump, were reduced to eggshell fragility by the rust. A can of tooth powder (a fastidious poacher, he would have been) had a patent date of 1899, the latest date we could find. There were two stoves: a collapsed box labeled only "Prize" on its front and a more hefty model still standing to the right of the front door, marked "Rock Island Arsenal, 1883, Army Wood Heater No. 1." The army stove, someone later suggested, may have come from a soldier station some miles to the north, brought either by the soldiers or the poacher after the station burned around 1917. It was the only obviously G.I. item in the place.

Stepping back from the cabin and looking around, we found it easy to imagine why the cabin was built here. Nestled back in the trees just far enough to be hard to see, the ridge to the east shielding his wood smoke from the nearest road (and probably from the fire lookouts on the high peaks to the east), the builder had a perfect spot. A few steps north or south would give him clear views of either of the two adjoining meadows (and their grazing elk?), and the narrow isthmus between the meadows carried a small stream from the southern one to the northern one. On the maps the stream was shown as intermittent, but it wasn't; it was reliable enough for the cabin. He had everything.

We tried to figure it out. If he was a poacher, why was the cabin inside the park instead of two miles west? Perhaps it was built by soldiers, then forgotten, then taken over by poachers who found it as safe and undisturbed as if it were outside the park. We enjoyed imagining that the reason the place was left fully stocked and supplied was because it was never left; that the builder died in his sleep (or in some appropriately colorful and desperate quarrel with a colleague) and lay right then under the ice-locked roof poles we couldn't budge. Frozen bones weren't part of our discoveries that day, but we were awakened, as Yellowstone people so often are, to the wonder of just how big the park is, and just how easily it can hide and save things. Here it is, a vacation mecca for millions, yet an hour's walk takes you into a wilderness so primitive and untraveled that it can swallow a man's home beyond all memory.

We never were sure about the cabin. Eventually one former employee, an aged ranger, seemed to recall there being a cabin over there somewhere, but we never knew who used it. If indeed it was army-built, it could have been revitalized by poachers, or it could have been built by them in the first place. It seemed to us improbable that the U.S. Cavalry would have been so casual about abandoning so many useful tools, utensils, and provisions.

However it got there, whoever had thawed frozen feet in front of its stoves (absently reading "Rock Island Arsenal" over and over again in the flickering warmth; melting more beeswax onto his skis for tomorrow's run; cussing when the coffee pot boiled over or burned his hand), it had been set aside by Yellowstone, in rentless storage, until a sharp-eyed ranger rode by. It rested, to borrow from Brendan Gill, "secure in the immortality of neglect."

Such is Yellowstone. As we use, enjoy, eat, and abuse it, it waits us out. It holds things back. When we say we are proud of our national parks we are saying we are proud of ourselves for having the decency and good sense to create them. But we should be proud of *them*, too. The Yellowstone that put that cabin away until everyone who knew of it was dead is the Yellowstone we should be most proud of. In giving us this lesson in the greater scale of mountain time, Yellowstone illuminates and deepens our appreciation of the short times we spend there.

Requiem for the Ranger

The ranger is among the luckiest of law officers. This is partly because of the work rangers do and where they get to do it, but it is also because of what people think of rangers. For even today, in a crime-ridden yet badge-fearing society, very few people think of rangers as police officers.

There was one occasion in my work where I even heard the comparison made. I was walking the boardwalks on the hot springs when a middle-aged man approached me to ask directions. He explained that "the cop down at the entrance station" had directed him here for more information. My response surprised me. I heated up and came perilously close to taking him by his lapels and telling him, loudly, that "We're not cops, we're *rangers.*" I realized, though, that "cop" is not a derogatory term to all Americans, as it is to me. I further realized, sadly, that as little as I liked it we probably are cops.

The national park ranger, in duty and appearance, was modeled in great part after the older Department of Agriculture forest ranger, whose flat hat and drab uniform had become standard some years before the park service was established in 1916. Yellowstone's first rangers were a mix, as they are now, some full-time, some seasonal. The full-timers were in many cases experienced Yellowstone men who had learned the park during the army days as soldiers or scouts. The seasonals were usually college students or young drifters. Because of the length of the season they were called "ninety-day wonders," and many were used only for entrance-gate duty.

Before World War II, in a time of simpler heroes and easier answers, the ranger was the epitome of rugged, self-reliant manhood (oh, there were a few women rangers in those days, but they were to most minds show-pieces and novelties, however good their work). The "Mark Trail" image of outdoorsy independence that charmed generations of young boys came into sharpest focus in the park and forest rangers, men of quiet strength and simple virtue, men fit subjects for Zane Grey or Walt Disney.

And looking back we can see that many of them were exactly like their image. Many weren't, but enough were to allow us to identify the type and watch its progress.

I admire (or, better, envy) the early rangers most for their versatility. Their duties included everything from fire fighting to motorcycle patrol to giving nature walks to chopping firewood (to heat their own drafty cabins). And in my envy I see how different it is today, for today each of those four tasks (I listed the first four that came to mind) is done by a differently titled employee. Most fire fighting is done by fire guards, not rangers at all though they have their own special badge and most closely approach the old ranger in the amount of hard work they must be prepared to do. Motorcycle patrols don't exist in Yellowstone now, but road patrol work is now done by law enforcement–specialist rangers. Nature walks, campfire programs, and other educational activities are conducted by "ranger-naturalists," a sepa-rate branch of the rangers who have become almost totally divorced from law enforcement, trail patrol, horses, and most of the other traditional "manly" aspects of rangerhood. And most of the time rangers don't chop firewood at all; their houses are heated by oil, and that kind of routine labor has been delegated to (or usurped by) the maintenance division—the crews of laborers who make things work and keep things clean in the park (and who often get paid a lot more than the rangers for their efforts).

Specialization has done some frightening things to the old jack-of-all-trades ranger. Mostly, specialization has made him impossible. There are still a few who are as good at identifying wildflowers as they are at search and rescue, or who can charm a bunch of kids as well as they can load a packhorse, but there will never be many now. There will always be a few, just because the work draws some exceptional people, but there simply isn't room for many. There is only room for specialists.

Increasing numbers of women in ranger uniforms have also been tough on the old image. Hardy woodsmen were, by definition, men. For old-timers who can't get used to being given tickets or getting rescued by women rangers, the old-time ranger is already irretrievably lost. The province of the outdoors, at least in the minds of the people who established the stereotypes, was not to be invaded by females; outdoor writing is still full of such attitudes, of hunters and fishermen escaping from their wives, of wives coming in and ruining a deer camp with lace curtains, and scores of other dreary attempts at a humor that should have died long ago. Like male rangers, some female rangers are better than others; some are great, some are lousy. It only takes one good one, however, to prove that a woman can do the work as well as a man. The narrow-minded old-timers might see it differently if they, like I, had been hiked into the ground a couple of times by perfectly dainty-looking young women. However totally their minds might be encrusted with Victorian ideas, an experience like that would at least shut them up.

Women or men, there are now two distinct subdivisions of rangers, known commonly as protectives and naturalists. The protective rangers do the police work. They take your money when you enter the park or a campground, and they patrol the roads in cars and the backcountry on horses. Naturalists are educators. They give campfire programs and nature walks, and they stand behind information desks at Visitor Centers, answering questions.

The divergent evolution of these two forms has been going on for many years, since the 1920s, in fact, and though the two are ever more dissimilar the process is not an even one. Within each strain there occasionally appear refreshing throwbacks: a protective with a field guide to butterflies in his pocket, or a naturalist who knows how to issue a ticket to some deserving fool. As time goes on, I fear, these aberrant types will become increasingly rare, not so much out of choice but because they just don't get the opportunity. Even as I served as a naturalist there was talk that the growing need for well-trained "law enforcement specialists" (read "cops" if you like) would soon compel the National Park Service to redefine the naturalists; as we became ever less well prepared to deal with law enforcement we would have to have some other title. We would cease to be rangers. Finally, and tragically, we would lose the badge. This was intolerable to us, especially those of us who liked to think we weren't all that bad at rangering in its broader context, and more than once I heard "if they take my badge, I leave. I'm a *ranger*." It was important to us.

But, backing up a bit, there is more to this schizoid tendency in the modern ranger. There is certainly a practical need for specialization, and we all have personal inclinations toward some kind of work we prefer; some people are good educators, some are good authoritarians. And, even more practically, the park service is so sinfully underfunded that it simply isn't possible to train people to do one job well, much less several jobs. As usual, money determines how the park is run.

Since the beginning, naturalists and protectives have maintained a rivalry, usually cordial but always a little destructive. Naturalists, even fifty years ago, were known as "fern fondlers" and "Sunday supplement scientists." Protectives were characterized as thugs with low foreheads and questionable personal hygiene. The rivalry has become a tradition, one encouraged by an administrative setup that keeps the two divisions from crossing paths often. When I started work there was virtually no communication between my supervisor and his equivalent in the protective division, though their offices practically adjoined, and therefore there was very little communication between us frontline naturalists and the frontline rangers. Both supervisors left in a year or so and were replaced by more friendly types; eventually we learned one another's names and even filled in for one another now and then. They even let me play on the ranger (read "protective") softball team, once they discovered that I could bat .500 and hit a home run now and then.

But the rivalry runs deeper than office-to-office. It is ingrained in the entire park operation. Everyone knows that naturalists are a little flaky. One night a couple of us were crawling around on the hot spring formations, trying to get some decent time exposures of the mist and reflected moonlight in the pools. We were dragging our tripods here and there, crouching for a better angle or to root through a pack for a different lens, and probably looking, from a distance, like a couple of misplaced saboteurs stringing up plastic charges. Headlights turned into the parking lot nearest us, a door opened, and a hefty voice demanded some explanation.

"What are you people doing up there?"

I recognized the voice. "Oh, hi, Larry, it's just Don and me, taking some pictures."

The response was predictable. As Larry got back into his car he muttered, "I should have known it would be a couple *naturalists.*"

Sometimes it became infuriating, when the phone would ring at the Visitor Center and some park employee would ask who was speaking. Whichever naturalist answered would hear the insult we most hated: "Oh, sorry, I was trying to get a ranger." Depending on how cranky we were, we might answer, "That's what the badge says, what do you need?" We probably couldn't help them, but we had to do *something* to remind them

that we mattered. The only trouble was, it happened so often that sometimes we wondered if we did.

And sometimes it seemed that everywhere we looked we were reminded of our odd status as non-rangers. The protectives had horses with
names like Apache and King. The naturalists' horses, when we had any,
were Roger and Jerry. Imagine it. Hi ho, Roger, away! The protectives had
new pickup trucks; we got their old ones. They even had fancier flash-
lights, the nice professional law-enforcement kind that had five cells and
could almost knock you over with the kick from their beam when you
turned them on. And radios—especially radios. The park radio system
involved typical units built into the vehicles, much like C.B.'s, and "handi-
talkies," very expensive little portables that you could hang on your belt.
The naturalist cars usually didn't have radios built into them, so we had to
carry the cast-off handi-talkies that worked only about half the time. They
were sure not to work when you needed them. It seemed that every time I
was out on some road needing to call in a report or request assistance, the
thing would stare back at me in mute unfunctioning disregard, as if to say,
"I only work for real rangers." It was so bad with the radios that it was a
matter of great pride with me that one winter I became influential enough
to get possession of one of the newest, smallest, and most powerful handi-
talkies. I would make sure I casually set it down for a moment whenever I
was in a ranger office, just so I could savor a little naked jealousy: "Hey,
that's one of those new five-watt units. How did *you* get it?"

"Oh, we naturalists are all using these now; not so heavy for us to carry
around, you know?"

The rivalry rarely came out into the open where it could be squarely
faced. It was a lot like sexism, and taught me just a little about the pain of
discrimination (what must it be like to be a *woman* naturalist?). There was
something sexual in the rivalry anyway. At worst it was our manhood that
was being questioned. Naturalists, even the men, peed sitting down. They
zipped their pants up the side. For a while in our sub-district, some of us
distinguished rangers as "front-zipper" or "side-zipper." Naturalists were
sissies.

But we had our moments, and we knew our advantages. We had elitist
snob appeal on our side, for one thing. It was harder to get a job as a
naturalist than as a ranger. You usually had to have more specialized
education. There were fewer of us. For all their condescension, it seemed
that quite a few rangers secretly hoped to transfer to the naturalist division
some day. We were much more the voice, and the face, of the park service

than any other group of employees. We had a lot to feel good about, and we enjoyed it. Maybe we even worked better and harder because of the rivalry; a little tension is good for the perspective, and it's often good for you to know someone doesn't quite respect you the way you'd like.

Whenever possible, a lot of us tried to broaden beyond fern fondling and learn something about what the protectives did. I sat in on as many protective training sessions as I could, and I learned a lot of things that I wished I'd heard about in naturalist training sessions. It was obvious there was a lot I was missing about Yellowstone and the people who come there.

One day the sub-district ranger held forth on general visitor relations, suggesting ways to best deal with the American tourist:

The average American does not like to be touched. If you've got to move some person, away from a domestic squabble for example, try to lead him, or make him feel like he's going of his own will. Once you put a hand on his arm, or his shoulder, you've violated his freedom of movement and started a kind of physical contest. He'll get defensive and harder to deal with at that point.

If you're trying to break up a fight in a campground or arrest someone, don't ever be afraid to back down if you're outgunned. This isn't the old west, and you're not being paid just to put your manhood on the line. If you think you can take the guy, that's your choice. But remember, he can't get away. There are only five roads out of here, and you can walk away from a bad situation and meet the troublemakers later with more rangers than they knew existed. The biggest guys get real quiet when they see six or eight uniforms.

We have preventive law enforcement here. You can always play cop and park on the side street out of sight of the traffic while you do your paperwork. That way you can catch someone running the stop sign. But here we want you to park on the main road, where they can see you. They won't run the stop sign, the law won't be broken, and you won't bond them. Be visible and be available.

I know you've all heard about chasing beggar bears from the road—one whack on the ass with your night stick and they're gone. You want to do that, go ahead, but I'm warning you not to. I know that Fraser here has been doing it for years, but one of these days he's going to get his, too.

Now, about the first class uniform. Wear it. The green jeans are okay for horse work, but the public wants first class. I remember once when Rob Yates, a seasonal patrol ranger, called me in the middle of the night to back him up calming down a drunk. I threw on my old jeans and met Rob, who as usual looked sharp in his first class uniform, at the hotel. We had a heart to heart with the drunk, and Rob handled it all. I just stood there being a second uniformed presence. As Rob was writing the guy up, he turned to me, looked me up and down, and said, "You must be one of them *summertime* rangers."

Don't let me catch you wearing those reflecting mirror sunglasses. To communicate with people you have to let them see your eyes, so don't wear those mirrors like Joe Highway Patrol. If you have to wear sunglasses, take them off when you talk to people.

And most of all, when you see someone doing something stupid—feeding the bears, cutting live wood, whatever—*don't get mad*. The worst thing you can do is take it personally. Unfortunately that's the easiest thing to do, too. Just keep in mind that they just got here, and that they don't know the rules. Be patient.

That last one is the purest form of wisdom. Nobody ever tells us naturalists things like that. We stop ignorant, perhaps even innocent, people from chipping away at the hot spring deposits and beavering down campground trees with cheap hatchets; we do it every day, and we grow impatient. We occasionally flare up and give someone hell, because we take it all very personally, as if the park were our property rather than everybody's. Vandalism is such a cruel act to us, such a slap in the face of what we want Yellowstone to stand for, that we become unobjective. And vandalism is so common that we have plenty of chances to get upset. Take the Boy Scouts. The Boy Scouts are known as the "green horde" for their habit of descending on a campground like so many olive-drab locusts out to win their pestilence merit badges. Giving a twelve-year-old boy an axe, or a trench knife, or a folding spade, and expecting him to act with discretion is a kind of generosity only the boy can appreciate.

And did you hear what he said about only five ways out of the park? That's terribly reassuring. A speeder can be flagged down at the next junction; a quick radio call ahead prepares a welcome for the moving violator. This is important because a chase in these mountains is terribly risky. One day the office radio unit came to life on Channel 2, the park-wide frequency. For an instant there was only the static and a faint siren, then a calm, quick voice said, "This is 115 Protto in hot pursuit at Dunra-ven Pass..." He continued, identifying his subject and requesting assistance to head him off at the next junction, but I doubt that most people listening heard more than those first few words, "hot pursuit at Dunraven Pass," after which we held a long breath, mentally following that chase through the hairiest stretch of cliff-hugging road in our part of the Rockies —one phrase of understated high drama, one moment of putting it all on the line with wailing siren accompaniment.

Naturalists hardly ever have to put it all on the line, and that single disadvantage (if that's what it should be called) assures our eternal under-dog role in the rivalry with the protectives. With the crowds Yellowstone is getting these days, the line is becoming a very busy place. Though it hurts me to hear of new protective rangers who genuinely dislike nature—who *want* to ride around in patrol cars with their flat hats cocked down over their eyes—I know we have to have them. But I'll never really think of them as rangers.

There is another way that rangers are subdivided, and it may be the reason that the rivalry between naturalists and protectives never gets violent, because it takes this same batch of people and reshuffles them into two completely different groups called seasonals and permanents.

Seasonals usually just work the busy season. In Yellowstone that's summer, and in Death Valley or the Everglades that's winter. Permanents work all year long. They are, simply, permanent.

But not really. The National Park Service has a career ladder that compels impermanence of many kinds. It usually requires transfer with promotion, so if you're a sub-district ranger in Yosemite and you're up for promotion, you'll move to be a district ranger somewhere else—Great Smoky Mountain, Glacier, Grand Canyon, wherever. The idea is that you end up with an exceptionally broad experience; you can do your work better, and the parks are constantly getting new blood and fresh perspectives. It is a good system, but it has its disadvantages. One does not move to the Valley District of Yosemite after three wilderness assignments and immediately know how to handle riots or drug busts (of course that's one of the things one is there to learn, but it's on-the-job training at best). One doesn't come to Yellowstone after working at Betsy Ross House and the Lincoln Memorial and immediately know anything about working with

bears. Bears, like riots, require some experience, and now that Yellowstone and some of the other parks have solved the worst of their bear
problems—that is, now that bear incidents and encounters aren't an
everyday experience—it's getting difficult to *learn* bears. The best bear
men are those who worked in the fifties and sixties, when a ranger could
easily be involved in dozens of bear problems each year, and could get lots
of practice at trapping, bluffing, or simply maneuvering around bears.
That level of practical education is no longer possible. Luckily, it's not so
necessary, either, but when it *is* necessary it's desperately so. As they
retire, the bear experts take something irreplaceable with them, a hard-
earned savvy that no amount of technology and classroom training can
replace. I recently heard a veteran Yellowstone researcher talking about
this problem, remarking rather wistfully that a certain Yellowstone ranger
was the last we had who could be counted on to know what to do if he had
to follow an injured grizzly into heavy cover with only a magnum for
company. Plenty of rangers have the guts to do it, but few have the sense
of a bear's moods—how the bear thinks—to do it and bring their guts
back with them.

You get some permanents who don't want to climb the career ladder.
They find a job and a place they like, and they stay. They never ask for a
promotion, and they refuse jobs if offered. They are known as homesteaders, and they make administrators uncomfortable, like a gummed-up cog in
the Xerox machine, because they don't take part in the musical chairs
occupational game that is the park service's hallmark. In parks like
Yellowstone—huge and complex in their wonders and hazards—the
homesteaders are the only ones who really know their way around. They
know that the woodstove at Skunk Cabbage Creek Cabin needs a periodic
whack at a certain place with a skillet to jar loose the flue. They know how
to shave three precious minutes off the ambulance run to Inspiration
Overlook when some old gent is suffering a heart attack there. They're
home. Some get stale, others just get better, but more than any other
full-time employees they're *permanent*.

There are other types of impermanence, though. It's common knowledge in the service (I've even seen studies of it, a rare case of common
knowledge also having facts behind it) that the mobility, combined with
life in tiny isolated communities (made up of intense, well-educated,
ambitious careerists, their homesteader mirror-images, and a healthy collection of provincial locals), causes serious mental stress. Psychological
maladies, divorce, and simple nervous fatigue are common results. This is

the paradox of being a park service permanent: there is little constancy in the life aside from the always exceptional surroundings.

Seasonals have an even greater mobility. Many prefer it, and would not become permanent. To the outsider both groups might appear so footloose as to be indistinguishable, but the differences, both bureaucratic and philosophical, are formidable.

The seasonal employee receives virtually none of the benefits the permanent does. The seasonal accrues no retirement money, is covered by no health plan but whatever commercial program he or she can afford, has none of the rights and prerogatives of the civil service wards on the inside; seasonals are second-class employees in every sense of the word except responsibility to the public. I was constantly reminded of Jerry Farber's celebrated tract on student rights, *The Student As Nigger;* we sometimes expected to be given separate rest rooms and drinking fountains.

Some of my fellow seasonals wanted in desperately. They traveled great distances to take government tests, scraped up enough money to put themselves through law-enforcement school or emergency medical training; they applied for every job that came available, no matter how grim. They'd pay a few years' dues conducting tours at Millard Fillmore National Outhouse for a chance to get back to the "good" parks later in their career. Incidentally, the urban parks and monuments look to be about half full of these people, frustrated naturalists and wilderness nuts who salvage their sanity by compiling "A Checklist of Birds Seen within One Block of Independence Hall, Philadelphia," or "A Preliminary List of Common Shrubs on the National Capital Mall."

Since the 1930s the National Park Service has had its mission complicated by assuming guardianship of scores of battlefields, monuments, urban recreation areas, and archeological sites, and as one moves up the career ladder, as I've said, one must log a certain number of years at these places or one is not considered well-rounded. Many seasonals were more than willing to do this work—some were even broad-minded enough and culturally advanced enough to like it (I'm not). Others didn't believe they had to be that well-rounded. They kind of wanted to keep a few of their pointy corners rather than have them ground off in the career mill. They liked nature, and couldn't see the need to learn crowd control or riot prevention.

There had always been a few such independents, but in the 1970s their numbers so increased that they came to identify themselves as a group. They preferred the freedom of the seasonal life, working only part of the year, or maybe working one park in summer and another in winter (Yellowstone had a small platoon of Yellowstone/Everglades seasonals). They traveled light and loved it. They were a new type. They were permanent seasonals.

More than that, they were professionals. They were experienced and well-educated. Though no generalization holds true all the time, I'd say that most of them were as sharp as they were *because* they were seasonals. Each season they were subjected to performance review; failure to measure up meant they wouldn't get rehired next summer. The weak ones were weeded out. This was a constant process, and with no job security (even if your rating was high, there was nothing to prevent the government from abolishing your job next season) the seasonals had a competitive edge, and a discerning eye for both opportunity and injustice.

For they saw that no matter how much the agency might talk up the high quality of their permanent employees, those permanents had job security. Once in, the pressure was off; one need not work as hard if one was not so inclined. One could slouch, lose one's mental or physical leanness, and know that the job would go on. This is not to say that many permanents weren't very good; only that, given the opportunity, a percentage of any group of people will succumb to the easier course. Seasonals were constantly reminded of this by the occasional outstandingly incompetent permanent, so deeply entrenched and fortified in his civil service battlements that nothing short of murder—his own or his commission of—would pry him loose from the job he was neglecting. The sight of these people and the lessons they inadvertently taught did more than anything else to galvanize seasonals into a self-aware group that at times was little less than a movement. Their rhetoric was self-righteous and often justified. They had pride. They had independence. They had no health insurance, but they had their souls. They were willing to fight for the parks, to follow orders, to preach the orthodox park service line, to get out their scissors when some fat administrator whose belly disgraced the uniform told them their hair was an inch too long ... they were true believers, but they weren't *permanents*.

Most permanents could never get clear around the idea that seasonals weren't just apprentice permanents waiting to get it. "Of course seasonals want to be permanents! That's how I got my start. I cleaned toilets in Death Valley for five winters before I was accepted at Indian Mounds National Cornfield. These young hotshots are just afraid of paying their dues, is all. They'll grow up eventually."

Not a chance, we said (yes, there I was, though certainly not the most militant, having had much more rewarding contact with many permanents than had most of the others). We are professionals. We are as good at the job as you. Some of us are better, and some of you know that we are already doing your jobs for you.

I've often wondered, since the summer when we stirred up so much unrest and dissatisfaction that the superintendent was moved to meet with us (it all reminded me very uncomfortably of dissident radicals having a showdown with the college president), why we were so fiercely proud of our independence. What we complained about to the superintendent was in fact how many of the federal bennies we *wanted*. We were professionals and we wanted to be treated like professionals, and so we wanted the things professionals got, like health insurance and job security. We were asking for the things we should have been most suspicious of. And the superintendent, a man of vast and sometimes painful experience in the parks, sat in front of us knowing how slowly the wheel would turn, knowing our complaints were just but would go unanswered, and knowing also, I suspect now, the irony of our desires. We were trying to institutionalize and formalize the very looseness that made us what we were.

I do know what I liked about the life, though. Scenes were always fresh, new times were always coming. Five months in Yellowstone, arriving with the springbeauty and leaving with the first snow, then on to the Everglades, or Saguaro, or a winter of school, or loafing cheaply through a dozen parks on a naturalist's lark. In those few moments found for reflection there was much to look forward to; old friends regathering every summer for a few months were better loved than friends seen year-round. We knew the migration routes, the shortcuts, the cheap campsites, the vacant floors. We epitomized an old and now-fading ideal first promulgated by the park service's premier director, Stephen Mather, who characterized the entire agency, with all its motion and change, as a family. The network of friends became more elaborate and entwined as the years passed: "He's in North Cascades now and he says you should look him up at Sedro-Wooley." "They're at Shark Valley until March and I'm going to be spending a few days with them on my way to the Keys." "I've got a cabin here at Big Meadow; come and visit and bring your guitar."

We got tired of roads, of packing and unpacking, of no pay or low pay, but we never got tired of the freedom. The freedom and the freshness, the welcomes we could count on and the cause that carried us, were inspiriting and driving.

But in my case, though I never gave in to the permanent's security, I must admit that one morning I awoke, my eyes still closed, and finally it was not amusing that I simply had no idea where I was. Usually when that happened I'd just lie there, eyes still closed, trying to remember. If I couldn't figure it out I'd reach over to see what was near (aha, a single bed . . . I'm not in my car), then reach up (oops, an upper bunk—must be government quarters somewhere). And at last I was just a little too tired, or a little sick of reaching over and finding nothing but the edge of the bed, and some of the romance was gone from the song that says "So many times now, Oh Lord I can't remember/ if it's September/ or July." And opening my eyes to the lumpy, buttoned-and-striped mattress of the bunk above me, I longed for something a little more, well, *permanent*.

The ranger, protective or naturalist, permanent or seasonal, must survive. The ranger must somehow weather the current identity crisis. I don't know how, but the ranger, at least something of the *old* ranger, must go on. The ranger is that important a figure and that valuable an institution. No other uniform in North America except for the red and navy of the Royal Northwest Mounted Police stands so singularly and so eloquently for good.

The uniform meant a great deal to me, much more than I thought any uniform could. Coming out of the Vietnam/university unrest/anti-Nixon subculture with a distaste for the stereotypical mindless faceless soldier, I had certain ideas about people who dressed alike and had insignia on their sleeves. But the ranger uniform had none of those unpleasant attachments, as far as I could tell. Putting it on didn't make my neck redden or my politics shift. I put it on knowing it stood for that higher good, and I was impressed at my capacity for accepting that as the simple truth it was. Rangers were Good, in uniform.

I soon discovered the universality of that opinion. People approach the flat hat with little paranoia. They open up. They trust. I didn't know any of that was still possible.

The children were best of all. Jaded by incredible toys and television, they still stood flushed and shy under a ranger's attention. It became a habit, being friendly with children, and parents loved it. Too much of a habit, perhaps, for when I left the park, or was out of uniform, I still had my lights on; I was friendly with kids the way people in small towns are, rubbing a little head as naturally as smiling. But without the uniform I was just another stranger. Both parents and children had their guards up.

But with the uniform on, the image was clear. Within the limitations of my slovenly tendencies (I sometimes forgot my badge, or put my name tag on upside down, and my shoes could become scuffed magically, sitting quietly by my bunk at night) I cared deeply for all those things the uniform made me responsible for. Some were simple, like standing up straight or not being quite as piggish as I would have liked (an overweight ranger is just another fat cop). Some were as complicated as the expectations and the needs of the people I was being paid to serve.

And I often wondered, from inside my sincerely projected image, about the less tangible elements of the ranger. Even though the job has changed, has been subverted and specialized into a committee of narrower officers, the image goes on. Rangers are some sort of heirs to frontiersmen. They have always been society's response to the need for a civilized woodsman. What's important about that is where it may yet lead. Under the new challenges and the new specializations there will certainly survive a public belief in, and a public need for, the ranger of hardy constitution and versatile craft. The tragedy of the modern ranger is that the Mark Trail woodsman is becoming a practical anachronism just as he is becoming a cultural treasure. The ranger, like the mountain man, the trapper, the cowboy, and the sheriff before him, has been so romanticized and glorified that few rangers alive could measure up to the standards of the image, any more than many cowboys could measure up to Wister's archetype in *The Virginian.* The difference is that we have a chance to preserve the ranger. The line need not die out or be replaced by more technological heroes like astronauts and truck drivers.

The chance we have is the national park system. The parks, whose welfare the rangers were created to defend, can now return the favor. By virtue of sixty years of service, and by virtue of the parks' perpetual need for certain services, the ranger could go on indefinitely. The way things have worked out, with wilderness becoming ever more islanded in the modern world, surely the ranger is one of the most important cultural achievements the national parks can aim to protect within their boundaries.

Is There Anything Here to See?

I first got to know the American tourist during an extended trip through Mexico and Central America just before I came to Yellowstone. In markets from Guadalajara to Chichicastenango to Colón, I saw us as we are, doing more damage to the American image abroad than the most incompetent professional diplomats ever could. Fat, lavender-haired ladies in electric aquamarine pantsuits, shrieking at patient shopkeepers, "How much is that in *real* money?" Bald, cigar-chomping old men in loud floral shorts taking pictures of a passing funeral or a beggar. Crowds of tourists bustling through the National Cathedral in Mexico City, photographing praying worshippers during an Easter Sunday Mass. The crimes of Kodachrome and ethnocentrism, at every place where local culture can be marketed.

Of course tourists are only as offensive as their hosts permit them to be; both can behave with sense and dignity. Moreover, I understand that the people who must consider such things (tour specialists, travel agents, and the like) no longer judge Americans to be the most obnoxious; we've been replaced by the Japanese, some say by the Germans as well. If this is true, America has lost world leadership of a sort we should not mourn, a leadership we've had far too long anyway.

In some professions that must deal wth large groups of travelers, "tourist" has become a pejorative. The word has come to stand for low-rate (as in "tourist class"), rude, boisterous, and culturally insensitive. In many circles in Yellowstone (especially hotel and store staffs and the less well-paid ranks of government employees) it has been largely replaced by "turkey." Tourist is more than a label, it's an insult.

Rangers are counseled not to use the word. With at least a little justification, park managers have decided that tourist is such a loaded word, so hopelessly colored, that it no longer serves its purpose. A tourist isn't simply a vacationing person any more. A tourist is a vacationing person who is very likely to do something silly. We can no longer help ourselves; we hear the word and we hear its implications. It's like expecting the average person to think of a female dog when they hear the word bitch. No, says the boss, you will not call them tourists. You will call them *visitors*. Here is a fresh, neutral name for them; use it well.

One would not expect this to work. One would expect that a tourist, by any other name, would still be a tourist. Changing the name doesn't change the creature; after all, the creature *earned* its reputation, souring the name as it did so. Won't the new name undergo the same character change? I once sat in a meeting where my bosses were trying to figure a way to get more visitors to stop at Grant Village, an unfortunate development in the southern part of the park. New signs, pamphlets, and all the usual things were proposed, without much hope, then the chief naturalist brightened up and joked, "I know! Let's change its name to Old Faithful!" I was the only one who laughed. A new name for an old thing seems like the silliest kind of self-deception, but I have to admit that it seems to work with tourists.

Visitors are everywhere now. A visitor has driven off the road into a bog near Norris; a visitor's dog has been parboiled in a hot spring at Mud Volcano; a visitor reports a herd of ostriches in Willow Park. The term has remained unloaded, probably because the old familiar "tourist" still travels the treacherous highways of our off-duty conversations. We have not abandoned tourists. We just don't deal with them at work. All day we direct visitors to the rest rooms, sell them books, give them fishing permits, and identify flowers for them. After work we tell tourist stories.

Anyone who deals with tourists for a while will develop mental images and stereotypes, though usually these are caricatures based on the outlandish rather than on the normal. We picture them in bermuda shorts (and give them mock taxonomy—*Touri bermudi*) and gaudy shirts. Sunburnt heads, instamatics perched on hard paunches. We see them frowning in confusion at an upside-down map, taking a tentative swat at dirty children who squirm and whine in the back seat. We see them buying tasteless souvenirs (they get little choice around Yellowstone): ashtrays that say

"Old Faithful, 300 feet" (that actually is the height of the Lower Falls of the Yellowstone River, but what's a little 100% error?); blue Indian war bonnets; little stuffed bears made in Hong Kong; plastic tomahawks; Smokey Bear masks; Naugahyde holsters for potmetal cap pistols ... in short, all the things to reinforce the twisted stereotype *they* have, of the West as a fairyland inhabited by talking bears, clockwork geysers, and the ghosts of gunslingers and braves. Romantic violence and Fenimore Cooper's virtuous savages. Disneyland with bears. Grizzlyland. Six Flags over Yellowstone.

They're conditioned by most of what they encounter before they get here—by television, by hotel ads, by childhood memories, by idyllic music—to expect fabulous improbable things, the more fantastic the better. But we have to believe they are like us—we know they're at least as smart—and our hope is to turn them on to the real Yellowstone, whatever that is. But their sheer numbers are a statistical certainty that we'll see plenty of flakes to nourish our most resented stereotypes.

It's a game we play, pretending these people, all two and a half million of them, are intellectual cripples, as if this great comic farce we perceive in their traffic is our personal entertainment. They help, frequently, by sending some especially hapless soul to give us a shock. A well-dressed gent hurried into the Visitor Center one day, map in hand, and spread it in front of me on the counter. "How do I get out of here?"

"Well, sir, you have five choices, depending on which way you want to go after you leave." I indicated the various roads on the map. "There are entrances on every side of the park. The closest is five miles from here—the north entrance." I pointed it out on the map, labeled, in bold, "North Entrance."

He was calm but frustrated. "Yes, yes, I see those entrances, but I want an *exit*. Where are the *exits?*"

I took a quick look, but there was no humor on his face, no tic of betrayal that this was all a flat joke on the ranger. This fellow was serious. He needed an exit.

"Oh. They just call them entrances because that makes more sense than calling them exits." At least it had until just now. "You can go out of them too."

"Oh. Okay. Thanks." He rumpled up the map and bustled out the door, and I wandered off in search of someone to tell my new tourist story to.

Bearings are easily lost far from home. As a child I watched my parents

take the wrong road now and then in strange country, and even then I knew
that my parents are pretty smart people. I use my childhood memories to
temper my impatience with questions I'm tired of. I remember the feeling.
This little boy with the melted fudgesicle in his hair is me. His mother—or
mine—is about to become the hundredth person today to ask if the sign out
front of the Visitor Center, the one that says "North Entrance, 5 Miles"
with an arrow pointing north, means that it's five miles to the north
entrance if she goes that way. *My* mother has always been patient with
me—how can I be less with her?

But forgive me, sometimes I am. I become a master of a sarcasm so
subtle, a condescension so beautifully understated, that only I have to deal
with its viciousness; it's totally lost on my audience. Only if someone else is
working the desk with me, a fellow sufferer, might there even be an
eyebrow raised questioningly in my direction when I blandly, oh, so
pleasantly, explain to a visitor that the rest rooms are right out there in front
of the building, right where they just walked in, right under the signs that
say rest rooms. Or that people do, indeed, live in all these houses (what did
they think lived in them?). Or that the animals they saw—"you know, the
ones with the ears?"—were probably elk, if they weren't deer, though both
are known to have ears.

It gets worse in private. In private many of us succumb more openly to
bewilderment and impatience.

"I wonder how some of these people find their way here?" I casually
remarked to a fellow ranger one day.

"Oh, I don't think much about that. You know what I wonder? I
wonder how many don't find their way home. I have this feeling that all
over America there are communities with an empty house or two. Ask the
neighbors and they'll just say 'Well, you know it's a funny thing about the
McPhersons; last summer they packed up and told us they were going to
Yellowstone, and they never came back.' I figure a lot of them get here, but
they wind up endlessly circling some big cloverleaf, yelling at their kids."

"Looking for an 'entrance' sign, maybe."

"Could be. Maybe they just buy a new house and start over, somewhere."

Though we deal with tourists all day, under many circumstances, the
Visitor Center is for us the heart of the dark side of public service. Out at the
hot springs, or on a nature walk, we have the double advantage of being
there ourselves and having something fun to answer questions about.
Inside the "V.C." (our Vietnam vets found the abbreviation especially

apt), it's just us, a few exhibits, and the visitor's bulging bladder. V.C. duty is dreaded as it begins, celebrated as it concludes. Here we learn what people really want.

The tourist in a hurry has a sense of responsibility to make sure that everything important is seen. Even a ten-second glance will save embarrassment back home, where no smug neighbor will be able to say "Oh, you should have gone over and seen the Prairie Dog Village—it was *much* better than the Reptile Gardens." This concern with logging all the essential attractions and vistas (and its corollary obsession with getting them all on film) simplifies the process of deciding what to do in Yellowstone. Just go to the Visitor Center and ask the ranger, "Is there anything here to see?" The ranger will certainly know whether his five hundred thousand acres of Yellowstone has anything worth a glance or a couple of inches of instamatic film. Even better, take your map along and point to the road from Mammoth to Old Faithful—fifty miles of towering mountains, glorious streams, and the world's greatest collection of geysers—and ask, "Is there anything along this road?"

The question really isn't all that unfair. What it says, at best, is "I'm new here, I only have a day though I wish I had a month, and I'd sure appreciate some tips on what I can accomplish in so little time." But after a long day the question doesn't come across that way. Other questions get asked more often—bears and bathrooms are the leaders—but this one is somehow most painful.

Sometimes I give in to their urgent need for a negative answer, their need to know that the neighbors couldn't have seen anything memorable on that road. I say, at my most obtusely ironic, "Nope. Not a thing on that road. What you want to do is get right on down to Old Faithful." Then, shocked by the magnitude of my lie, I take a shot at recovery. "But don't just wait around for Old Faithful to erupt. There's an easy trail (the damn thing's paved, getting ready for your great-grandchildren who will have motorized roller skates emplanted in their feet at birth) out to Castle Geyser. It'll only take a little while, and (here I play to their need to have one on the neighbors) you'll see some great thermal features that a lot of people miss." The balancing act of summarizing two million acres of wilderness against their insanely short average visit is itself balanced against my relief that they all *can't* stay a month, my sympathy with the hopelessness of their situation, and my desire to get them into at least one breathtaking *personal* encounter with Yellowstone. Out of the car. "Hands on," as the educators say.

But only the gifted and patient few can maintain the commitment needed to do the questions justice. The gifted few can turn a request for a bathroom into a mini-seminar on wildflower appreciation, the visitor forgetting the demands of his kidneys in a trance of nature lore. I get cynical. I start to study them.

One summer I discovered that several of us were into the same game: trying to guess what the question will be before it's asked, as they come walking through the door. You have to be quick—you only have a couple of seconds to read the person before he reaches you. This man isn't carrying a map or a camera; he wants the bathroom. The guy with the "Old Milwaukee" T-shirt wants to see a bear ("The kids want to see one," he explains, as if he didn't buy two pounds of marshmallows to throw to the bear). This lady in the heavy powder wants a hotel. The kid who just walked past the drinking fountain wants to know if there's a drinking fountain in here. And here come three people, almost visibly reeking of wood smoke, who clearly want a backcountry permit. This guy is . . . wait, he's got a field guide, and he's holding it open to a certain page! He's going to ask me something about nature! What a break, I've only been here two hours and already a question about nature! I wonder if I'll know the answer . . . Let's see, bears are the big brown ones and flowers are the little yellow ones . . .

The questions go on. Do we sell film? stamps? post cards? (No ma'am, the hotel company won't let us. I don't understand it either, but I guess they were here first.) bumper stickers? window decals? ashtrays? Where can I get a patch like yours, ranger? (Wait a few minutes, kid, you can have mine.)

When it gets busy, it approaches theatre, one minidrama after another. America on the Road. A middle-aged couple, the man angry and the woman near tears, report she left their camera at a picnic table—a vacation tainted for the rest of their lives, it will never be discussed without a triumphant shrug from him and a contrite grimace from her. Two young couples disagree, nearly quarreling, over a route to Glacier Park. The ranger guarantees bitter resolution to the disagreement because his answer will unavoidably prove someone wrong, someone right. A young, happily unmarried couple trudge in from a week in the woods, and ask with fearful hope if there is a pay shower in the area.

A family—man, wife, two children—approach one day and report a wolf sighting. I automatically disbelieve wolf sightings until some questions are answered. "Have you ever seen a coyote?" Yellowstone, if it has any wolves at all, is coyote heaven, and though we dearly hope for some reliable wolf sightings, most people don't know the difference, so we must be strict. The man almost convinces me; it was "very big and *dark*."

Coyotes are light. Then he falters, asking his boy for additional information. The kid remembers it as a very *light* animal. The man, embarrassed, mumbles he was driving and didn't get a very good look. He asks his wife. She didn't see a thing, was reading the map, seems to have some doubts about the kid having seen it either. They all leave in embarrassment, and for the hundredth time the Holy Grail of Yellowstone wildlife sightings— a bona fide wolf—slips through my fingers.

An attractive lady in her forties asks where she can show her children some Indians. I bridle, answering too sharply that the reservations aren't like zoos for the entertainment of tourists. She is smarter and better spoken than I thought, and her hurt look tells me I should not have assumed she was an insensitive gawker. Taking in her bearing and bright expression, I reread her as someone with at least some interest in native American culture, and make a few suggestions.

People ask about "that big earthquake a few years ago in the park; you know, the one that killed all those people?" I explain that it was west of the park, in 1959, over beyond Hebgen Lake, and I shiver at what I see in some eyes. They aren't interested in earthquakes. They want to go see where an entire campground full of sleeping people was buried by a landslide. I'm tempted to play with them, to suggest that if they look around they might find jewelry or even teeth, but I'm too afraid their eyes will light up even more. I give them a pamphlet about earthquakes, hoping that when they toss it, unread, into the back seat maybe one of their kids will learn something from it.

Complaints are often the most pressing and interesting minidramas, and are usually easy to handle. We're told in training that the best thing to do with an indignant visitor is to get out a complaint form. Getting it in writing, putting it down on an official form, dissipates a lot of anger. Once thus defused, they can usually be talked into solving their problem.

Complaints. Not enough campsites; we drove from Calgary and there's no place to stay, where can we stay? Too many campsites; for God's sake why cater to all these tourists? Why not save some forest? Food's terrible at the hotel. (Forget it, sir, I've been complaining about that for years and it doesn't help.) Food's terrible in that little town we just came through. Where are all the bears? We were here ten (twenty, thirty, a million) years ago and the bears were *everywhere!*

And, the most appalling complaint ever heard in a national park: The television reception is terrible down in the campground! How am I going to watch the game tonight?

Some complaints are just expressions of disappointment, the most touching of which involve return visits. "I was here in 1937 and, boy, the hot springs were really something back then. Too bad they've all dried up like that."

"I was here in 1953 and Old Faithful was a lot bigger then. Is it true it's dying?" (Only of embarrassment, sir.)

"I worked here in 1944 and it sure wasn't crowded then." (No sir, I'm sure it wasn't. It wouldn't have been even if everybody hadn't been off fighting World War II.)

Embellished memory is wonderful. A child sees Old Faithful a thousand feet high, sees one grand hot spring and spends thirty years magnifying it into a vast mountain range of colorful fountains. Old Faithful varies greatly in size from eruption to eruption, so seeing fewer than a dozen eruptions leaves you unequipped to evaluate it. Overall, it's pretty much the way it's been for a century. So are the Mammoth Hot Springs; one dries up here, another starts up there. People don't like to be told they've remembered inaccurately; it sounds too much like creeping senility. But it's a natural and common response to a favorite memory. I try to break it to them easily, but fall back on a century of documented evidence if I have to. "Old Faithful will die some day, that's for sure Ma'am, but you aren't a witness."

After a few months of V.C. duty one comes to terms with the numbing effects of answering the same question, if only by succumbing to the numbness. "Where are the bears, ranger?" "Well, let me tell you about that, sir... " Click, the tape recorder is on, and the message rolls out one more time, word for word just like it was yesterday. If all else fails, there's always martyrdom—oh, no, not another question about the bears! How will I last until lunch?—which at least offers the sweet indignation of a burden nobly suffered.

But we know we have nothing to complain about. We get America at its best and most stimulating. Many people come to us already fired up about the park, and we get to deal with them when they are most receptive to new ideas, most willing to be taught, most wanting to be liked. As a wise supervisor points out to me, patiently and repeatedly, "Paul, I know it's the thousandth time you've heard the question, but remember, it's the first time that guy has asked it."

And keep in mind, Paul, that when you lock up the V.C. and go home, you're sleeping in Yellowstone tonight, the one, the only. And that tomorrow, when that poor tourist who wanted to feed some bears is halfway back to Fort Wayne you'll *still* be in Yellowstone. And, as you know, there *is* something to see here.

Fear and Loathing
at Indian Creek

Yellowstone campgrounds, even the small ones, become communities at night. Every evening a new set of neighbors settles in, a new pack of dogs harass the ground squirrels and chipmunks, and a new pack of children whittle and hack away at the trees. It's an accelerated version of the mobile American society we hear so much about, where the people move daily instead of every three or four years.

The place is a little more factious than your average community. Next to the forty-thousand-dollar mobile home laden with dignified retirees is a literal commune of one- or two-person tents, suffused in a light haze of illegal smoke and heavy music. Next to the Mormons, the Episcopalians; the Democrats, the Birchers; the gun nuts, the bleeding hearts. It's not a melting pot, but it's a hell of a mixing bowl, and a great place for conversation. You might hear, or see, almost anything as you walk the campground.

For all their ostentatious comforts, the well-heeled campers aren't the ones that I found the most intriguing. I was always interested in what was going on next door, where the Great American Counterculture had pitched its tents. The counterculture presents some telling self-portraits when it goes on vacation (perhaps they have another, less bourgeois, word for it; tripping, I suppose). They are inclined, both philosophically and economically, to camp in the old sense, in tents and sleeping bags. They rarely have televisions, but they often have mighty stereos. With these they blithely flood the campground with Led Zeppelin, guilty of a dormitory mentality that bewilders me. Choice of music isn't the point; they could be playing Mozart and I'd still be appalled at their lack of consideration. More important, I can't understand their deafness to the natural sounds (I won't insult, or dignify, natural forest sounds by calling them music). Wilderness settings provide a contrast to our usual cultural (or countercultural) trappings. Why drag along so much artificiality that we drown out the freshness?

One night after my campfire program I could hear vintage Jefferson Airplane chopping holes in an otherwise sweet mountain evening. Fifty yards down the road I walked into a campsite with a microbus (the vehicular emblem of the vacationing counterculture, the people's Winnebago) parked to one side. It was too dark to see faces, but two orange dots glowed companionably over near the fire pit. The air suffered with a cloying scent I remembered immediately from my collegiate days on the edge of various countercultures.

My sudden appearance, flat hat providing an authoritarian silhouette, cleared the air a bit, startling a young couple from their reverie. The glows disappeared; perhaps they swallowed them.

I greeted them brightly. "Hi! Actually, I've always admired Jefferson Airplane, but it's getting late and the sound is carrying clear across the campground. Mind turning it down?"

"Huh?" The realization that this was not a bust soaked in slowly. "Oh. Yeah. Sure, no problem, be glad to." The young man rose, hurried over to the bus, and turned off the music.

The counterculture wasn't always so pleasant to deal with. One afternoon, while driving through the campground, I spotted a prone body sprawled across the entrance to a vacant campsite. I parked and walked over to an incredibly disheveled (and keep in mind that I have a high tolerance for sloth) young man whose ratty hair hung over his face into an unspeakably colorful puddle of vomit. I reached down and tapped him on the leg. "Excuse me, are you all right?" It seemed like the best question, rather than "Are you alive?" or "Are you for real?"

His eyes opened (Whew, he's alive! I'd hate to have to do anything with this body that involved touching it). He raised his head a few inches, his hair stirring in the puddle, and tried to focus on me through whatever mental fog he was dealing with. "Yeah, I'm okay."

Doubting the reliability of his judgment on a matter of that sort, but relieved that I didn't have to drag him back to my truck, I rose to leave. "Fine, just checking." Back to the truck, and away, as his head settled back into the same spot.

Between that sordid extreme and its opposite in the aluminum mansions-with-wheels is a world of characters: your neighbors and mine, you and I, "goin' campin' " in Yellowstone. Most of them are fun, sensible, well-meaning folks, perfectly forgettable except for a lingering assurance they gave me by their sameness, a feeling that I live in a country that is largely populated by people I like. Given half a chance I'd warm to them enough to want to do more than tell them the short-cut to the rest rooms. I'd suggest a good place to see some elk, or tell them where groceries were cheapest (anyplace outside the park, compared to anyplace inside the park). A few would even get a hot tip on local wild strawberries. After several years of dealing with the public, when I was generally burned out on the work, I was still a sucker for a nice friendly family.

The campgrounds have always been a prime target for what the park service calls "interpretation," a high-flown term for education. Every night in almost every campground there was a campfire talk, or program, or something. The kind of something depended on the size of the campground. The really large ones had huge log-seated amphitheaters that would hold five hundred or more, where formal slide programs and loudspeaker systems allowed one ranger to talk to truly big mobs of campers. A vestigial campfire was safely ensconced off to the side in a little masonry pit, where its modest flickerings wouldn't interfere with the slides being projected onto the screen. The smallest campgrounds had a few simple log benches in a semicircle around a fire pit; they were small enough that a campfire talk still had something to do with a campfire.

We preferred the small ones. We knew that the big ones, where we stood up there with a necklace microphone and a handheld remote control unit, reached the most people and were the only practical way to handle that size crowd. But the small ones were more fun, and much more stimulating. After you'd given your slide program about half a dozen times you could pretty much put yourself on autopilot and run through it, jokes and all, without any deep feeling. But to stand up in front of thirty, or fifty, or eighty random Americans and announce by your unencumbered presence that they should pay attention to you—no props here—*that* was something to stir your spirit.

After five years I was tired of the formal presentations. There came an evening when, somewhere near the middle of my program, droning along in all sincerity, I suddenly realized I had no idea where I was in my talk. It was as if I'd been sleep-talking and had just then been awakened. I had achieved robothood. Luckily the slide then projected was the sort that I could have allowed to linger on the screen for a few extra seconds for the audience to admire, so the pause, while I studied the picture and figured out what I was supposed to say next, was not awkward.

The wearier I grew of the formal presentations, the more I enjoyed the informal talks. About six miles from Mammoth is Indian Creek Campground, a small one with a cozy little fire circle off in the woods behind the campsites. Here, where a talk was supposed to last thirty to forty-five minutes, we would often chat with the crowd for two or three hours. Here, far enough away from the nearest real settlement so that it probably attracted a different type of camper, the campfire talk survived and flourished.

Dealing with the campers, week after week, year after year, was probably the closest I'll ever come to knowing what's on America's mind. Keeping always in mind that park visitors do not include America's fifty million impoverished and immobile souls, and that people who stay in campgrounds carry a different set of conceptual baggage than those who stay at the hotels, I found myself always on the lookout for attitudes, especially for animosities.

Take the bears. Rare was the camper who, once the reasons behind prohibiting roadside feeding of black bears were explained, didn't immediately nod heartily in approval, if not enthusiasm. Only once did someone object beyond expressing disappointment. I'd just gone through my spiel about the bears, explaining that back in the 1960s when roadside feeding of black bears was being permitted, an average of twenty-four bears were destroyed every summer—some hit by cars, some shot by rangers when the bears became impatient with abusive, pesky tourists and started clawing people. Usually that twenty-four-dead-bears story was the clincher, proof that the price of the show was too high; eyebrows would raise, opinions would shift, anger would dissipate. A well-dressed man toward the front of the group was unimpressed by the story. In the casual atmosphere I tried to encourage at a talk, he announced, "That's okay with me. I want to see some bears!"

With more composure and maturity than I thought I possessed, I calmly responded, "You don't mind the bears being killed?"

"Of course I mind, but I'm willing to let it happen if it will give me the chance to see a few bears. I don't get much chance to see them, living in a city. You guys who live here, you have them all the time."

A swirl of glib answers—given a choice the bear would rather live; have you ever seen a bear eat a foil film wrapper?—raced to my tongue, but once again I acted like a grown-up. Seeing that glibness would not reach him, I just answered that I was glad that the people in charge of the bears didn't agree with him. Neither, it seemed, did the audience. Several protested, encounter-group style, to his attitude, almost shouting him down and breaking the tension I'd felt and permitting us all to smile about our sudden feelings and the bears that caused them.

Other attitudes, bigger ones, troubled me more. My first few years in the park coincided nicely with the decline, fall, and hermitage of Richard Nixon. In those years I think I saw America sour a bit. I don't want to overdo this, because there were too many immeasurable variables, not the least being my own changing attitudes about myself and my work; the first couple of summers I ran on pure missionary zeal, then I slowed down a little and grew wiser (and maybe a little cynical) as I learned more about the past and future of the environmental movement. I believed, always more deeply, in its importance, but I became skeptical about its chances and therefore about my chances to help it. I became a political realist.

But what I heard and saw those years, talking to America daily, conducting scores of campfire talks, couldn't have been only the result of my own changing outlook. I trust my perceptions, and heard about it from enough of my friends who had similar experiences, to know that I saw America get mean.

As the revelations about political infighting, payoffs and graft, and unprincipled executives flowed from Washington, and as Americans suffered the quiet outrage of an unworthy leadership, my evenings by the campfire changed. Most obvious was political talk. The hourly newscasts about Watergate kept everyone stirred up, and more than once I had to interrupt a discussion of some constitutional point when two of my audience would get sidetracked. Watergate came on vacation to Yellowstone, and for once the bears were replaced as the number-one visitor obsession.

Most of the change was subtle. People seemed uneasy, or unhappy—somehow unsatisfied. They were quicker to complain, harder to amuse. I knew several people of my father's generation who had trusted and admired Nixon for twenty years. Something in them died when he went down. Some evenings it seemed that every park issue we discussed brought out some greater national issue. Violation of park speed limits grew into the ironies of a political system whose prime rule was "don't get caught." Bear-feeding lectures turned into seminars on national security.

Worst, the skepticism and disillusionment were directed at me, a federal officer, some woodsy representative of that awful mess in Washington. I have notes to myself written then: "Is it me? Is it just that I'm getting tired of repeating my messages, losing the pleasure of spreading the good word? Or is it these people? Am I really seeing a change in mood? Are this year's questions cast in a more suspicious tone? They seem to be, as if people are less willing to trust anyone now... " One evening there was enough despair in the crowd that I burst out, "Listen, I didn't even vote for him! And the park service is too poor to be guilty of graft! You want to know my salary? Let's talk about bears!" Everyone laughed, and the gloom lifted, but what an effort we made to enjoy what once had been easy.

Though the experience was shorter, I think I also saw a little healing of spirit when Nixon was finally gone. We didn't have to approve of Ford's politics to feel a lot better about the country, and the following summers seemed to witness a slackening of suspicion, whole weeks going by without a single sour remark about Washington politics.

By my final summer in the park I gloried in Indian Creek talks. I didn't always want to do it, but like jumping into cold water it was easy once I got started. With years of park life behind me and an ungodly amount of academic research beginning to pay scholarly dividends, I got cocky. I knew the answers to the questions, I enjoyed myself, and my fund of bear stories was well-nigh inexhaustible. At its best a good campfire talk was as exhilarating as a dramatic performance. I knew several rangers who were better at it than I, who were more eloquent or inspirational. I only talked, probably a little too homespun in tone, but that was who I was and my homework was done well. There was one evening, with an audience of about sixty. After forty-five minutes of jokes, debates, and stories I informed the group that they had fulfilled their obligation and were free to go, but that I was glad to throw some more wood on the fire if anyone wanted to stay and talk a while longer. They were a nice group, somehow nicer than most, and it was a compliment of the highest order to me as a ranger that not until an hour later, after a full-dark chill had settled on us, did the first person from the group finally leave. I don't remember what I said, or what it meant, only that I didn't tell any lies and that in simple conversation and shared experience we were joined in an utterly honest little celebration of companionship. No Nixon, no disillusionment, no worry, just a small group of refugees from tomorrow, gathered by chance and interest for a couple of hours, wanting just the joy I wanted to share. It was rarely that good, that warm, but even once in six years would have made it all worth it.

Chance played a big part in how an evening went. Sometimes an elk would wander by only twenty yards from the campfire, an unparalleled visual aid for a wildlife talk. A couple of my friends had bears walk right in and look around, only yards from the thrilled, petrified crowd. My own best was an animal we didn't even see. It was late dusk and I was sermonizing about some park policy when a pack of coyotes began to yap and howl to the north, across the meadows toward Panther Creek. The group didn't need my suggestion that we take a few moments and listen to the song. It was an energetic chorus, one of those freewheeling, ringing jubilations that have so little to do with the old cliché about the "lonesome coyote's howl," and it went on, lifting then fading then lifting again, for several minutes. It left us all shivering a little. Just when it seemed the medley must end—could not be encored in any imaginable way—there was a new voice over the others. A deep powerful call, drawn from greater lungs, rose over the tenor yowls of the pack, silencing them and soaring full and smooth in a steady ascent that dipped only slightly when it abruptly ceased. It left the woods still, and my group visibly shaken. I can't say, and have no way of proving it, but if there is yet one wolf in Yellowstone, one gray-bearded old roamer in search of his vanished kin, we heard his proud song that night.

I feel about campfire programs the same way I feel about rangers. Whatever happens to the parks, whatever political ills befall them, this faltering institution—the old campfire circle—simply must go on. Even when bloated and electronically sterilized, it is one of the unexpected blessings of a visit to Yellowstone, a touch of what's best about sharing the woods. Philosophers emphasize the solitariness of wilderness experience, and I approve; the renewal and stimulation to be had alone with nature is priceless. But national parks are more than wilderness. They are outposts on the edges, from which people can go, or at least peer, in. And the outposts, be they campgrounds, museums, or even hotels, can be enriching too. People brought together with a ranger share a knowledge and a joy that, though they are no replacement for a walk in the wild, are a valid, even essential accompaniment to it. They learn there, of wilderness, its pros- pects, and its risks. More personally, they learn of its possibilities. Even if they are too rushed or timid to take it on themselves right then, they know it's waiting for them. And, if the ranger is any good at his work, if the fire crackles and crumbles hospitably as they sit, and if the smoke that stings their eyes that night surprises them a few days later when they next put that coat on, their Yellowstone campfire will never go out.

A Post of Honor

Park Headquarters at Mammoth Hot Springs was a military post, Fort Yellowstone, from 1891 to 1918. The U.S. Cavalry was sent to Yellowstone in 1886 to patrol the park, a "temporary expedient," everyone imagined; it lasted more than thirty years, and is one of the most unusual episodes in American military history. This huge natural reservation was managed and protected by soldiers in a legal arrangement so bizarre that no one ever really got accustomed to it. The commanding officer of Fort Yellowstone, with anywhere from one to four troops under him (but scattered in small units here and there about the park) took his orders from the War Department, sometimes from a western office but quite often directly from the Secretary of War in Washington. At first the officer was a captain, but later, as the post grew and became more prestigious, he was more likely to be a major or a colonel. What made the assignment so unusual was that he "wore a second hat," as acting superintendent of the park. The civilians who had tried to run the park from 1872 to 1886 had been called superintendents; the "acting" prefix was part of the notion that the army would not be here long. When serving as acting superintendent, this officer took his orders from the Secretary of the Interior. Two distinct sets of records (correspondence, reports, etc.) were kept, and they are as lively and engaging as documents without lurid illustrations can be. These relatively low-ranking officers responded to this peculiar arrangement with remarkable vision and adaptability. Rather than spin wheels fighting a dual command, they accepted orders, even from the civilian Secretary of the Interior, almost as if they liked it.

There were some good reasons for their enthusiastic cooperation. For one thing it was an exceptional assignment. Even in the 1890s the army was so large that rare was the captain, or colonel, who ever heard much from the Secretary, much less heard from him every week or so, much less had equally frequent dealings with the Secretary of the Interior. I've wondered if it was more than coincidence that several of these Yellowstone men went on to distinguished careers (three were Congressional Medal of Honor winners; S.B.M. Young was Theodore Roosevelt's commander in Cuba and later his Chief of Staff). Fort Yellowstone was a post of promise.

A second reason was the fort's traffic. The army lavished architectural gifts on Yellowstone, especially in the last wave of expansion at the post, from 1909 to 1912, because someone noticed that Yellowstone received more foreign visitors than any other army post, with the possible exception of West Point. Fort Yellowstone was a post of eminent visibility.

Another reason was "the cause"; the American military was full of vigorous sportsmen who were just then leading the fight for wildlife conservation. Several of Yellowstone's officers were members of the exclusive and influential Boone and Crockett Club (the archives in the park contain numerous letters from Theodore Roosevelt and George Bird Grinnell, co-founders of the club, who checked in frequently to see how things were going). Most of the officers recognized Yellowstone as a shining light of hope in a murky era of resource waste. Captain George Anderson, acting superintendent in the 1890s, funded winter poacher patrols from his own pocket and wrote articles (including a chapter for a Boone and Crockett Club book) on Yellowstone's problems. In short, Yellowstone under the military began to generate a self-sustaining and vital sense of cause. The military made some mistakes, but only because they were trying hard to do the right thing when nobody was quite sure what the right thing was. The acting superintendents of Yellowstone are neglected heroes of the American conservation movement. Fort Yellowstone was a post of honor.

The soldiers, on the other hand, weren't as certain this was all a good idea. They didn't like such isolated duty, and they weren't too crazy about the weather. My favorite Yellowstone quotation, from Frederic Remington, was attributed to these troopers, who said that Yellowstone has three seasons: July, August, and winter. Many of the soldiers were raw recruits, with no notion of mountain life. Others wanted more excitement, though what with the Indian wars winding down (like many later military posts, Fort Yellowstone was just several rows of buildings without a protecting stockade), there weren't many untended Indian children left to be slaughtered for Old Glory. Military excitement was getting hard to come by, though occasional tawdry opportunities, such as the Philippines and Cuba, still came up.

Yellowstone's "temporary expedient" status worsened the problem, because each year new troops were assigned to the park, so that most soldiers, even those who warmed to the assignment, had little chance to learn the job. Not until 1914, when volunteers were solicited to serve at Fort Yellowstone, did the park get soldiers who really wanted to be there. The idea was that two troops, Yellowstone Park Special Detachments Troops One and Two, would form the core of the ranger force scheduled to come in when the National Park Service was formally born in 1916. (It didn't work out that way; political problems kept the service so underfunded that rangers weren't brought in until 1918, by which time the Special Detachments had been disbanded and many of the best men had drifted off.) But until 1914 it was potluck for Yellowstone assignment. The desertion rate was so high that in 1908 a special board of inquiry was held to determine the cause. Among the most common complaints from the troopers was that they didn't like the mountains.

By 1970 this whole colorful story was nearly lost. The standard Yellowstone histories said little about the army, and scholars were just coming to terms with how important the thirty-two years of army administration had been. The cavalry had brought order to the abused park, and had brought creative energy to the interpretation of the park's original legislative mandate. Much management policy, as I've already talked about, was developed by the army, for better or worse.

As the park's debt to the cavalry was recognized, it occurred to someone that we ought to tell the public about it. Thus was born the Fort Yellowstone Walk. A few evenings each week a naturalist led a group of visitors on a tour around the fort, pointing out the stables (now garages), the barracks (now offices and warehouses), the guardhouse (now a residence), and the rest. The buildings were all in use, so it was a pretty sterile performance, not going in any building or seeing any structure restored to its original state. Worse, we had hardly any information; we carried an hour's worth of stories to tell, and we didn't even believe some of them ourselves. Because we knew so little we were afraid to encourage the group to ask questions. The only ones we could answer with confidence involved the location of nearby rest rooms. It was grim, dry, old-fashioned education.

At the end of the 1972 season we got the word that next year Fort Yellowstone would become a "living history" activity. Living history is a term for a mildly theatrical presentation in which the naturalist is dressed in period costume and deals with the audience as a character from some past time. Colonial historical sites are good examples; visitors encounter a 1650 housewife churning butter on the porch of a replica colonist's house, and she regales them with stories of her hardships and joys. The Civil War battlefields (known on the inside as the "Cannonball Circuit") present living history at its most attention-getting, with battle reenactments. Ragtag bands of volunteer locals get out on the battlefield and try to act like twenty-thousand troops running through hell. Many educators now deplore this reenactment business, referring to it as "boom-boom" education; they say it is shallow and pointlessly sensational, admitting even the historical relevance of hearing the cannons that shredded so many of our forefathers.

Nothing so grand was envisioned for Fort Yellowstone. We would get a couple of noncommissioned officers' uniforms and sidearms and give the walk wearing them. The only other difference was that we would pretend it was 1915 and we were actually noncoms in the Special Detachments, out for an evening to show some visiting dudes the fort. Same stories, different uniform. For one hour it would be 1915; all conversations would be in terms of 1915. The President's name was Wilson; his vice president would be best remembered for having said, "What this country needs is a good five-cent cigar."

The assignment seemed as improbable as the army's. Besides our ignorance and total lack of acting ability, we faced an imposing logistical challenge: bringing 1915 to life while surrounded by the 1970s. We had no props except the ones we wore. All the buildings were in use for modern purposes, and we couldn't enter them. The fort fronts on a major park intersection and there is a noisy flow of traffic. We were leading groups of people through a residential area, across the backyards of park employees. For an hour it would be entirely up to the naturalist/soldier to provide the mood and setting of 1915. It all sounded impossible.

It came down to carrying the whole show on strength of personality, of talking such a good game that something of the army days was briefly revived. In the vernacular, it came down to being bullshit artists. Luckily, the three of us who got the assignment (no volunteering here) happened to have that in us. In spades, some said.

We found, as well, that we could make the difficult surroundings work for us. In 1915, the year we were portraying, cars were first permitted into the park. When a big tour bus would roar by, spreading fumes and ill will over us all, I'd act as if it was a Model T or a Hupmobile and remark from my 1915 perspective, "Goldang auto*mo*biles! I hate those things, they just scare the devil out of the horses." Then, turning to my group of "dudes," I'd make a little prediction. "You folks mark my words, someday we're going to have more of those blasted flivvers in this park than we'll know what to *do* with." Anyone paying attention would chuckle, and on we'd go.

In 1974 I became involved in a research project that eventually yielded great amounts of information for the Fort Yellowstone Walk. I spent my winters cataloguing, organizing, and microfilming the park archives, dealing directly with the original records of the army administration. Before long, and without even wanting to, I knew the hotel rates (with or without a bath), my monthly pay, the cost of freighting grain for the horses from Livingston, Montana, my commanding officer's company, the cost of a dozen eggs, and an appalling collection of equally trivial stuff that fascinated visitors. The additional information made the walk far more realistic and fun, and my own confidence (not to say arrogance) about my facts seemed to give the group more confidence too, so they'd play along. We argued, eventually, about President Wilson ("T.R. was *my* man in 1912!"), Indian policy, the war in Europe, feeding bears, shooting coyotes, whatever seemed interesting at the moment. The walk became, according to many visitors, an unexpected highlight of their visit. As we found ways to bring the story to life, our own interest and enthusiasm flourished too. Though in a park so blessed with natural wonders historical education should probably never become much more than a novelty act, we made the Fort Yellowstone Walk fit, and made it fun as well.

We even won an award. Word reached us—I don't remember how, probably through an anonymous phone call—that some office somewhere in the park service, somewhere to the east of Yellowstone, had decided that our living history program was outstanding. Naturally, we were curious. Are there trophies? Plaques? Certificates? Will there be clippings we can send to our mothers? Amazingly, we never found out. We asked everybody we could find—our bosses, friends, strangers in the halls of the administration building—what is our award? *Where* is our award? It became, that summer, one of the ongoing mysteries of our government service, something we'd shake our heads and laugh about in resigned bewilderment. Somewhere, we knew, somewhere in the great nether bureaucracy of the park service, some bastard was enjoying *our* certificate (was it embossed? who signed it?) hanging on his wall. I hope he got a nice frame for it.

Fort Yellowstone became enough of a showcase to get attention when political heavies came to town. The Secretary of the Interior has an Advisory Board on National Parks, composed of legislators and prominent citizens. They occasionally visit the parks, where they are wined, dined, and shown the sights by carefully selected rangers who are unlikely to say anything meaty or disturbing to them. My only acquaintance with the committee was during a visit they made to Yellowstone, a visit that kept the park's staff hopping for days making sure everything looked better than it was. (I've never understood this tactic of putting on a good face when things are going to hell; those people are supposed to be there to learn what's wrong. There must be some wisdom in it, though, because every Yellowstone superintendent has done it that way, and some have been savvy politicians.) The best-behaved ranger was sent to show the committee the famous confluence of the Firehole and Gibbon rivers, where the Madison is formed. I figured that only this guy, of all of us, could be counted on to tell the committee the heartwarming myth (long ago disproved and discarded by historians) about the group of explorers who camped here in 1870, and, in a fit of improbable altruism, decided to work to set the area aside as a national park. Any of the rest of us would have giggled too much telling this story. In all directions, things were spruced up, shined, or repainted. Female personnel were made especially visible, dragged, fingers still tapping, from their typewriters, to which they could be returned when the committee left.

Mammoth was one of the last stops on the tour. We heard unconfirmable reports that some members of the committee preferred the hospitality of the hotel bars to the scenic wonders, but as far as I could see they were putting in some very long days.

The day they were to arrive at Mammoth, my immediate supervisor, John Whitman, and I received word that we were to be ready to show them Fort Yellowstone. There was to be a reception at the superintendent's house about six-thirty, followed by a large community dinner nearby. John and I suited up at five o'clock, arguing over who got the revolver and who got the .45 automatic, and then stood around the office trying not to get wrinkled or soiled; the heavy wool of the two-tone blue dress uniform is stiflingly authentic.

Conflicting reports reached us. The committee had arrived and were getting settled at the hotel. Many were very tired. Some were thirsty. We would have an hour to show them Fort Yellowstone. We would have half an hour. We were canceled. We were on again, but we had only forty-five minutes. We could invite the public to join us. The public was to be avoided. The committee would come all at once (we still didn't know how big the committee was: ten? twenty? five hundred?). The committee would arrive in two groups and we would each take half of them.

Around six o'clock we learned that a few of them were about to show up. We plotted possible courses through the fort, looking for ways to avoid colliding with the other's group, then we went outside to the porch of the Visitor Center, immediately attracting a small crowd, some of whom were members of the committee freshly arrived from the hotel across the street. John took charge of them, yelling soldierly orders about double-timing up the street and watch out for the stagecoaches, and led them off down officer's row. In a moment, my group arrived, and as I introduced myself I attracted a few more tourists.

Looking around I recognized only the two most famous, Lady Bird Johnson and her companion Ann Morton, wife of the Secretary of the Interior. Blathering along convincingly about life here at the fort, I rushed them off across the lawn before too many tourists showed up to confuse me.

In half an hour I showed them the most important buildings, concluding the tour without mishap behind the administration building, where I gave my favorite sermon on the Cavalry's neglected contribution to conservation and the responsibilities we all share for the park's future. I don't remember a word I said, having fallen for Lady Bird instantly. Not only was she a distractingly gracious presence, she played along with obvious interest, asking me intelligent questions about the soldier's life. I wasn't terribly nervous about my presentation, being so overburdened with historical trivia, but I dreaded some untoward intrusion, perhaps a drunken reeling tourist suddenly recognizing her and demanding an autograph. I didn't want the mood to shatter.

It didn't. It held just fine, and after thanking the group for coming along I told the tourists how to get back to their cars and led my group of VIPs up the alley behind the superintendent's house.

As we approached the back of his house, something occurred to me that I will always be grateful for but will never understand. From somewhere, some neglected recess of my mind, clawing its way frantically over the vast clutter of less useful information, came a startling insight concerning the propriety of my present course. Offhand, still only faintly aware of the significance of the realization, I remarked to Lady Bird, who was walking by my side, "Y'know, I bet I should take you in through the front door."

In her sweet, musical Texan she assented, "Yes, I imagine so."

Thus I came within an ace of leading a First Lady through the mudroom, past the boots, garbage cans, and moprags. If the superintendent somehow failed to kill me for such a gaffe, his wife surely would have.

Instead, I led my little band around to the stately front porch and into the waiting crowd of Select Company, where John and I stood around looking like streetcar conductors at a butler's convention. I located myself ideally, within reach of the cookies and within sight of Lady Bird, who graciously endured a string of puffed-up local dignitaries as politely as if she were shaking hands with princes regent at some state dinner. I was in love. A well-placed and thoughtful friend eventually led me over to her and introduced us formally, and we chatted briefly. I suppose the only time that day that I saw a sharper look of interest on her face was when during our talk about park visitors I observed that though one occasionally saw black families as guests at the hotels one rarely saw them in the campground; but before I had an opportunity to display my peculiar sociological acumen, social conscience, and lack of proper blandness she was whisked away to meet some more overdressed and prominent citizens. I didn't even have a chance to ask for her phone number.

During the Bicentennial, the National Park Service put your tax dollars to work in hundreds of special programs, from historical movies to traveling troupes of actors portraying historical figures (Lincoln, Twain, and so on) who gave skits at parks all across the country. Yellowstone, in some minds already its own National Park Service anyway, geared up with many programs, culminating in a visit from President Ford in August.

Five naturalists were selected to prepare a special pageant, a one-hour skit about the past and future of Yellowstone, and about what that future might mean to America. Dressed as a mountain man, an early explorer, a soldier from Fort Yellowstone, an early tourist, a modern ranger, and a modern backpacker (I know that's six, but two parts were played by one person), they presented their skit at campgrounds for several weeks, polishing it until it was quite entertaining, even moving. In an hour they exposed visitors to the history and color of the park, with lots of laughs and a few stronger lessons (the trapper confronting the ranger with "What kind of wilderness is it where a man can't kill his own buffler?" or the 1920s lady enthusing over the fun of watching the bears at the garbage dump). It was a good show.

Bicentennial fever peaked during the President's visit. The announcement that some major political figure would arrive in a few days always put everyone in high gear, as I said before. Soon everything was being painted, washed, and so on, and female employees were again brought out into the open, squinting in the unfamiliar sunlight. The preparations for the President's visit were unparalleled. He was going to make a major policy statement; it was rumored that he was going to bless us with a first magnitude campaign promise, a great financial boost for the always ailing park service.

At one of the last minutes the word came down from the superintendent that prior to the President's speech at Old Faithful, the historical pageant would be presented to the waiting crowd. The actor-naturalists had concluded their scheduled tour some weeks earlier and resumed their normal duties. Now, even as presidential panic gripped the bowels of the park administration, the pageanteers looked around at one another, paused, then looked again; sure enough, someone was missing. Bob Jonas, who played the intrepid explorer Samuel Hauser, had already left the park for winter work elsewhere. A moment's frightened hesitation ensued, then someone perked up and announced, "Paul will do it! Let's get Paul," followed later by "Don't be silly, Paul, sure you can do it. You've seen the thing a couple times, haven't you? Just ad lib! We'll give you cues."

Of course there was no saying no. It was a command performance. A more immediate problem, however, was my costume. Its most important elements were a stove-pipe top hat and a formal black dress coat, both 1880s vintage (Samuel Hauser later became territorial governor of Montana, a fact I would come to regret). Bob had worn these well, with great dignity and aplomb, but Bob and I were uniquely dissimilar in shape. Mostly, I was a lot bigger. Nothing fit, and there was no time to get replacements from Salt Lake City or Denver or wherever they rent 1880 explorers' outfits in larger sizes. The solution was clear: Paul will only breathe *out* while wearing the coat.

Meanwhile, down at Old Faithful a large platform was built on the boardwalk in front of the geyser so that the President would speak with Old Faithful as backdrop. Loudspeakers, sound trucks, and miles of wire appeared on the gray flats around the Visitor Center. Technicians scurried here and there, advance units of the Secret Service walked purposefully about, blending into whatever they stopped in front of. Up in Mammoth we had no idea what we were getting into.

The morning of the speech we drove down to Old Faithful, familiarizing me with the script on the way. "Okay, after you discover the park, I catch the poachers." "Then she feeds the bears?" "Right." "Then I argue about it?" "No, he does that . . ."

When we arrived we learned that the whole plan was academic. We were told that, depending on the President's arrival time we would be told at the last minute ("The last minute! What's this right now?") if we would have an hour, or forty-five minutes, or half an hour. Maybe only fifteen minutes ("Fifteen minutes! I won't even have time to discover the park!").

But a bigger problem was evident when we looked around. The place was crawling with overarmed strangers: mounted rangers, flown from California to act as a special honor guard; Yellowstone rangers, more than I knew existed, all conspicuously armed; National Capital Park Police, the huge storm troopers who do the cop work at all the monuments in Washington, D.C.; and the legendary Secret Service. These last, the agents of the President's own little police force, were the most intimidating of all, partly because at first glance they were so, well, normal looking. They were all of average height and build: trim, well-dressed, with passionless faces and eyes that never stopped moving, even when the agent paused to whisper something into his coat-sleeve microphone.

Old Faithful is a security nightmare: a broad, open plain surrounded at comfortable rifle range by forested slopes and large dark buildings with hundreds of upper-story windows. This alarmed us even more than it alarmed the Secret Service, because in a few moments we would replace our ranger uniforms with outlandish theatrical costumes, and, looking like the original Merry Pranksters, we would attempt to walk out to the podium for our skit. It didn't matter that the President wasn't there yet. The very idea of us, looking like a band of fugitive marionettes trying to find the way to Oz—and bristling with antique firearms—moving anywhere among this horde of centurions seemed foolhardy at best. At the slightest sign of trouble, little guns not much bigger than an electric drill, that can shoot an impossible number of bullets in a second, can materialize from somewhere on each agent's person; at that point the trouble runs into real trouble.

Before changing our outfits, we rushed around grabbing any authoritative person we could find, hoping to make sure all the right people knew we would suddenly appear and were harmless. Friendly, even. We finally insisted on an escort, from our dressing room to the stage, dragooning a large ranger into the job. Then we went to change.

When we emerged twenty minutes later, transformed into Yellowstone history, Old Faithful was packed. There were six thousand people already gathered near the podium and pushing against the rope barrier an hour before the President was to arrive. Hiding as well as we could behind our one-ranger escort, we moved around the edge of the crowd to the boardwalk that led to the podium. An agent immediately zeroed in on us. I wondered if a single ranger was adequate proof of our trustworthiness (I could see the headlines: "Violent Demonstration Narrowly Averted; Secret Service Guns Down Heavily Armed Crazies"). The agent checked each of our guns—the mountain man's Hawken, my revolver, the soldier's automatic, which the agent flashed through various stages of disassembly like a magician shuffling cards—then let us go on.

The boardwalk followed one end of the crowd, and the Secret Service were stationed evenly along the crowd. Each agent gave our weapons a look so chilling I was afraid to touch the metal. West District Naturalist Dave Pugh showed us how to get through the crowd to reach the podium. "The President's supposed to arrive in thirty minutes. I'll give you the signal when you have ten minutes left and you can wrap up the presentation just before his helicopter lands." Dave's signal was very important to us, because otherwise we might finish too soon or be right in the middle of the show when the choppers appeared.

It should have been predictable that we never saw Dave again that day. As soon as he was a few feet behind us, he was lost in a swarming chaos of Hawaiian shirts and cowboy hats. One moment we were standing quietly, if conspicuously, at the edge of the crowd, waiting to be sent on, and the next we were marching theatrically toward the center of the podium, John Whitman yelling soldierly drivel at me about park regulations. The show was on.

It was not a good stage. With six thousand people you need a sound system. All we had was the President's microphone, mounted on his podium. This forced us to maneuver constantly, like players in a bluegrass band moving up to the microphone to take their twelve-bar breaks, so that whoever was talking could use the microphone. What had been a rather loosely staged presentation became a series of little speeches, an indifferent audience sweating impatiently in the bright sunlight. The advantage of the microphone was that we could talk to each other, discreetly, without being heard by the group. Occasionally, when someone else was holding forth at the podium, I'd sidle up to John and whisper, "Where the hell's Dave?" or "What do I say next?"

Small helicopters passed over every few minutes, each one distracting the crowd, but these were just security forces checking the area for leftist bears.

Finally, just as we were winding up our little show, someone strolled past me and remarked, "Here come the choppers." Without being obvious about it, I found a reason to turn to the north, down the valley of the Firehole River. Sure enough, here came three tiny dots that were rapidly growing larger. From the elevated podium we had a visual edge on the crowd; they couldn't see as far, and they wouldn't hear the motors for at least a couple of minutes. As our modern-day ranger made one last speech we congratulated ourselves on a bad show well given, and then smiled politely at the scattered applause as the dots resolved themselves into those industrial-strength helicopters we always see in news films of the White House. The crowd finally saw them as we stepped from the podium and hurried toward the back of the crowd, where we expected to find some space by the press stand so we could watch the speech. An agent immediately had us. "Where are you going?" he asked our weapons.

"Oh, we're just gonna go back to the press stand and watch the speech."

"What about the guns?" he was now talking directly to Don's Hawken.

"Oh, we'll just hold them. We don't mind. It's okay."

"No. There's no way you can have those things here." He said "no way" with such absolute certainty that I involuntarily started to hand him my revolver. "No. I don't want them. If you're going to stay they have to go. Get them out of here." We snagged a passing naturalist and convinced him to haul the weapons back to the car, then found places to stand in our dampening woolen getups.

The President's part of the show is even more blurred in my memory than my own: "Ruffles and Flourishes" blaring incongruously from the loudspeakers and out across the geyser basin, his daughter's blond hair shining warmly in the sun, his remarks about his own summer as a Yellowstone ranger back in the 1930s, about stories he told his kids so often they begged not to hear his bear stories any more, his grand program for the restoration of the park service budget to a realistic level (lots of applause here), Old Faithful quietly erupting as hoped for right in the middle of his speech, the full-bottomed lady ranger right in front of me . . . and then he was done, and the crowd applauded with sincere generosity. I applauded that I was about to take this outfit off and breathe in again.

As we hurried to the dressing room we were headed off by orders not to change yet. "There's a dignitary's picnic over by the river, in a fenced-off area; you can go if you stay dressed in your outfits."

"Food, you say? A barbecue? Which way?"

It was at this barbecue that I sort of met the governor of Montana. I was happily scarfing roast beef at a shady table, breathing out contentedly, when John Whitman marched up. "Paul, get your top hat on and come with me."

Now you must understand that after five years of friendship I admired and trusted John enough to follow him to hell if he knew the way, so I automatically grabbed my hat and took off after him.

"What's up, John?"

"Just come on, you'll see." His corporal uniform looked great in the afternoon sun, and his pace was determined.

He led me through the scattered picnickers to a small group of people, maybe five, standing in a circle. They were all well-dressed and deeply involved in a conversation. One tall man in shirt sleeves looked vaguely familiar, like I'd seen him on television or something, and my roast beef stirred uneasily as it dawned on me what was about to happen.

Bustling officiously up to the group, the picture of military splendor and respect, John interrupted them in his best army voice. "Excuse me, folks." All eyes were on him; surprise, a little curiosity, no trace of annoyance or fear. John was rolling now, no backing out.

"Governor Judge, I'd like you to meet Samuel Hauser, the first territorial governor of Montana." Remembering who I was dressed to portray, I gave him my best political saunter and handshake, suddenly knowing that this was a horrible mistake. It wasn't working at all. Nobody was smiling. The governor was polite in his greeting, and there it ended. We were not a hit. We were merely silly, not even worth calling a bother. Chagrin washed over me like a damp breeze, and the entire group, in unison, gave us a cold stare as we stood there grinning like the phenomenal asses we were.

We made our escape then—I felt like crawling except that it wasn't fast enough—and found excuses to finish up our roast beef and get out of those outfits quickly. For days, weeks, afterward, I'd suddenly ask John, "How could you do that? How could you walk me into that? Did you see how they looked at us? How could you do it?" And he'd grin back at me, and shake his head in confusion. "Paul, I just don't know. It seemed like a good idea, you know?"

Snowmorcs and Pig Rigs

About halfway through the army's stay in Yellowstone they published a small volume we now call the "little red book." It was only a few dozen pages, in a red binding, but it contained all the important instructions for scouts, officers, and enlisted men on duty in the park. Many of the copies that survive in the archives are concave from having been carried in hip pockets for so many years. I once tried to get the park to republish it for sale to modern visitors, it's that charming. They declined the suggestion, fearing with some justification that some visitors would misunderstand and try to apply the rules and regulations to their stay in the park today.

The book contained some durable advice about winter. The park closed up by October then, and winter tourism was virtually unheard of. Winter was poaching season, the animals being especially easy to kill when they moved to lower country and were trapped in heavy snow. In the little red book the public was dismissed in a sentence:

All persons traveling through the park from October 1 to June 1, should be regarded with suspicion.

One thing I'll give snowmobiling right off is that when you're getting ready to take a trip of any length there's a real feeling of setting out—almost a feeling of expedition. My first "solo" from Mammoth to Old Faithful, about fifty-five miles, was like that. Packing the machine at the end of the plowed road just south of Mammoth, it was as if I was being launched into another world; with my heavy oversuit (handi-talkie tucked safely somewhere between loose inner layers) enveloping me, my skis strapped like an asymmetrical outrigger to one side of the machine, a backpack full of clothes and food (to wear and eat when I got to Old Faithful, where I would be working a few days), I was a self-sufficient little recreational vehicle. With such preparations the trip was essentially dangerless—thousands travel the park far less well prepared, and usually only the drunkest get hurt—but still the extensive readying gave an added kick to the trip.

It's a quick climb from Mammoth to Golden Gate, a few minutes' uphill run through the tumbled limestone Hoodoos. Though it was calm this day, the Gate is sometimes a giant wind tunnel where snow, ice, duff, and small rocks whip about in bitter winds, thus heightening the feeling of breaking through from the lower park to the upper plateau. I cruised out of Golden Gate Canyon onto Swan Lake Flat, suddenly into a winter that hadn't reached Mammoth. Everything was white and still. Off to my right, beyond the snowy lumps of sage and the frozen lake, the Gallatins— Holmes, Antler, Little Quadrant, Electric, and the rest—seemed new and strange in white. The stillness was a strong presence despite the noise of the machine.

It is twenty-one miles from Mammoth to Norris, and south of the flats the road is almost always in forest, the "great piney woods" of the mountain men: rank on rank of lodgepole pines, their bows clogged and piled grotesquely with mounds of snow. Occasional breaks in the forest—the meadows bordering Indian Creek, Beaver Meadows opposite Obsidian Cliff, North and South Twin Lakes—only punctuate and emphasize the solid procession of forest. I rode steadily, forgetting that on a long drive like this it's better for the machine if you vary the speed now and then. It's easy enough to average thirty-five, even forty-five, beyond which I'm uncomfortable. Fifty, when you're this low to the ground and the track has even the smallest irregularities, is exhilarating. Sixty requires too much energy and attention to be fun. I realize that many people routinely go much faster, but they like snowmobiles in the first place.

Hot spots, where a warm spring or subterranean channel of hot water is near enough to the surface to keep the road bare, are covered regularly by maintenance crews with wood chips. Because the front ski-runners on the machine get no purchase on anything firmer than snow, you lose maneuverability on pavement. When you come to a hundred feet or so of bare pavement you approach it dead on, aiming the machine for the middle of the snowy road beyond it. If you miss your aim, or if the bank of the road leads you off target, you end up on the berm and must get off and wrestle the front end of the machine around so it faces your goal again.

Glare ice, I think, is worse. Not only can't you steer well, the ice does not resist your forward motion should you find yourself heading in the wrong direction.

Norris Junction gives you choices. You may turn left and go east to Canyon, drive straight ahead to Madison Junction and on to Old Faithful, or turn right and go to the geyser basin at Norris. I stopped only briefly, to cool the machine and stretch my legs. On an earlier trip, with several people in a park service Thiokol, I'd spent some time in the basin, an eerie, steamy place in winter, often impossible to see because of the dense fog of steam and spray that hangs there. The Thiokol, a pair of wide-set tracks (like a tank's, in principle) with a little box of a cab perched above and between them, lumbered along at ten miles an hour, making the trip to Old Faithful, what with stops for sightseeing and fuel (getting only two to four miles to the gallon) at Norris, pretty much an all-day affair. Boredom is more or less impossible on such a trip as this, but the Thiokol promoted it. The cab's windows frosted up immediately except for a small circle directly in front of the driver, kept unfogged by a little caged fan mounted near it and by frequent applications of soggy mitten. The tracks operate independently of each other; there are two levers that, when pushed forward, accelerate either track. To go backward, pull them back. To turn left at a corner, make the right track go faster so it outruns the left one and brings you around to the left. To spin in one spot, push one lever forward and the other backward. And do it all very slowly.

The Thiokol, now that I think of it, wasn't all that simple. The tracks weren't in tune. At full acceleration (such as it was) one went faster than the other. For a reason having something to do with the welfare of the clutch, this problem couldn't be corrected simply by pushing the two levers to points where each moved its track at the same speed. You had to push them all the way forward, which meant that gradually, as the faster track outran the slower one, the Thiokol edged toward the side of the road. When you got to the edge of the road you made a correction, aiming it back out toward the middle again. Thus you inscribed a gentle series of frescoes as you moved through the snow, humming along with the droning engine and squinting through the iced-up windows.

There was no denying the advantages of my snowmobile for sightseeing. As I accelerated up the hill from Norris Junction my field of view was limited only by my helmet and the lodgepole forest that had again closed in on the road. Out across Elk Park (no elk in sight) and then Gibbon Meadows (no gibbon either) and into the canyon of the Gibbon River, down past the steaming cascades; as I entered the canyon a bald eagle joined my parade, following along high above me for a mile, as if in escort of anyone silly enough to be out here on Christmas morning.

The forest closed in again, the Gibbon winding back and forth under the road and through the trees, with dark boulders snowy and wizard-hatted rising from the current. At Madison Junction I passed the road in from West Yellowstone, the small community on the west boundary that, like any number of similar communities in Michigan, Wisconsin, and Minnesota, bills itself as the snowmobile capital of the world. The traffic became heavier here, as most people just ride the lower part of the park, from Madison to Old Faithful to Lake to Canyon to Madison. Slowing only to glance into the dark waters off the Gibbon River bridge, I rattled up into the Firehole valley, now only twelve miles from Old Faithful.

The Firehole, like the Gibbon, is warmed enough from hot springs and geyser runoff to stay open and bare-banked all year. Against the flashing snow the river was black over its volcanic bedrock and weed beds. A great blue heron stood rigid and unexpected along the opposite bank, and I wondered what protection those long stick-thin legs had against the cold. Turtling down into the warm layers of the suit in sympathy, I followed the river and turned onto the old Fountain Flats Drive. The main road continues off to the east, but I preferred the old one that followed the river. Out on the more sparsely wooded flats I figured I stood a better chance of seeing a few of the bison and elk that winter in the basins. The snow was well trampled in the meadows where bison had used their huge muzzles to push it aside and reach the grasses. Here and there fresh-frozen buffalo chips broke the whiteness.

No bison appeared, though I watched some trout finning in the river below Ojo Caliente Spring (the Firehole is ideal for trout, staying comfortable for fast growth most of the year) and thought I saw a cow elk for an instant in the clearings beyond Goose Lake.

There's a little iron bridge just before the old road rejoins the main one, and you don't see it until you're almost on it, especially if you happen to be gawking around for wildlife. All at once there it was, and the best I could do was stop my machine and kill the engine as it nosed against the near edge of the bridge. It was the best I *had* to do, because the entire far edge of the bridge was blocked by an immense bull bison. He was standing broadside to me, staring at me with that bovine expression of interest that seems always about to become sleep.

Now there's an old saying about the bull bison. If he raises his tail it means one of two things—charge or discharge. The saying came to mind immediately as I sat there astride a vehicle with no reverse, and I sensed the saying's ultimate inadequacy. One need not examine the rear end of so formidable an animal in order to determine what the rest of the animal will do.

I rose slowly from the seat so that I stood straddling the machine, my feet still on the running boards. If I needed to climb a tree, I decided, the machine was on its own; I would not take it with me (there's a story in Yellowstone of a ranger who while out skiing encountered a bear awake out of season and actually climbed a tree without pausing to remove his skis).

Bison are not hurriers, and to his scale of things the wait was insignificant. He was wet, so I figured he'd just climbed up from the stream. Perhaps he was considering how cold it was to get out of 50° water into 0° air. I hoped that he would not be put off by the experience. Evidently he wasn't, and presently he ambled off, leaving the road clear. Encounters like these are almost always harmless, but the thoughtful person does not take them for granted. I was glad to leave him behind.

I had no sooner turned onto the main road when some of his friends showed up. Being sensible, the park's mammals travel on the roads whenever they can in winter. On the park's only plowed road, I've driven along for miles behind a trotting moose. I get the feeling that they aren't really going anywhere in particular; that after fighting deep snow for a few days they just enjoy making such good time. Throughout the park in winter, on the roads that are groomed and packed by snowmobiles, the animals travel regularly. I was now confronted by such travelers, maybe a dozen bison—cows and calves—who stopped, as I did, for a session of confused staring and milling. They turned and pawed indecisively. I rose and cased the nearest trees. We vacillated. We considered. Then a whining rattle behind them heralded the arrival of three brethren of the frozen thumb, an impatient, beery trio who stopped their machines directly behind the anxious herd only long enough to confer for a few seconds before dismounting and rushing at the animals, roaring like football players at a public scrimmage.

I'd like to think they hadn't seen me, parked directly in the path of the bison they were trying to stampede out of the way, but I'm sure they did. I could see them, right down to their porcine, windburned faces. Luckily the bison were not willing to confront me (must have been the park service insignia on my helmet), and they fled from the shouting morons into the deep snow at roadside, wading with painful wallowings down toward the river. The three gallant riders were back on their machines and screaming by me before the bison were clear of the road and long before I could get enough clothes off any portion of my body to make a recognizable gesture of contempt.

I proceeded, in an ill temper, the rest of the way into Old Faithful, finally convincing myself not to let them spoil the rest of my day. The cavernous old Inn, buttoned and boarded for the winter, looked frozen cold, but there were warm lights from other smaller buildings. Now that I was here I could travel by ski.

At first sight, the snowmobile seems like a great idea, a vehicle that does for winter what the trail bike does for summer. But then not everyone is happy with what the trail bike has done for summer. Snowmobiles, perhaps even more than trail bikes, inspire either intense excitement or raging fury in observers. My trip to Old Faithful provided ample proof of the good the machine can do. I had a glorious, if interrupted, day on a maintained roadway, and did the park no real harm. But despite that and other good trips, I'm not convinced about snowmobiles. Part of my doubt stems from the machine itself, and part from the way it is used.

Take the noise, for example. It's as if the people who invented the chain saw and the trail bike got together and decided it was possible to invent something that would make an even *more* objectionable noise. And so they replaced the confident throaty roar of the saw—the powerful gut-shaking howl of the bike—with the anemic clattering whine of the snowmobile, succeeding beyond their wildest expectations in discovering a whole new dimension in offensive sound. I have yet to hear one make a noise I would call pleasant (and I do think some loud machines have nice noises—I enjoy a good air hammer), much less trustworthy. There's something in the timbre, in the vibrating sloppiness of that little engine that just screams "treacherous unreliability" at me.

But noise is more than a matter of a rider's confidence, or a rider's aesthetic sensibilities. It's an intrusion on the surroundings. When I'm skiing near a road I find myself relaxing a little when I move far enough into the woods to be out of range of the snarling parade. I tell you that on a still day that can be very far indeed.

I know that among my friends, some of whom are far more anti-snowmobile than I, it is this penetrating whine of the machine that irritates them most. I'm not sure, though, that even if the machines were utterly silent my friends would approve of them. There are other considerations. To their way of thinking the "polluter scooter" epitomizes the worst in inappropriate use of the park.

Like most pastimes, from surfing to crapshooting, snowmobiling has its own subculture, with magazines and celebrities and everything to appeal to the joiner instinct. It is this subculture that has most deeply offended the skiers, whose own subculture is its opposite.

The stereotypical snowmobiler is, in the minds of my friends, a slob—an overgrown, probably fat, kid. Obviously it's not valid, but it's easier to find objection to a snowmobiler at first glance than to a cross-country skier. Snowmobilers of necessity dress heavily; they face fifty-mile-an-hour winds all day. They move awkwardly and can wear themselves out if they have to trudge very far in all that gear. They are dependent on their machines for motion. Skiers, on the other hand, are the antithesis of technological dependence. They look trim in their light wool, even if they are not. They move smoothly and quietly over the snow. They seem efficient in their surroundings.

The naturalists at Old Faithful—most being skiers by interest and snowmobilers by professional necessity—coined the word "Snowmorc" to replace the longer, unwieldy "snowmobiler." It combined the "snowm" of snowmobile with the "orc" of Tolkien's *Lord of the Rings* trilogy. Orcs are big, sloppily constructed goblins with terrible manners and vicious, simple minds. Snowmorc stuck. Perhaps it's still used.

Like so many pet outrages, the snowmorc is based on a type specimen, the worst of the species. We ignored all our friends who owned and enjoyed the machines—we forgave them, I suppose, knowing they were otherwise reasonable—and aimed our disdain at the faceless slobs who buzzed skiers, chased wildlife, trailed empty beer cans, and generally missed the point of why the park was open to them. We remembered the times we'd seen a group of machines parked at some glorious overlook, the owners oblivious to the view, either all clustered around the trailer sled that held the beer or huddled nearby discussing the latest in leopard-skin upholstery.

One day I was doing the desk at Old Faithful Visitor Center when a small group of snowmorcs shuffled through the door and stood around huffing and clapping and dripping. I was working over near the fireplace, that being the warm spot in the building. As a group of skiers slid past the huge glass front of the building one of the snowmorcs separated himself from the bunch and came over to me. Indicating the skiers moving by outside, he asked, with just a little defiance in his voice, "What are they doing?"

The question seemed so stupid that I nearly ignored it, but there was something about this guy, for all his gruffness, that appealed to me. In my most innocent sarcasm, I answered him. "Well, it looks to me as if they're skiing. You know, moving across the snow?"

"But why?"

"Well, some say it's fun." I looked down at my too-flashy ski boots and nonregulation homemade gaiters. "You know, good exercise, fresh air, nature?"

"Looks like lots of hard work, not fun."

"Oh, I kind of enjoy it, and I've never been known for my love of work." There was still something about him that made him seem worth this little effort. As he began to speak again I realized what it was. Through his partly opened suit I could see that he was still big, though not fat, and probably very strong. "Listen, I work in a foundry six days a week. I get *lots* of exercise. When I get a day off I like to have some *fun*."

I said something polite and lame about there being different kinds of fun, and went back to work. I still haven't figured out why he resented those skiers; it was resentment, I'm sure. But it taught me that the door swings both ways. Up until then I had always assumed that snowmorcs were oblivious of us, and that we were the only ones strong-minded enough to feel any hostility.

Glacier National Park managed to exclude snowmobiles from most of the park, something at least a few people would like to see done in Yellowstone. In fact a minor park service hero came out of a snowmorc incident in Glacier. It seemed that a couple of snowmorcs were seen driving on a road that was closed to them and didn't have much snow on it. The ranger on duty was able to pursue them in his truck, and he finally caught up with them. The story we heard in Yellowstone was that the ranger hit a snowbank at one point in order to avoid hitting the snowmorcs, who evidently tried to circle around behind him despite his clear signals to stop. Glacier at this time was having poaching problems, and the ranger had reason to worry about his own safety. His solution was to fire his revolver into one of the machines, to disable it and keep the driver from escaping. A few of the local papers up there, always on the lookout to ridicule the park service, jumped on the story and twisted it around in their best tradition, turning it into a Keystone Kops routine with a silly ranger as the star and two innocent snowmobilers as victims (no one could explain away the presence of the snowmorcs on a closed road). Some of us in Yellowstone saw it otherwise. The ranger had just done what we all had wanted to do, many times. Shooting the machine, someone remarked, was even better than shooting the driver. There was no question in our minds that the man was a hero. There was talk of taking up a collection and buying him a magnum. And a few days after the incident, a little note appeared on the ranger office bulletin board:

> Snow machines will not be shot.
> They will be live-trapped.

The irony of our attitude about snowmorcs is that in Yellowstone, if you ignore the very real temporary damage done by their noise, they are probably doing the park less harm than the skiers. Legal use of the machines is restricted to roads, and except for the ones who can't resist an untracked meadow of snow, most snowmorcs do little worse than some occasional sidehill gouging, running up steep embankments along the road for a little-kid roller-coaster kick. Like cars, their paths are restricted. And, like cars, they don't bother most of the wildlife, who quickly learn where the paths are. Most of the elk and bison I pass don't even bother to look up as the machine goes by. They get used to the noise more quickly than I do. They've learned that the noise is not a threat to them in the park, however threatened it may make me feel.

Skiers, on the other hand, go everywhere. They *love* wildlife. Studies conducted in recent years reveal that the elk, bison, and other wildlife in the Firehole drainage spend a distressing amount of time dodging camera-wielding skiers who don't appreciate the caloric demands they are placing on the animals when they follow them around for pictures. Winter is no time for park animals to have to put up with much of that.

Snowmobiles are probably going to be using Yellowstone for a long time. Snowmorc clubs are politically powerful in the region, and park administrators are probably smart to let them have their fun rather than waste energy fighting with them. Some park administrators are too fond of snowmobiling themselves to even want to fight with them. It costs a lot of money to maintain and groom the roads for the machines, as well as to patrol the roads they use; some say it would cost no more to actually plow the roads clear of snow all winter so that cars could come in. If snowmorcs and skiers would agree on anything, it would be that cars in the park in the winter are a mistake; a most precious element of winter in the park is breaking loose of conventional habits and feeling some isolation.

So I'll admit that snowmorcs have some reason to be in the park, and I'll admit that skiers can't wholly justify their holier-than-thou attitude about snowmorcs. Still, when a long line of thirty or forty big black machines comes snaking with a deafening scream into the parking lot next to Old Faithful, and the leader loops his chain of growling articats or whips or doozie-scooters or whatever through a couple of flamboyant figure eights around the lot (like a long, long dog circling its bed before lying down) as a prelude to lining them up to race engines a bit more before shutting down, and when as the noise finally ceases to dominate my senses and I watch the fumy purple smoke that trailed in behind them drift heavily out across the cone of Old Faithful, and when the riders in their ponderous outfits that match not only their fellows but the upholstery on their machines waddle hastily to the rest rooms and then back to their machines, and when all this happens in the middle of a stunning natural setting and the setting goes unnoticed by the riders, I must wonder why they need a national park for what they do, and why a national park must spend so much money to enable them to do it.

Therefore, like my military predecessors, I will always regard at least these persons traveling through the park in winter with suspicion.

The round trip to Bighorn pass took a short day, from mid-morning to late afternoon. It was a bright, deep-breathing sort of day to be in the high country, and we ate lunch at the pass with strong breezes slipping up to us over cool snowbanks. As we dismounted back at Indian Creek and helped trailer the horses, I couldn't have felt better about the day except for this trouble I have with horses that I probably should explain.

A good horse and rider are a beautiful sight. They are such a combination of fluid motion and singleness of spirit that together they become one genuinely lovely thing. But when I consider my limitations as a rider—my inability to find familiar or welcoming contours on a saddle, and my knees' firm reluctance to pivot in more than one plane—I must conclude that the horse does not exist who has such sterling qualities that he can make the two of us, him and me, a lovely thing. Well, he may exist, but I'm pretty sure the government doesn't own him.

Yet I like horses. A friend calls them "a thousand pounds of stupid," and at times it seems so, but when I keep my expectations reasonable I suspect that horses have more often found disappointment in our dealings than have I. Trouble has been, I never spent enough time with any horse to establish sufficient team dynamic so that I could know the satisfaction of good horsemanship. I'm a bad horseman to begin with. That, especially, was the problem as we dismounted behind Indian Creek that day. I had announced to Les earlier in the day that perhaps eighteen miles was a bit much to ride after a year out of the saddle. By the time we dismounted "perhaps" had become "damnsure," and I was lost in happy anticipation of an evening of elevated feet and sublime sloth.

Still flexing saddle-stiff joints, we piled into the pickup and wound out of the campground to the main road, heading north to Mammoth. As the truck rolled out onto Swan Lake Flats, we picked up speed, that being one of the few places in the park where the parkwide maximum speed limit of forty-five seemed inadequate.

Then, just as my backside was adjusting to the seat, someone asked, "Is that dust coming out of the canyon?"

On the north end of the flats the road drops into Golden Gate canyon, where a roadway was cut into the west side of the canyon wall, or buttressed over an attached shelf, before the turn of the century. It is the winter passageway to the interior of the park that I spoke of earlier, and though it has been modified and rebuilt since the first construction it still has a precarious feel. It causes many ladies, looking down into the canyon below, to shiver and scoot closer to their husbands. And, as I already knew from an experience with a stalled tractor-trailer, anywhere in the canyon a single motorist can create an impenetrable traffic jam.

As the dust rose in a brownish column, someone wondered if it was a rockslide, a horrible thought to anyone acquainted with the canyon's road. The truck's playful speed became purposeful. In seconds the cloud darkened. "It's not dust. It's smoke. There's a fire."

The smoke blackened and towered as we bounced into the last pullout this side of the canyon and piled out on a run for the canyon.

The run was just long enough for me to fall behind the others, and just demanding enough that, despite the adrenalin-inspired preoccupation with the unseen fire, I had time to be impressed that I wasn't really all that far behind guys I'd always assumed were twice as fast as I was. You sometimes think almost abstract, certainly irrelevant, things like that when something important is going on. Then we reached the mouth of the canyon, a narrow little opening in the hills into which the road disappeared in a quick drop along the left wall of the canyon in front of us. The source of the smoke was a large recreational vehicle, burning furiously about midship, with an occasional popping sound as volatile contents exploded.

The R.V. was almost perfectly placed to do the most harm, on the tightest part of the stone-walled bridge, so close to the canyon wall that already the cliff above it was blackened. There were a few cars backed up on our side of the fire, and we assumed there were as many on the downhill side. We couldn't see any people in or near the R.V., and as we reached it the people in the nearest car told us that the occupants, a family, had received various degrees of burns and were hurried into another car and rushed north to the clinic. The ever-more violent fire gave us no time to feel relieved; among their other features, many R.V.s have absurdly large gas tanks, and several of the cars were far too close to the fire should there be a big explosion. Another park service truck arrived about then, the "honey wagon," a tank truck used to pump out outhouse reservoirs. The driver joined us and we went to work on the traffic. We directed the threatened cars to back away, and assigned ourselves duties, mostly involving traffic control. We were in no position to do anything about the fire except give it lots of room. As I worked my way back up the road, cars were already backed up out onto the flats, a few dozen vehicles in only a couple of minutes. Other rangers began to arrive with fire-fighting gear, and the next couple of hours were spent flagging and redirecting traffic, waiting tensely for that one big blast that never came, and helping fire crews scrape up little melted blobs of R.V. from the road. All that remained of the thing was the bottom frame, a few low panels, and a charred skeleton that outlined its former walls. Apparently the fire started when the driver tried to prime the carburetor on a stalled engine, spilling gas on some hot surface, and it worked through the gasoline bit by bit. The body and contents were simply gone—not on the road, not anywhere—melted or seared into smoke, cinder, and oblivion.

Another moment of abstraction occurred as I ran back up the hill to start working on the traffic when we first arrived. I was shouting directions at gawking tourists, getting cars moved here and there, and generally making good sense, when a stationary figure across the road from me caught my eye. I looked over, still waving and shouting at the busy cars, and saw a frumpy, balding, Bermuda-shorted little man taking my picture. Some things never change.

To most minds the fire was a terrible tragedy and no more. To mine there was something else here. The next day, putting aside for a moment the terrible misery and suffering (the little boy was burned badly), I was not entirely sorry to look upon the blackened skeleton of the R.V. I don't wish pain on anyone, and I wish it all hadn't happened, but I couldn't help feeling good that at least one of these big aluminum bastards had gone to hell.

The modern recreational vehicle, a self-propelled mobile home, is as objectionable in some circles as the snowmorc. They are called "pig rigs," and to the militant environmentalist they symbolize the worst in society's delight at conspicuous, energy-squandering consumption. If, as Edward Abbey has said, Detroit's huge sedans are "iron mastodons," then these rolling palaces are surely aluminum dinosaurs. Their luxury surpasses anything in our community of *im*mobile homes (there might be some jealousy in our distaste), and we never become accustomed to their vastness:

"I got invited into one of those big Winnebagoes after my campfire talk last night."

"Yeah? How was it?"

"Pretty amazing. I didn't actually get any farther than the main lobby, but I got a pretty good look around. From where I stood I could see a lot. It looked like it was raining down in the servants' quarters."

Huge mobile homes are not new; I've seen pictures in the park files of converted trucks, vans, and buses of sixty years ago, and the park's earliest campers were known as "sagebrushers" because they just parked their buckboards in the brush for the night. The phenomenon of the modern land-yacht is different, though. The biggest ones push against every legal and emotional limit to cram more and more comfort, household, and weight into one moving unit.

It is the emotional limits they most test. We see the pig rigs, like the snowmorcs, in stereotype. The type specimen is a badly balanced monstrosity, overflowing with veneer and pile carpet, trundling slowly over a mountain pass seemingly oblivious to the parade of overheating cars behind it ("They're just old retired people who don't care if they ever arrive anyway," moan the outraged young turks). It is also a lovely primitive little campsite next to a small brook whose gurgle is drowned out by the generator of the rolling condominium that squats nearby, awning, lawn furniture, and barbecue spread across its temporary front yard. It is also one of these swollen boxcars rumbling along with an equally huge and even more sumptuous trailer in tow, both tower and towee being adorned here and there with trail bikes, canoes, and go-carts. The type specimen for our distaste is this nightmarish energy sump, a total isolation booth around its occupants, a dripping, air-conditioned fortress against the elements, whose driver will proudly announce to anyone who asks that they are "going camping." With, as a last slap in the face of whatever is right about enjoying the outdoors, a name like "Wilderness Wanderer," the type specimen is easy enough to hate.

Of course the stereotype doesn't hold up. As much as I might prefer the blind satisfaction of simple outrage, I can't fall for it totally. Nice people, people my mother would have over for dinner, keep stepping out of the pig rigs. People who get excited about Yellowstone.

"We retired five years ago. The kids were grown and there wasn't any point in just pooping around in Fresno listening to our arteries harden, so we sold the house and bought this R.V. ("Hiram's Hideaway," or "The Two of Us," or something equally innocent has been painted on the side.) We haven't stopped moving since. We visit the kids every year, but not long enough to be a burden. I like to fish, and the little woman collects butterflies. . . . Come on in and have some coffee, won't you, ranger?"

Some are even sensitive to the waste, if not to the conspicuous consumption. "Oh, I know it uses lots of gas, but hell, we're not heating the house while we're away, so I figure it evens out. And once we get parked and set up, we use the bug to get around." He points to a little Volkswagen hitched to the back like a dingy behind a schooner. "I worked for forty years so I could afford this freedom, and I'm going to enjoy it, energy crisis or not."

It isn't really the people, it's the machine. It has an offensive presence that angers us. Most are boxish, with no smooth or rounded outlines. They always stick out a little farther than they should, just beyond the boundaries of courtesy, wherever they are parked. Most parking lots weren't made for them, so they park sideways, occupying six or eight spots, or park in some side lane and block traffic there instead. Wherever they go, they don't quite fit.

And they know it, and they resent it rather than apologize. "Why don't you build park roads wider? This place is huge, and a couple more feet on each side of the pavement won't hurt your precious wilderness."

I don't entirely disagree. If we accept that Yellowstone should permit pig rigs in, we might as well make it practical for them to move around. Of course the real answer is that even if the park service wanted to do it, they can't afford to keep the roads in good shape at their present width, much less make them wider. Putting that aside, the demands that pig rigs make on the park are not all that extreme. No one has established that the occupants produce any more trash, or sewage, or drink any more water, or use more of any other part of the resource, than do other visitors. They just use what they use in greater comfort. The backpacker certainly takes more management attention per capita, more tax dollars per day of park use. The rig rider uses more gasoline, but he doesn't have to pay for a shower as a backpacker does. Both use hot water which, one way or another, takes energy. Most park campgrounds do not have hookups for electricity, sewage, and the like, and the self-contained rig can carry its own facilities and provisions, thus lightening pressure on the public ones.

But still, after all the justifications and rationalizing, the rigs still don't quite fit. It's more than a physical squeeze; they simply aren't what we have in mind for Yellowstone. It's arrogant, but we're suspicious, and I think rightly so, of all that luxury and appliance when the park is supposed to be offering simpler joys. Some do not consider butane stoves and smoky campfires joys of any kind, but the rustic element of the park experience is too far along, and too well proven, to be so lightly compromised. I don't say we need weight limits on park vehicles, and I don't say there aren't people whose physical limitations necessitate greater vehicular comforts, but I do believe a horse, even a federal one, is better than a pig rig, and I'm sure the park is better enjoyed with less aluminum and plate glass rather than with more.

Winter Nights

Winter night is a place, as much as if it were on a map. One goes out onto a lake, or out to a patrol cabin, or out to the hot springs... or out into the winter night. That sense of place is so strong with me that I gather memories of winter nights as I gather them of rivers and ridges. It's a conceptual eccentricity, an emotional luxury, that I allow myself because in Yellowstone, with Yellowstone people, it has been so patently true.

Darkness does not seem, when I am in it, like the absence of light. It must seem like a tangible, physical thing, like the ether of old; else how could I feel that I am *in* it? And, therefore, when darkness is chilled and thickened by great cold, when it is salted with hoar frost, and when its palpability and density seem to make even the breathing of it harder, I am persuaded that winter nights are not altogether hospitable places, at that.

At their strongest, when subarctic winds sweep over the Gallatins and darkness falls during business hours, winter nights can be oppressive. I succumb to glumness, not because I miss the light but because the winter night presses in on the walls and threatens to push in the windows if I reduce the equal pressure exerted from the inside by glaring electric lights.

Often I am drawn, thoughtless, onto the porch. For a moment I listen to the wind clank the cord latches against the flagpole. Presently a pair of elk, sheltered from me in the one-way mirror of darkness yet disturbed by my sudden appearance on the porch, resume their desultory sparring. I

198

hear the dry clacking of their antlers and an occasional squealing grunt. Usually that's all that reaches me from beyond the island of porch light, though occasionally the wind carries faint sulphurous traces from the springs, or drifting howls of the local coyotes, their song cut and twisted on eddies of breeze. In only moments the cold drives me, hands in pockets and lungs full of dark air, back inside to my guitar, good company on more winter nights than I could say, some of them spent more socially.

We skied the half mile from the residence area to the Old Faithful Snow Lodge, Jo with her fiddle sticking from the top of her pack, I with a heavy guitar case in one hand and my ski poles in the other. The lodge wasn't busy, maybe twenty people in the restaurant and bar. The rooms were dark and warm. As we walked in with our gear, some of the people seemed wrong for the music we had in mind, and Jo, knowing my dislike of playing for strangers, glanced over one shoulder with a look somehow both concerned and reassuring. I had doubts, but no choice now.

Once through the restaurant and into the bar, we met friendlier faces. Cook, always unreasonably exuberant, lifted Jo off the floor with a big hug, not having seen her for at least two hours. There were a few musicians sitting at the corner of the bar, only one of whom would matter—Jeff Cobb, veteran Yellowstone winter person, gas pumper, skier, and proprietor of the only bass fiddle in our corner of the Rockies.

Jo shines in a crowd; she generates joy and warmth and gathers happy people at will, with a totally unaffected enthusiasm for whatever she's doing. Music is her special magic. She weaves a campfire program around performances on fiddle, flute, saw, harmonica, and guitar, and I've seen two hundred people fall in love with her and seen her direct that love toward the park. She naturally took the lead in the Snow Lodge, pulling up a bar stool, sawing a bit on her fiddle, and suggesting a tune to Jeff.

I hesitantly unpacked the Martin and took a seat by Jeff's bass, so that the three of us were a small triangle facing each other. People stirred uneasily.

You never know how it will work when you play with a new musician. Jo and I were attuned, and she kept me at ease—probably kept me from packing up right then and fleeing all these strangers (I'll talk up a storm to a thousand strangers, but over the years I'd come to keep my music for a few friends).

About a minute into Jeff's first song I knew it was all right. I was among friends. His bass lines were professional and solid, and his voice on some hill tune or other, had the perfect combination of strength and twang. The barriers dropped, and I picked out a basic background, looking for an opportunity to offer something flashier and already warming to the whole idea. Jo's fiddle carried the breaks, and Jeff was our leader instantly.

There's a feeling a musician gets, if lucky, a sense of touching the audience. When the music is right, and the listeners are ready, the communing—the feeling of reaching into another's heart—is strongly felt whether there's a visible response or not (and if it doesn't work, the feeling of loneliness is devastating). In the lodge that night, a few warm hearts, brought to that quiet, drifted-in little island of firelight, reached and touched so that we all seemed musician and we all listened as audience. Knowing that Jo, through vastly superior musicianship, could follow us anywhere we might venture, Jeff and I explored what common musical ground we had and found some we weren't aware of. At one point it came to my turn (an intuitive decision made by some group consciousness) to provide the instrumental break between the verses of some song—"Old Slewfoot," perhaps—and I found myself spectator to my hands, watching them run through a melody line and a syncopation that I hadn't dreamed was in me. Such was the power of this group musical spirit. As the song wound back into the next verse, I recovered enough to look over at Jeff, who was still gaping at my guitar, and I said, "I didn't know that was possible."

And as his bass notes rolled up to meet the verse he drawled, "It isn't," and on we went.

Somewhere after midnight, beyond the bluegrass, the Hank Williams, the various folksy patter that Jo and I knew, and Jeff's extraordinary reserve of hill music, I hunkered down around the Martin and coaxed tired fingers into one last drill, the old Merle Travis classic, "Cannonball Rag." Through the half-light, beer, and general emotional haze that had settled over us, Jeff identified at least the genus of what I was after, and the sweet rich treble of the Martin was lifted and driven on the rhythmic hum of his bass. The small room was a second sound box, a resonant giant of a guitar, played from the inside. Somebody spun in an impromptu dance, and as I slipped down a three-octave run far more cleanly than I had any right to, Cook hooted with glee. Playing without thought or care, I looked up into a small group of faces without names, all with me, then finished the song, momentarily resting my head on the Martin as the last full chords hovered and faded inside.

* * *

Foremost subject among geyser gazers is certainly Old Faithful, and of the time spent gazing at it, most seems to have been occupied in a quest for an ever finer understanding of its faithfulness. They're not so much concerned with why it's so faithful; that is a matter of geological circumstance. What really absorbs most of their intellectual energy is more practical and, in some very human ways, more predictable. What they really want to know is how to quantify this fidelity; how to predict the next eruption. They seek to take this natural treasure and reduce the most endearing element of its character to mathematical certainty. To their credit, they don't have any great plans for the information once they have it. After all, the rangers at the Visitor Center have for many years had an excellent formula for predicting the next eruption. Based on stopwatch.timing of one eruption, they can tell the impatient tourist the time until the next eruption within a minute or three (the tourist then asks, "Think it's worth waiting another twenty minutes for? We have to be to Cody by dark."). No, the really hard-core Old Faithful student wants the information because, well, we ought to *know*, oughtn't we?

I suppose. I'm a great believer in science and have that same insatiable compulsive curiosity about a few things myself, and I don't doubt that the information has some ultimately useful application, but personally I don't care when Old Faithful will erupt again. It's enough that it erupts at all.

The most fanatic, dedicated, and inventive Old Faithful–gazer I ever knew lived for quite some time watching it day and night, sleeping where and when he could (setting his alarm to get up to time each eruption at night). Summer and winter, his patience and devotion were religious. The park service finally recognized his talent, as well as the worth of what he was learning, and gave him a permit to study the geyser more formally: to use certain government facilities and gear, for example. The permit also freed him from restrictions that the general public could not be without. Possibly foremost of these was permission to go up on the cone. Which brings us, roundabout and a little late, to another winter night.

I'd never been up on the cone before, and my experiences with lots of other fragile depositions convinced me that I didn't need to go there. But John invited me to go with him and time an eruption, up close, and it sounded like a good idea. You see, in the winter the steam from the eruption is so dense that it's difficult, at best, to time the actual eruption. There's too much steam coming out of the vent before the eruption begins;

you can't see when the water starts to come out. Same problem at the end of the eruption; too much steam to tell for sure when the lessening flow of water actually ceases. Darkness makes the difficult impossible. The answer, if you're legal to do it, is to get right out there next to the vent, where the whooshing column of water is at your fingertips. This is what John did, nightly, and I took heart from his generally unboiled appearance. "Sure, let's go."

From a distance, the cone looks smooth, like a coolee hat with a gently rounded top. That's how it looks from the boardwalk where the crowds stand to watch eruptions in the summer. As you cross it, you find that it's pocked with cracks and bowls. Ridges of sinter have formed, with shallow pools behind them. The conventional wisdom in a geyser basin is "walk on the hard ridges." The soft deposition behind the ridge (and the feared thin crust one expects momentarily to break through) is supposed to be more dangerous. Walking on the ridges also does less damage to the deposits because you leave fewer footprints.

Though I'm bored with the overused allusions to hell—all the geothermal features named "The Devil's Thumb," or "The Devil's Kitchen"—there is no denying that on a windy midnight, with ragged shreds of sulphurous mist shrouding my path, and John fading and reappearing in it as he moved along ahead of me, the impression was satanic. John seemed to know his way, moving quickly, casually warning me now and then not to fall into some especially wicked-looking pool as we threaded our way to the top of the cone. He carried a small pocket computer with him, constantly poking at it with authority, occasionally muttering about the "indicator," a small side vent that releases the first water and signals the imminent eruption of Old Faithful.

We arrived at the vent just in time. The ground did not shudder, but it passed along to my feet a feeling of vibrant power that was somehow more impressive than any mere quaking would have been.

John was poking at his computer full time now, absorbed in mathematical anticipation. I did not share his calm.

"John, from the looks of the wind, I think we're gonna get wet standing here."

"Um. No problem." Poke, poke, beep, click.

The geyser was roiling and sloshing vigorously, like a huge subterranean laundromat, all the machines about to break down from having been brutalized by too many depressed bachelors.

"John, I think we're bound to get wet here. Look at how the wind is."

He didn't even point out that one doesn't *look* at wind. "Hmm. Wind is okay. No problem." Poke, poke, click, poke, poke, click.

"Boy, listen to that water. Uh, John . . . I, uh . . . John?"

Poke, poke, click. Beep.

A final rushing roar, not terribly loud but prodigiously imposing, was too much for me. I turned, and as the water burst up I picked my way hastily about twenty yards down the cone, turned, and looked back. John stood, as before, nosing his little computer. Poke, poke, click. He was drenched. But as the water poured from his shoulders I realized that in principle he'd been right. After the splashy disorder of the initial gushing the geyser settled into a more reliable jet whose mist was blown away on the far side of the cone.

For the first time my curiosity got the better of my caution, and I hurried back to the vent. The column of water, from arm's length, was improbable at best. A few years ago, as a ditch digger, I worked with any number of recalcitrant fire hydrants and got a healthy respect for the kind of pressure it takes to drive water any distance vertically. It takes lots. What I saw here was imponderably greater, a solid tree trunk of racing steaming water, a yard or more thick, a volume and shape of flow that I resigned myself to worship rather than understand. Its quiet rushing noise heightened the wonder of it. After a moment, with John now completely forgotten in my fascination with this solid-liquid form that stood unmoving before me, I raised my eyes and followed the column's course upward. The water climbed effortlessly, not becoming less than a solid tower until nearly a hundred feet tall. At that level, in the drifting clouds, steam, and vagrant spray, I lost it in the broken moonlight of the winter night.

*   *   *

It's an easy ski, maybe twenty minutes over one low ridge, from the road to the cabin, and with full dark by four-thirty in the afternoon a good moon is welcome light. Four or five cars are left at the road by the dozen of us, arriving two or three at a time. Shouldering daypacks full of food, wine, and clean plates, we slide over the bright snow, around the barricade across the old service road, and up the easy slope. At the top, with a tall black grove of evergreens obscuring the creek bottoms to our left, we pause to soak in the view.

The small creek winds between sage-covered slopes, its willow-lined banks vaguely smokelike in the moonlight. Just up from the creek sits the cabin, with a small barn off behind it. The barn and its corral are dark and vacant, but a warm golden glow from the windows of the cabin softens the light of the moon and turns patches of snow under the windows a warm cream. There is no sound, no movement but the wind, but the cabin is lively and beckoning.

Skis are stacked noisily against the south wall, boots are stomped clean of clinging snow, and the kitchen is crowded with greetings, shufflings, and laughter as smells of stew and wine mix with those of ski wax and wet wool. Dinner is a feast of lamb stew ("There may be some elk in there, remember that party?"), unexpected salads, heavy bread, and hearty wines, with coffee and "the best of all talk" afterward. The stories are mostly new—it's been a long summer—with a few old favorites ("When was it you saw that cougar?") and an occasional tidbit of local gossip or news mixed in.

In the end a volume of Robert Service is produced—the first time I've seen it at a party here. In the fading heat of the stove everyone is quietly perched on bunks, trunks, and stools, as favorites are read.

> The wind's getting real ferocious; it's heaving and
> whirling the snow;
> It shrieks with a howl of fury, it dies away
> to a moan;
> Its arms sweep round like banshees,
> swift and icily white,
> And buffet and blind and beat me. Lord! it's a
> hell of a night.

The stove is barely keeping itself warm as the book changes hands.

> Then I ducked my head, and the lights went out,
> and two guns blazed in the dark,
> And a woman screamed, and the lights went up,
> and two men lay stiff and stark.
> Pitched on his head, and pumped full of lead,
> was Dangerous Dan McGrew;
> While the man from the creeks lay clutched to the breast
> of the lady that's known as Lou . . .

The romance of Service's simple rhymes, an anachronism in so much of the world today, is alive and well at the cabin on the Blacktail Plateau.

They have cradled you in custom, they have primed
    you with their preaching,
They have soaked you in convention
    through and through;
They have put you in a showcase;
    you're a credit to their teaching—
But can you hear the Wild?
    it's calling you.

Let us probe the silent places, let us
    seek what luck betide us;
Let us journey to a lonely land
    I know.
There's a whisper on the night wind,
    there's a star agleam to guide us,
And the Wild is calling, calling . . . let us go.

Finally Bob Haraden undertakes "The Cremation of Sam McGee," his soft downeast accent a fresh counterpoint to Service's forceful verse.

There are strange things done in the midnight sun
    By the men who moil for gold;
The Arctic trails have their secret tales
    That would make your blood run cold;
The Northern Lights have seen queer sights,
    But the queerest they ever did see
Was that night by the marge of Lake LaBarge
    I cremated Sam McGee.

The poem ends, the book closes, and it's obviously time to go. Leftovers are divvied up (bachelors moving to the front of the line), someone regrets the shortage of huckleberry pie, bottles are stoppered, and the stove is tended to. Someone slips away quickly, mixing and crossing eleven pairs of skis—short with long, fat with skinny—so that as the rest of us leave and grope for our skis the night rings with mock outrage, confused giggles, and the clatter of colliding wood. Then, with a clouding midnight sky giving the terrain little visible relief, and only the faintest starshadows tinting the snow as we pass, we top the ridge and glide softly back to the cars.

*   *   *

Night is much more common than day in the winter here, so it's no surprise I dwell on it; anything that takes that much time to pass must be offering me something. Mostly, now, looking back with a memory that has selected only the occasional bright tidbit for preservation, I'd say that winter nights have been special for offering contrast to warmth. Frostburns across the ridge of my nose, where the metal rim of my glasses pulled away the skin on a thirty-below night, always reminded me of how easy it was to keep warm on those nights by skiing with no haste. They reminded me as well of how little adjustment is necessary for comfort while skiing, when, if I get feeling too warm, merely raising my balaclava an inch on my forehead straightens out my thermostat.

The nights have heightened the times spent in them, and the times spent secure from them. One such night, about an hour before dawn, I walked drowsily through Mammoth, bundled in down, still feeling the tingling pressure of a last warm sleepy embrace on my chest. The sky had traces of morning: the stars were dimmer and the clouds had that distinctness they get when it will soon be light. I crunched across the snow, wanting to get back to sleep before I woke up too much, past the storehouse and over behind officer's row. The bull elk were bedded down in depressions in the snow between the bunkhouse and the superintendent's house. Their heads were up, and each sent a plume of white breath straight up in the windless air. Their eyes sparkled darkly at me as I passed (Don't think too hard about why *they're* awake, Paul; just get home). The faint yap of a lone coyote reached me as I crossed the porch, but I had completed the walk before the cold penetrated my heavy clothes and woke me any further. This was no time to pause for a serenade. Quickly undressing, I curled up for a last hour of sleep. The radiator clanged tentatively, and just before I dozed I heard the early plow truck scrape by on its way east.

Of Hope, and Memory

Whatever of my social conscience that survived college occasionally interrupts my preoccupation with the joys and trials of Yellowstone and its future. It confronts me with questions about the world: When millions of your fellow human beings are starving and the lady down the street buys enough cat food to feed a whole suburb of Calcutta, when a thousand environmental crimes are destroying us, when we're under so many guns—nuclear, chemical, population, and the rest—that no one sleeps well, and when you're barely making a living instead of getting a nice job in some respected profession; when all these things are true, how can you spend so much time worrying about Yellowstone's wilderness?

I am always a little cowed by this confrontation with my self, but I know the answer. I do it because of my social conscience, not despite it. Yellowstone's wilderness suffers most because it is immeasurable and therefore difficult to quantify or define in terms society is comfortable with. It always seems that a little more can be sacrificed (just here at the edge, where nobody will mind). And, always, or usually, it is done openly, with due process and legal sanction from some agency or other. This is terrible because if we ever do get the world straightened out, or even stop it from getting worse, we're going to need Yellowstone very badly to help show us the way back. From the way we treat the world it is obvious that we don't even respect our own existence value, much less Yellowstone's.

Ultimately, anyone who cares about places like Yellowstone must wonder how much more can be lost. When does civilized negotiation, environmental journalism, and legal bickering lose its worth, and when must principles finally be defended? When will I, or anyone else, finally join the Monkey Wrench Gang and act more firmly to stop the loss? Will we ever? It does seem to me that there has to be a final wall, and it also seems to me that our backs are getting pretty close to it right now. We're being talked out of resources and ideals that matter very much, and we have been losing ground for years. The direction is clear; the aim of the people who prefer development to wilderness is quite surely to develop everything. They have never shown a capacity to be satisfied with anything less than everything, and we have no reason to expect them to change. As hard as I try to be hopeful, and as carefully as I try to reason through the problems, at least a part of me knows that there has to be a point beyond which they can't go around me but will have to go over me. It's that important. Yellowstone constitutes such a point, but the place can be wrecked and philosophically gutted without even entering it, by up-to-the-boundary development and airborne pollution. The romantic last stand, a few people pushed to the limit and crouching on the edge of the last wilderness with deer rifles, waiting for the bulldozers to get into range, is almost impossible because this is not a conflict with fronts. Like the Vietnamese War, where people didn't stand in straight lines and defend constant borders, there are no sure stands to take. There are no straight lines to be had, and by the time the developers reach the borders it's already too late.

I am told that the crayfish swims backward. I've seen them do it. This, conveniently, saves their looking over their shoulders at whatever is chasing them. They have to watch it close in. The parks are defended in the same way—backward-looking flight. We are so necessarily occupied with what's chasing the parks that we can't always see where they're headed. They're just trying to escape.

Yellowstone is being closed in on, very quickly, from many directions. The odds increase that Old Faithful will not die a natural death, that geothermal development on the west boundary of the park will sooner or later foul up the tangled pressure systems of the geyser basins, leaving the geysers dead and still, irretrievable victims of human avarice. The odds increase that ranchers, condominium owners, skiers, backpackers, and the rest of us will do in the grizzly bear, and that in a hundred less glamorous ways Yellowstone will be diminished. Those are the odds, but they aren't yet inevitable, and my social conscience demands that I try to help the park. However bad things are elsewhere, we still need the pure and undisturbed, if only against which to measure our general decline. The park serves social purposes in civilization by presenting nature's alternative to human control of the world.

But the park is not enough. We do not preserve Yellowstone just to salve our consciences about despoiling other places. Yellowstone is betrayed if by its existence we justify the abuse of other lands, or other beauties. We cannot apply all the values by which we judge the health of Yellowstone to the rest of the world, but we can hope that the respect we show the earth in Yellowstone will rub off on us when we go back to Fort Wayne, or Birmingham, or Tucson. In our efforts to convince people that Yellowstone is not just another Disneyland, not just another roadside attraction, we must show them that it does more than merely entertain or divert. We must show them that it teaches ecological unity of a sort that *can* be applied to the rest of the world, that it reveals fabulous uncultivated beauty, and that it enriches our lives as it heals our spirits. It does these things at grave and constant risk to its own welfare.

A friend of mine says that Old Faithful, half-surrounded by boardwalks and hotels, fails at being Disneyland in a Disneyland setting; that it does not live up to the expectations that setting inspires in people. They don't know for sure what they thought they'd see, but it was certainly something else than a little spurt of water; why, that old hotel over there is more impressive than that! My friend thinks that the geyser, come upon without its grand architectural backdrop and without the fanfare provided by any festive audience, would leave people staring at an exhausted vent in wonder rather than walking away halfway through the eruption.

I think he's right, but I also think that even in its present setting the geyser could mean more to people if they were properly introduced to the place. And I think that all Yellowstone could mean much more to people if they were properly introduced to it. They could find wonder where now they find only curious restlessness or disappointment. I think they could find it because I have found it, and when I came here I was as unprepared as any of them.

I have found it unexpectedly and at random; experiences do not form themselves into neat artificial units like chapters of a book. We must reshape them, consciously saying, "There, in that experience, is a story I want to tell; it begins here and it ends there, and I will lift it from my life and set it aside to enjoy and share." Without that segregation, they remain only undifferentiated episodes attached to others, but they are the form in which I most remember Yellowstone. Chance, as Pasteur said, favors the prepared mind, but chance does not provide a table of contents. It only provides the moment, the brief glimpse through the gifted eye, and the opportunity for some greater vision.

The search for that vision is easily sidetracked. Like the photographer who is so absorbed in proper exposure settings and foreground framing ("Let's not stop here; the light's no good for pictures") that he never pauses to enjoy the subject, I risk missing the present in my concern for the future. A friend who saw that risk in me once observed, toward the end of a particularly nice day we'd spent together, "I'll bet you're really looking forward to looking back on this, aren't you?"

It just happens to be my personal demon, that I worry about holding onto the moment. How does one absorb these days and store times that seem so mightily important and yet pass so quickly? When a sunstruck bat loops crazily above my lawn in broad daylight, plops in the dust, then flutters and dips away over the sage, I want to sit and hold the sight, not just its surprise and melancholy amusement but its implications and possible moral, that daylight (my world) is as unfamiliar to the bat as dark (his world) is to me. When a rainbow trout drags my line into the dusk over the Madison River and sends a sweeping slow-motion arc of golden spray across my vision with its tail, I hold that endless instant of sunbow in my sight as I turn to leave the river, and I drive home with it hovering over my headlights. When at dusk we at last find the calypso orchid in the cradle of a grassy hillside seep under dark trees, I want to strain to get this rare blossom into my mind, to hold it in memory as I leave it in the gloaming.

But the pictures change. Memory's vision transforms and enhances the original like a hand-tinted postcard so that I know my own memories are not accurate and I rely instead on less changeable memories, especially of feelings: the breath-catch of any unexpected wonder that may confront you when you're open for it.

Though I suppose it's greedy and unreasonable I sometimes feel a little panic when these moments pass so quickly. I want them to be caught and still, so that I can call them up any time for review, but that would kill them. Once, skiing out of Slough Creek canyon, we paused over a single coyote track. The foot had compressed the light snow so that it was packed firm, then a wind had come and blown away the looser surrounding snow; the track stood up like a tiny mesa, an inch above the remaining snow. As we turned to go a single coyote, then the whole pack, began to howl on the ridges above us. The calls carried across the narrow valley and ricocheted through the darkening sky until it seemed there were hundreds of coyotes above us, taken flight. When it faded we were shivering and still, and another euphoric moment was gone, some part of the feeling of it filed in memory for later enjoyment.

It's these unexpected moments that most reach me. It's true that I forget the mosquitoes and the blisters, the cranky tourists and the lonely nights, just as I forget the fishless hours on the river. It's also true that I'm always questioning my perceptions and my ability to do justice to the moments when they happen. But even when I feel prepared for the chance it twists around and gives me a surprise. We went up to Swan Lake Flats one evening to watch the swans and to look for elk. We stood on the hood of the truck for better elevation and after watching the swans on the lake for a while we turned the other way to look for elk or moose. As we were looking, three swans rose quietly from the lake and flew south, passing directly over us just a few yards up. That was the surprise in the moment, when we heard the approach and fade of the soft whistling rush of wind through the primaries of flying swans. It was a sound of almost cosmic richness, like the first laughter of a new woman. It is what I remember best of that day. I didn't know I was so well prepared for it, and would never have known it was what I was there for. And, typically, I want its like again and again.

I envy the scientists who have spent years studying lichens, grizzlies, and geysers; the rangers who have hiked every trail; the historians who have studied every document; the fishermen who have fished every stream. I want to be all of them, but I succeed only in being a little of each of them. And, though it doesn't make me content, I know that is enough.

I left the park one fall to take another job, consciously deciding to be permanent at something, though just as consciously deciding not to be permanent in the park service. I knew I'd only begun to do the park justice, but I was sure I should go. I was spending most of my free time in the library or in my office with the archives, obsessed with a more formal learning and a need to become more than I thought I was. I was therefore already gone in a sense, having forfeited direct contact with the wilderness so that I could study its past and its prospects.

I packed up the car one more time, on a November evening, getting set for the cross-country trip I'd made so often before between Yellowstone and all the other places that mattered less. I gave away some things that wouldn't fit in at the last minute, already having lost the illusion of mobility I'd prided myself on when I had to mail fifteen boxes of books (the millstones of learning) to my new office in Vermont.

When I drove down the Gardner Canyon on my way out of the park the next morning, the river was steamy and dark. A few deer were moving up from the river toward Sepulchre, but the sheep must have already gone up to McMinn Bench for the day because I didn't see them. It seemed likely to snow soon, and a hell of a time to be leaving Yellowstone, but I couldn't imagine a good time to do such a thing.

In the canyon I pulled over across the opposite lane and parked overlooking the jumping water. The cartwheel churned steadily in the dull light; the sun wouldn't hit it for half an hour yet. No trout jumped while I watched—I knew it was early in the season for them to be jumping, but I had to look—but an ouzel dipsey-danced with nimble sureness over the slick rocks at the very edge of the torrent. I watched him and felt a need to wave good-bye. Even in the mountains, there never seems to be enough time.

Acknowledgments

The stories I tell in this book celebrate as well as I can my gratitude to Yellowstone friends; we shared it, and we will never forget it.

The essays in Part 2 have grown out of my research in the park's history and natural history, but I have considerable conceptual debt to several people. The bibliography that follows suggests the breadth of the material upon which my learning is based, but some of the most provocative ideas in the book arose from discussions with Don Despain, Douglas Houston, Mary Meagher, and John Varley, all biologists with the National Park Service. My debt to other park friends and co-workers, especially naturalists Don Arceneaux, Dick Follett, and John Whitman, is also a pleasure to acknowledge. I have always treasured my friendships with these people, but in writing this book I have discovered how much I also benefited from their wisdom.

My historical work in Yellowstone was made possible at various times by the support and encouragement of naturalists Tony Dean, Alan Mebane, and John Tyers. I feel a special debt to the late John Townsley, superintendent of Yellowstone during most of my time there, who fought the good fight for adequate management of Yellowstone's superb historical collections: the archives, the library, the museum collections, and the photographic collection.

Jerry Phillips of the National Park Service helped with materials concerning the tort claims system and its history. Norton Miner, of the U.S. Fish and Wildlife Service, provided several important reports on the eagle translocation project discussed in the chapter "As the Eagle Flies."

The encouragement of many people was important to me during the two years of occasional effort it took to produce the manuscript and the additional year it took to find a publisher. The late A. Starker Leopold was a patient listener to my sputterings about park management philosophy, and encouraged me to write this book when I was still trying to imagine its form. Nick Lyons and Craig Woods offered the kind empathy of fellow writers. John Merwin, Rick Rinehart, Martha Roth, Steve and Nancy Schullery, and Christina Watkins all provided sympathetic attention while the book was being written.

The manuscript was read and commented on by Doug Houston, Tom McNamee, Mary Meagher, and John Varley.

Susan Sindt, fellow ranger-naturalist, first suggested to me that I would write the book, back before I left Yellowstone in 1977.

My wife Dianne Russell provided, through her enthusiasm and support, an incentive roughly equivalent to a publisher's contract. For that and more enduring reasons the book is dedicated to her.

Some months after I finished writing *Mountain Time* I was surprised to discover that title staring back at me from the shelves of a used book store. Bernard De Voto used it for a novel (a very nice novel, by the way) that was published in 1947. Authors often work very hard to come up with decent titles for their books, and so I feel compelled to acknowledge that though I did indeed think up my title myself, someone else thought it up earlier. If I must be preceded, I am grateful it is by a writer of De Voto's skill.

Bibliography

This might appropriately be called a "Suggestive Bibliography" because it does little more than skim across a great many topics and reveal some possibilities. What I hope it suggests is the wonderful breadth of reading matter available on the park. What I hope it provides is encouragement for you to explore that huge informational resource. The list is just representative. Rather than list all the important papers on a topic I offer only a few; the interested reader can easily find more in the bibliographies of the ones listed. I would love to give you about 500 titles with extended commentary, but even a list as long as the following one is unusual for a book of this sort.

It is tempting to provide commentary on even these few titles; I'd rather not give the impression I wholeheartedly recommend all of them when actually I think a few of them are wretched. But then I wrote some of them myself, so my opinions are probably as suspect as anyone's. We each have to evaluate everything we read for ourselves anyway.

There is one I will recommend, however, because it is timely. If *Mountain Time* succeeded in arousing your concern about the welfare of the Yellowstone country, your next book on the subject should be *Greater Yellowstone*, by Rick Reese. The full reference is in the bibliography. This book will give you a good summary rundown of the problems the area faces, something *Mountain Time* was not intended to provide.

Abbey, Edward. 1977. *The Journey Home*. E.P. Dutton, New York.

Albin, D. P. 1979. Fire and Stream Ecology in some Yellowstone Lake tributaries. *California Fish and Game* 65:216–38.

Aune, Keith Edward. 1981. *Impacts of Winter Recreationists on Wildlife in a Portion of Yellowstone National Park, Wyoming*. M.S. Thesis, Montana State University, Bozeman.

Baden, John, and Richard Stroup. 1981. Saving the Wilderness, a Radical Proposal. *Reason*, July, pp. 28–36.

Barbee, Robert. 1984. *1983 Annual Report of the Superintendent Yellowstone National Park*. Yellowstone Park.

Bartlett, Richard. 1974. *Nature's Yellowstone*. University of New Mexico Press, Albuquerque.

Blonston, Garry. 1983. Where Nature Takes Its Course. *Science 83*, November, pp. 44–55.

Bromely, G. 1965. *The Bears of the Southern Far East of USSR*. Isdatel'stvo "Nanka" Academy of Sciences of USSR, Siberian Branch, Far East Subsidiary, translated by Canadian Wildlife Service.

Bryan, R. B., and M. C, Jansson, 1973. Perceptions of Wildlife Hazards in National Park Use. *Trans. N. Am. Wild. Nat. Resour.* 38:281–95.

Bryan, Scott. 1979. *The Geysers of Yellowstone*. Colorado Associated University Press, Boulder.

Cahalane, Victor. 1939. The Evolution of Predator Control Policy in the National Parks. *The Journal of Wildlife Management* 3(3):229–237. 1950.

————. A Program for Restoring Extirpated Mammals in the National Park System. *Journal of Mammalogy* 32(2):207–210.

Chase, Alston. 1983. The Last Bears of Yellowstone. *The Atlantic*, February, pp. 63–73.

Chester, James. 1976. *Human Wildlife Interactions in the Gallatin Range, Yellowstone National Park, 1973–1974*. M.S. Thesis, Montana State University.

Cole, Glen. 1978. *The Elk of Grand Teton and Southern Yellowstone National Parks*. National Park Service, Yellowstone Library and Museum Association, reissue of Research Report GRTE-N-1, 1969.

————. 1970. An Ecological Rationale for the Natural or Artificial Regulation of Native Ungulates in Parks. *Transactions* of the Thirty-Sixth North American Wildlife and Natural Resources Conference, the Wildlife Management Institute.

————. 1975. Nature and Man in Yellowstone National Park. Yellowstone National Park Information Paper No. 28.

Connally, Eugenia, ed. 1982. *National Parks in Crisis*. National Parks and Conservation Association, Washington.

Corbett, Jim. 1946. *Man-Eaters of Kumaon*. Oxford University Press, London.

Craighead, Frank. 1979. *Track of the Grizzly*. Sierra Club Books, San Francisco.

Craighead, John. 1980. *A Proposed Delineation of Critical Grizzly Bear Habitat in the Yellowstone Region*. The Bear Biology Association, sponsored by the University of Montana, U.S. Fish and Wildlife Service, and the Wildlife Management Institute.

Craighead, John, Frank Craighead, Robert Ruff, and Bart O'Gara. 1973. Home Ranges and Activity Patterns of Nonmigratory Elk of the Madison Drainage Herd as determined by Biotelemetry. *Wildlife Monograph* 33, Wildlife Society.

Craighead, John, J. Sumner, and G.B. Scaggs. 1982. *A Definitive System for Analysis of Grizzly Bear Habitat and Other Wilderness Resources*. Wildlife-Wildlands Institute Monograph No. 1, Missoula.

Darling, F. Fraser, and Eichhorn, Noel D. 1969. *Man & Nature in the National Parks*. The Conservation Foundation, Washington.

DeSanto, J. 1964. Bird Kills in Poison and Stygian Caves. Mimeo, Yellowstone Park.

Despain, Don. 1972. Forest Insects and Diseases. Yellowstone National Park Information Paper No. 18.

————. 1972. Fire as an Ecological Force in Yellowstone Ecosystems. Yellowstone National Park Information Paper No. 16.

Dorf, Erling. 1980. *Petrified Forests of Yellowstone*. National Park Service, U.S. Department of the Interior, Washington.

Eastwood, John. 1980. *Backcountry Use in Yellowstone National Park*. M.S. Thesis, University of Wyoming, Laramie.

Follett, Richard. n.d. *The Birds of Yellowstone and Grand Teton National Parks*. Yellowstone Library and Museum Association, Yellowstone Park.

Haines, Aubrey. 1977. *The Yellowstone Story*. Colorado Associated University Press, Boulder.

Hamilton, Wayne. 1982. Geological Investigations in Yellowstone National Park, 1976–1981. Thirty-third Annual Field Conference—1982

Wyoming Geological Association Guidebook.

Hampton, H. Duane. 1971. *How the U.S. Cavalry Saved Our National Parks.* Indiana University Press, Bloomington.

———. 1981. Opposition to National Parks. *Journal of Forest History* 25(1): 36–45.

Hardin, Garrett. 1968. The Tragedy of the Commons. *Science* 162: 1243–48.

Houston, D. 1971. Ecosystems of National Parks. *Science* 172:648–651.

———. 1973. Wildfires in Northern Yellowstone National Park. *Ecology* 54(5): 1111–1117.

———. 1983. *The Northern Yellowstone Elk: Ecology and Management.* Macmillan, New York.

Huth, Hans. 1957. *Nature and the American.* University of California Press, Berkeley.

Institute of the American West. 1984. *Parks in the West & American Culture.* papers from a symposium, Sun Valley.

Keefer, William. n.d. *The Geologic Story of Yellowstone National Park.* U.S. Government Printing Office, Washington.

Kellert, S. 1979. *Public Attitudes towards Critical Wildlife and Natural Habitat Issues.* U.S. Fish and Wildlife Service, Washington.

Knight, Richard; Blanchard, Bonnie; and Kendall, Katherine. 1982. *Yellowstone Grizzly Bear Investigations: Report of the Interagency Study Team, 1981.* National Park Service.

Knight, Richard; Brown, Gary; Craighead, John; Meagher, Mary; Roop, Larry; and Serveheen, Christopher. 1983. *Final Report, ad hoc Committee to Investigate the Need and Feasibility of the Supplemental Feeding of Yellowstone Grizzly Bears.* Committee report, National Park Service.

Krutch, Joseph Wood. 1952. *The Desert Year.* William Sloane Associates, New York.

———. 1956. *The Great Chain of Life.* Houghton Mifflin Company, Boston.

Leopold, A. S.; Cain, S. A.; Cottam, C.; Gabrielson, I.; and Kimball, T. 1963. Wildlife Management in the National Parks. *American Forests,* April.

Lund, Thomas. 1980. *American Wildlife Law.* University of California Press, Berkeley.

McAvoy, Leo, and Dustin, Daniel. 1983. In Search of Balance: A No-Rescue Wilderness Proposal. *Western Wildlands,* Summer, pp. 2–5.

McCool, Stephen. 1983. The National Parks in Post-Industrial America.

Western Wildlands, Summer, pp. 14–19.

McNamee, Thomas. 1984. *The Grizzly Bear*. Alfred Knopf, Inc., New York.

Mantell, Michael. 1979. Preservation and Use: Concessions in the National Parks. *Ecology Law Quarterly* 8(1): 1–54.

Meagher, Mary. 1971. Winter Weather as a Population Regulating Influence on Free-Ranging Bison in Yellowstone National Park. Paper presented at the American Association for the Advancement of Science Symposium on Research in National Parks, December 28.

———. 1973. *The Bison of Yellowstone National Park*. National Park Service Scientific Monograph Series Number 1, Washington.

———. 1974. Yellowstone's Bison: A Unique Wild Heritage. *National Parks & Conservation Magazine*, May, pp. 9–14.

Meagher, Mary, and Phillips, Jerry. 1980. Restoration of Natural Populations of Grizzly and Black Bears in Yellowstone National Park. Paper presented at the Fourth International Symposium on Bears, Their Biology and Management.

Murie, Adolph. 1940. *Ecology of the Coyote in the Yellowstone*. Fauna of the National Parks of the United States, Fauna Series Number 4, U.S. Government Printing Office, Washington.

Nash, Roderick. 1982. *Wilderness and the American Mind*. rev. 3rd ed. Yale University Press, New Haven.

National Parks and Conservation Association. 1979. *Citizen's Action Guide to the National Park System*. National Parks and Conservation Association, Washington.

National Park Service. 1973. *Final Environmental Statement, Proposed Wilderness Classification, Yellowstone National Park, Wyoming*. National Park Service, Midwest Region.

———. n.d. *Yellowstone Master Plan*, preliminary draft. National Park Service, Washington.

———. 1977. Tort Claims Guidelines. In-house report, National Park Service, Rocky Mountain Regional Office, Denver.

———. 1982. *Final Environmental Impact Statement Grizzly Bear management Program*. Yellowstone Park.

———. 1984. Bear Information Book. In-house photocopy, used for employee training.

Neimeyer, Carter. 1980. Final Report Montana Golden Eagle Removal and Translocation Project. U.S. Fish and Wildlife Service.

Pelton, J. R., and Smith, R. B. 1979. Recent Crustal Uplift in Yellowstone National Park. *Science* 206:1179–1182.

———. 1982. Contemporary Vertical Surface Displacements in Yellowstone National Park. *Journal of Geophysical Research* 87, No. B4: 2745–2761.

Reese, Rick. *Greater Yellowstone, The National Park and Adjacent Wild lands.* Montana Magazine Montana Geographic Series Number Six, Helena.

Reiger, John. 1975. *American Sportsmen and the Origins of Conservation.* Winchester Press, New York.

Rinehart, John S. 1976. *A Guide to Geyser Gazing.* Hyperdynamics, Santa Fe.

———. 1972. 18.6-Year Earth Tide Regulates Geyser Activity. *Science* 177: 346–347.

Robbins, William et al. 1963. *A Report by the Advisory Committee to the National Park Service on Research of the National Academy of Sciences National Research Council.* National Academy of Sciences, Washington.

Rogers, Bob. 1982. Elk—Yellowstone's Growing Dilemma. *Western Outdoors*, April, pp. 25–26.

Romme, William, and Knight, Dennis. Landscape Diversity: The Concept Applied to Yellowstone Park. *Bioscience* 32(8):664–670.

Roszak, Theodore. 1972. *Where the Wasteland Ends.* Doubleday & Company, Garden City.

Runte, Alfred. 1979. *National Parks: The American Experience.* University of Nebraska Press, Lincoln.

Russell, Carl. 1933. A Concise History of Scientists and Scientific Investigations in Yellowstone National Park. National Park Service mimeo.

Sax, Joseph. 1980. *Mountains Without Handrails.* University of Michigan Press, Ann Arbor.

Schullery, Paul. 1975. *The Yellowstone Archives: Past, Present, and Future.* M.A. Thesis, Ohio University, Athens, Ohio.

———. 1976. "Buffalo" Jones and the Bison Herd in Yellowstone: Another Look. *Montana, The Magazine of Western History*, Summer, pp. 40–51.

———. 1980. *The Bears of Yellowstone.* Yellowstone Library and Museum Association, Yellowstone Park.

———. 1979. ed. *Old Yellowstone Days.* Colorado Associated University Press, Boulder.

———. 1983. ed. *American Bears: Selections from the Writings of Theodore*

Roosevelt. Colorado Associated University Press, Boulder.

Smith, R., and R. Christiansen. 1980. Yellowstone Park as a Window on the Earth's Interior. *Scientific American.* 242(2):104–117.

Stegner, Wallace. 1954. *Beyond the Hundredth Meridian: John Wesley Powell and the Second Opening of the West.* Houghton Mifflin, Boston.

―――. 1962. *Wolf Willow.* Macmillan, Toronto.

Stroup, Robert. 1979. Conservation and Capitalism. *The Libertarian Review,* October.

Sumner, Lowell. 1967. Biological Research and Management in the National Park Service—A History. Mimeographed. National Park Service.

Taylor, Dale. 1973. Some Ecological Implications of Forest Fire Control in Yellowstone National Park, Wyoming. *Ecology* 54(6):1394–1396.

U.S. Fish and Wildlife Service. 1982. *Grizzly Bear Recovery Plan.* U.S. Fish and Wildlife Service, Denver.

―――. 1979. Report to the Assistant Secretary of the Interior, Review and Evaluation of National Park Service Fisheries Policies and Practices March, 1979. Ad Hoc Fisheries Task Force, Washington.

Varley, John, and Schullery, Paul. 1983. *Freshwater Wilderness: Yellowstone Fishes and Their World.* Yellowstone Library and Museum Association, Yellowstone Park.

Weaver, John. 1978. *The Wolves of Yellowstone.* National Park Service Natural Resources Report Number 14, Washington.

Wirshhorn, James. n.d. *Climate of Yellowstone Park.* Mountain States Weather Services, Fort Collins, Colorado.